NICK COHEN is a columnist for the *Observer* and *Evening Standard*. Since the publication of *What's Left?* he has proved himself to be a necessary and excoriating voice of the Left. He is the author of three previous books: *Cruel Britannia: Reports on the Sinister and the Preposterous*, a col-lection of his journalism, *Pretty Straight Guys*, a dissection of the Blair leadership, and *What's Left? How The Left Lost Its Way*, a polemic against the hypocrisies of Western liberalism.

www.nickcohen.net

From the reviews of *What's Left?*:

'Exceptional and necessary ... Do not feel you have be leftist or liberal to read it, because it engages with an argument that is crucial for all of us, and for our time'

CHRISTOPHER HITCHENS, *Sunday Times*

'A roaring polemic of outrage against the moral and political crisis of the liberal tradition. It is already one of the most discussed current affairs books of the year'

MARTIN KETTLE, *Guardian*

'Angry and splendid'   DAVID AARANOVITCH, *The Times*

'Cohen's re-evaluation of everything that has ever animated his vastly political being says many, many things that really do need to be said'   DEBORAH ORR, *Independent*

'This book is much more than a mere denunciation of old left-wing friends and colleagues. It is also a moving account of a long personal journey carried off with wit, verve, considerable literary skill and compassion. Cohen is at his best as a painstakingly forensic officer and he marshals his evidence with flair and rigour' PETER OBORNE, *Observer*

'[Cohen writes with] a genuine passion and human sympathy about people who have experienced appalling suffering' MICHAEL BURLEIGH, *Evening Standard*

'Of wide reference and great brilliance' JOHN LLOYD, *Financial Times*

'If Cohen's aim is to discomfort the many whose self-righteous resentment of Blair and Bush has dulled their moral judgements, he succeeds brilliantly' *Economist*

'One of the most powerful denunciations of the manner in which the Left has lost its way ... Cohen's is a brave voice' MICHAEL GOVE, *Spectator*

Also by Nick Cohen

What's Left? How The Left Lost Its Way
Pretty Straight Guys
Cruel Britannia: Reports on the Sinister and the Preposterous

NICK COHEN

Waiting for the Etonians

Reports from the sickbed
of Liberal England

FOURTH ESTATE · *London*

First published in Great Britain in 2009 by
Fourth Estate
An imprint of HarperCollins*Publishers*
77–85 Fulham Palace Road
London W6 8JB

LOVE THIS BOOK? WWW.BOOKARMY.COM

A catalogue record for this book is
available from the British Library

ISBN 978-0-00-730892-7

Typeset in Minion by G&M Designs Limited,
Raunds, Northamptonshire

Printed in Great Britain by Clays Ltd, St Ives plc

Mixed Sources
Product group from well-managed
forests and other controlled sources
www.fsc.org   Cert no. SW-COC-1806
© 1996 Forest Stewardship Council

FSC is a non-profit international organisation established to promote the
responsible management of the world's forests. Products carrying the FSC
label are independently certified to assure customers that they come
from forests that are managed to meet the social, economic and
ecological needs of present and future generations.

Find out more about HarperCollins and the environment at
www.harpercollins.co.uk/green

To A-M for sustaining and supporting me

CONTENTS

PART 3 – *Oh, Comrades!*

PART 4 – *Tyranny and the Intellectuals*

PART 5 – *The Silence of the Hams*

Contents

PART 9 — *Waiting for the Etonians*

INTRODUCTION

Looking Back at the Ruins

Men, it has been well said, think in herds; it will be seen that they go mad in herds, while they only recover their sense slowly, and one by one.

CHARLES MACKAY, *Extraordinary Popular Delusions and the Madness of Crowds, 1841*

TWO YEARS AFTER the Great Crash of 1929, the American journalist Frederick Lewis Allen looked back on the Jazz Age of the twenties as if remembering a dream. The daring flappers, abandoning their corsets and lifting their skirts 'far beyond any modest limitation', the swaggering investors, who 'expected the Big Bull Market to go on and on', ought to have been fresh in his readers' minds. But Lewis knew that the bank failures and mass redundancies of the Great Depression had made the recent past utterly foreign. The optimism brought by prosperity was now as far away as a distant star. Wondering what to call his book, Allen hit on a title which was also a reminder, *Only Yesterday*.

After a deluge, nothing seems as remote as the day before it came. The thirties and the eighties have more to say to us now than the Britain of eighteen months ago. Across the centuries, historians of bubbles have reached for metaphors from fantasy worlds and lunatic asylums when they have tried to describe how crashes twist the linear progression of past to present out

1

of shape. They talk of manias, lusts, fevers and delusions in make-believe lands that people take to be real until the sound of the roof falling in wakes them to face a bleak new world. Alexander Pope spoke for all sceptical historians when he wrote of the South Sea Bubble that ruined early Georgian England, 'they have dreamed their dream, and awakening have found nothing in their hands'.

For this generation to think about what it was like before the Great Crash of 2008 will take the same mental wrench as the thirties' generation needed to see back before the Great Crash of 1929. Only yesterday, level-headed young couples took mortgages of four or five times their joint incomes to buy hutch-like apartments in streets which estate agents described as 'up-and-coming' and their friends described as 'scary at night'. Only yesterday City dealers in nightclubs threw handfuls of notes in the air for giggling girls to catch, as waitresses marching to the theme tune from *Rocky* brought £500 bottles of vodka and methuselahs of champagne to their tables. Only yesterday, Her Majesty's Government encouraged speculators from every part of the globe to settle in London by so under-regulating finance capital that NatWest bankers and media moguls involved in scandals as notorious as the Enron affair of 2001 and the collapse of Conrad Black's empire in 2003 could not be brought before British courts. American prosecutors took the alleged fraudsters to the US for trial, and confessed that Britain's lenient treatment of serious crimes baffled them. They did not understand that only yesterday politicians and civil servants had boasted that the City's economy was booming because of their 'light-touch regulation' of speculators whose number included potential swindlers. As a few of us noticed at the time, the politicians and civil servants never went on to argue that the inner-city economy might boom if the authorities applied a similarly light touch to the policing of the slums whose inhabitants included potential drug barons.

After the crash, Americans trying to find their bearings could at least hold on to the thought that George W. Bush's right-wing government presided over the bubble. As was to be expected, it did not intervene when sharks more interested in pocketing commissions than the principles of reputable lending sold millions of Americans mortgages they could not hope to repay. The Bush administration, like Herbert Hoover's Republican administration in 1929, believed that the market knew best and did not worry when financiers offered derivatives of such obscurity no one understood their risks. The conservatives' neglect made ideological sense. All of the great crashes occurred under politicians who accepted laissez-faire, such as Hoover, or politicians the moneymen corrupted, such as the Georgian oligarchs of 1720 who took the bribes of the South Sea Company.

Until yesterday, that is, when Britain broke the mould. When the bubble reached its peak in the summer of 2007, Texan oilmen and former investment bankers did not govern this country. Nor were our leaders enriching themselves with bribes from the City. The British dreamed their dream under a relatively honest, social democratic government, many of whose members had been fiercely sceptical of finance capital.

Those from radical families learned the histories of the Great Crash and Great Depression at their mothers' knees. At university in the seventies and early eighties, moderate leftists clutched the works of Lord Keynes and J. K. Galbraith to their breasts, while the extremists quoted Karl Marx and Antonio Gramsci.

By prejudice and well-grounded conviction, the left had always been wary of 'funny-money men' and 'spivs'. In 1975, while still at Edinburgh University, Gordon Brown edited *The Red Paper on Scotland*, a collection of essays that dreamed of radical transformation. He endorsed the vision of the early socialists who wanted to abolish 'the split personality caused by people's unequal control over their social development – between man's personal and collective existence – by substituting communal co-operation for the divisive forces of competition'. A better world could come only if the public accepted 'the necessity for social control of the institutional investors who wield enormous financial power both in fostering privilege in our social security system and in controlling the economy'.

Three decades on, Gordon Brown and his Labour colleagues allowed the 'divisive forces of corruption' and the 'institutional investors' to engage in an orgy of speculation. For the first time in financial history, one of the great market manias that punctuate the history of capitalism was presided over by a centre-left rather than a centre-right administration. Like the most gullible investors in the Wall Street of the twenties, social democrats thought 'the Big Bull Market would go on and on', and did not see the crash coming.

Think back to yesterday, and you will remember that they were not alone.

THE FINANCIERS COULD no more imagine the coming disaster than the politicians. They applauded the hospitality of the Labour government, along with the tax breaks it offered foreign dealers and private-equity buyers, and went on a speculative bender.

Men 'go mad in herds', declared the Victorian journalist Charles Mackay, as he looked at the stock-market crashes of the eighteenth and nineteenth centuries. He might have been writing of the twenty-first. Bankers, drunk on cheap money, packaged and traded in supposedly high-yielding, mortgage-backed securities, unaware or unconcerned about the possibility that poor 'homeowners' might default and leave them with worthless assets.

Why should anyone be anxious? The bankers said that they had spread the credit risk on the securities they sold to investors by slicing and dicing mortgages, so that good-quality loans were bundled in with riskier debts. Even if the diced borrowers had lied about their income or been bamboozled into debt by commission-hungry brokers, house prices were rising around the world, and politicians and central bankers were saying they had abolished the booms and busts of the business cycle. If individual borrowers fell ill or lost their jobs, they were entitled to sympathy, but lenders could always repossess their homes and sell them for more – often far more – than the value of their mortgages. Property guaranteed profits.

Meritocratic theory holds that the rich are rich because of their keen intelligence and hard work. They are not the beneficiaries of inherited wealth or good luck, but deserve their fortunes. Instead of seeing the potential for catastrophic failure in the financial system they were supposedly managing, the British rich engaged in the most conspicuous consumption since the Gilded Age of the late nineteenth century. The Candy brothers became commercial celebrities for meeting the exacting requirements of the global plutocracy. In 2007, they announced that they would soon be offering properties in a development near Hyde Park, with prices ranging from £20 million for ordinary apartments to £100 million for a penthouse that the press described without exaggeration as 'the most expensive flat in the world'. The brothers provided luxuries humanity had never known it needed before – a 360-degree 'memory mirror',* a purified air system, a tunnel from the car park to a nearby Michelin-starred restaurant, a floor-to-ceiling fridge and a 'panic room' (which, I admit, was prescient).

Creative entrepreneurs produced work to match the times. In 2007, Damien Hirst displayed the world's most expensive

---

* Although it looked like a full-length mirror, it was in fact a video screen with a time-delay function. Why would anyone want such a thing? Well, with a memory mirror you did not have to put yourself through the momentary inconvenience of looking over your shoulder to see if a dress fitted neatly over your bottom. You could turn around and study an image of your haute-coutured derrière taken ten seconds earlier without the risk of cricking your neck.

piece of contemporary art, a diamond-encrusted platinum cast of a human skull. The memento mori had been a staple of Western art since the Middle Ages, so Hirst won no prizes for novelty. All that concerned onlookers was Hirst's asking price of £50 million. His work created a sensation because of its sale-room rather than its aesthetic value. The following year, on 15 September 2008, he proved that the triumph of the art sale over the artwork was complete. He auctioned at Sotheby's pieces he cheerfully admitted his employees had mass-produced in his studios. The buyers did not care, and gave him £100 million. Even the critics did not pretend to be interested in what message, if any, he had for his public, but reported the sale like business journalists covering a soaring stock.

As the buyers made their bids, Lehman Brothers collapsed.

Until then, £50 million for a kitsch skull had not appeared beyond the reach of the richest of the super-rich. The Office for National Statistics reported that annual bonuses in the City had risen by 30 per cent to £14.1 billion in August 2007. The overall level of British bonuses, which included payouts to CEOs, senior managers, the new breed of commercialised public servants and up-market car and property dealers, as well as City financiers, reached £24 billion – a figure that comfortably exceeded the entire British transport budget.

To accompany apartments with secret tunnels to Michelin-approved chefs and objets d'art peppered with diamonds, were ever-more sumptuous versions of traditional luxuries. A Poole-based boatbuilder produced Britain's first 'super-yacht'. For £8.75 million the buyer received a 37-metre boat, fitted out with American black walnut furnishings, sleeping quarters for twelve (plus eight crew), a king-size bed in the master stateroom and a bar, dining area and hot tub on the sky deck.

The astonished children of England's upper-middle class started to talk about the vertiginous gap between the 'haves and the have yachts'. It was not only that they could no longer keep up with the Joneses – or the Abramoviches or Mittals, as their more successful neighbours were more likely to be called – they could no longer keep up with their parents.

Sebastian Cresswell-Turner remembered that when he was a child in the seventies almost everyone he knew 'lived in a large house in the country or in one of the better parts of London'. His father was a moderately successful architect and his mother did not have a career, but they could still afford to buy a converted rectory and send their children to private schools. When he was growing up, 'London' to Cresswell-Turner and his school friends meant Kensington, Chelsea or Hampstead. 'Battersea and Clapham were entirely off our radar, Stockwell another country, and Brixton, Peckham and Streatham simply unheard of,' he wrote. 'Now, with a few exceptions among those who are notably rich or successful, the next generation of the same families I grew up with is living in just these areas.'

Unless they were working in the City, they could not think of living in the type of homes their parents had brought them up in, or sending their children to the type of schools their parents had sent them to. 'Career choice is now all-important,' said Cresswell-Turner, who was a writer and had therefore made the wrong one. 'Go into the City, where they encourage and feed off the very process that is putting such pressure on the rest of us. As my host at an Oxfordshire dinner party said the other day: "A generation ago it didn't make much difference what one's chums did, whether they went into the army or the City or publishing or whatever; but now it's a make-or-break decision."'

Couples from the old bourgeoisie worried about how much they needed to earn to become like their parents – an ambition which would have appalled them when they were teenagers but was now looking more desirable by the day. What was the cost of a house in a sought-after area, a manageable mortgage, regular foreign holidays and places in smart schools for their

children? The breathtaking annual income of at least
£250,000, and preferably £500,000, the *Sunday Times* told
them in early 2007. If they wanted to be truly rich and afford
the central London town house with Britart bric-a-brac on
the walls, holiday homes in exotic resorts, access to a private
jet and accounts at the chi-chi stores, they would need to
make at least £2.5 million – preferably £10 million. Rachel
Johnson, who reported the findings, wasn't exactly a poor
little match girl, she was the sister of Boris Johnson, who
became the first Tory mayor of London in 2008, but she
concluded:

> When I look around my normal, as in non-City, contemporaries
> they are all working their socks off, hamster-wheeling, both the
> husband and the wife (only one in 10 women of working age
> can now afford the luxury of staying home unwaged to raise her
> children). They are raiding their parents' nest eggs to keep their
> heads above water, remortgaging their houses to pay the school
> fees and, if they go abroad at all, they head off to eco-turismo
> communities in Sicily where several families share a swimming
> pool (if there is one) and all eat pasta together. As the super-rich
> are getting richer all the time, they are driving up the prices of
> the things that we middle classes used to be able to afford on
> one income, but now can't manage with two.

In a wicked world full of suffering, the complaints of the shabby
genteel were not pressing concerns for busy people with limited
supplies of compassion. Nevertheless, I thought them worth
listening to because I have found that spectators on the edges
provide the best descriptions. They have the access to a privileged milieu, and can see what outsiders cannot; but unlike the
truly privileged, who socialise only with fellow insiders, they are
not lulled by routine into thinking that the freakish is normal.
In the case of the bubble world of 2007, the dazzled and envious

commentaries of those on its margins also performed the essential public service of blowing away consoling illusions.

THE GREATEST PROPAGANDA success of its rich men was to convince the rest of society that they were not plutocrats but 'middle class'. Indeed, not only were the rich meant to be middle class, so was everyone else. The working class, once the object of implausible hopes on the left and unreasonable fears on the right, and the upper class, once the object of surly contempt on the left and abject deference on the right, disappeared from the national conversation. 'We're all middle class now,' declared the media, and hardly anyone noticed that it was talking twaddle.

The proletarianisation of manners explains why. The old ruling class was almost a caste. It had separate schools, separate tastes, separate newspapers and, occasionally, separate countries when its members were sent to govern the Empire. When the Empire fell, so did its legitimacy. The last upper-class prime minister was Sir Alec Douglas-Home. Educated at Eton, he was the only British prime minister ever to play first-class cricket. He ruled briefly from 1963 to 1964, before being shoved aside by Harold Wilson, a new man, who had not been born into privilege, and promised to forge a meritocratic Britain in the 'white heat' of technological revolution. The Tory Party responded by promoting meritocrats of its own. Margaret Thatcher, a provincial grocer's daughter, so preferred clever Jews to the landed gentry that traditional Conservatives moaned that she had 'more Estonians than Etonians' in her cabinet. When her colleagues deposed her in 1990, they decided that Douglas Hurd's Eton education made him too aristocratic to be her successor, and elected John Major, the son of a former trapeze artiste. Educated at Rutlish Grammar School, he was the only British prime minister ever to run away from the circus to become a politician.

The producers of popular culture confined aristocrats to the society pages or pilloried them as embodiments of all that was devious and dangerous. In a time of multiculturalism, they supplied the solitary stock character Hollywood felt it could denigrate safely. The Germans were long gone and the Soviet empire had fallen. The West was under attack from radical Islamists, but writers and directors worried that it was 'Islamophobic' to be beastly about them. The English upper class filled the gap in the market. You only had to hear a cut-glass accent in a Hollywood film or British television thriller to know it belonged to the villain.

The new rich never aroused the same class hatred as their predecessors because they lacked caste distinctions and seemed more at ease with the modern world. The bombastic figure of Philip Green, the shopping tycoon, exemplified their ordinariness. His fortune was beyond the imagination of most – in 2005, he paid himself a dividend of £1.17 billion, the largest payout to an individual in British corporate history. As impossible for the masses to emulate was his ability to avoid paying the same taxes as the little people who shopped or worked in his stores by ferreting away much of his wealth in the Monaco tax haven. But his tastes, like those of most of the rest of the new elite, were those of the common man. For his son's bar mitzvah in 2005, he spent £4 million on a three-day party for his guests and hired Destiny's Child to serenade them. A few years before, for his fiftieth birthday, Sir Philip had hired Tom Jones and Rod Stewart to perform at another three-day party, a toga one this time. On his fifty-fifth in 2007, George Michael and Jennifer Lopez did the honours. Given the same resources, the overwhelming majority of his compatriots would have paid to have Stewart, Jones and Michael croon for them if they were old, or to have Lopez and Destiny's Child impress their friends if they were young. Culturally, the rich were no longer different from you and me. With the exception of the intelligentsia, 'we' could all seem the same.

To pretend, however, that 'we were all middle class' was wishful thinking when anyone who looked at Britain could see that 'we' were more segregated than at any time since the early twentieth century. At the bottom were the poor. Journalists and economists put much effort into maintaining that poverty no longer existed in Britain. The argument's propaganda value lay in its ability to persuade the wealthy that they need not allow twinges of guilt to spoil the enjoyment of their riches – a remote possibility, I grant you, but one which free-market enthusiasts felt the need to warn against.

But although widespread hunger had been unknown since the thirties, the bottom 25 per cent of households, who could not afford to save £10 a month or pay for an annual holiday, were hard up. Those at the very bottom of the heap, living on an income of £8,600 or less, and unable to afford even £3 for a school trip without cutting back on food or heating, were poor by the standards of the rest of society.

The poor appear in these pages cooking the dinners and looking after the children of the wealthy, or cleaning up after the bankers and journalists of Canary Wharf. Inevitably, their role in the crash was to be its victims when their jobs went – assuming they had jobs, that is: the government was content to leave many vegetating on unemployment or incapacity benefit.

On the next rung up was the 50 per cent of the population which Danny Dorling, a cartographer of the English class system at Sheffield University, described as the 'normal' British. They had single incomes of £13,400 to £29,600 and joint incomes if they were in couples generally running into the forty thousands. They could afford school trips for their children and annual holidays. They also had the money to play the apparently unlosable housing lottery. For all their desire to be owner-occupiers, no previous generation would have described them as truly middle class. They were what we used to call the respectable working and lower middle classes.

The top 25 per cent of society was wealthy: couples with a joint income of more than £60,000, and a mortgage on a house whose price was rising faster than their salaries – faster, indeed, than they dreamed possible. As the complaining upper-middle class proved, even couples bringing in £100,000 to £150,000 did not feel rich, although those who complained about how hard it was to pay school fees were among the richest in the land. (A mere 7 per cent of parents educated their children privately.) Only the super-rich surpassed them. They did not worry about paying school fees, but, as Dorling nicely put it, 'worried about being kidnapped'.

With China pumping out cheap goods, the standard rate of retail price inflation, and the interest rates that tracked it, stayed low. With Chinese savers pouring their capital into the international money markets, anyone who could make a half-credible case for a loan found a receptive audience among bank and building society managers.

A glut of cheap money produced rocketing asset prices, and a new generation of investors discovered the wonder of leverage. Everyone from bankers to young house-hunters could borrow cut-price to play the financial or property markets. When they sold, their asset had shot up in value while the size of their debt had merely increased with its interest rate. Few thought about the possibility of their assets shrinking in value while the size of their debt continued to increase with its interest rate. The horror of deflation was yet to come. For if the politicians, the speculators in the investment banks and the rich did not see what was about to hit them, neither did the once staid high-street bank managers – or all the eager customers who grabbed their loans.

THERE WERE PROPERTY and credit bubbles in America, Australia, much of Europe and Russia. Britain's was up there with the best of them. Although everyone wanted to blame the

Americans for the crash when it came – blaming Americans was what Europeans did best, after all – house prices rose faster in Britain than in the US, as did personal debt. While American household indebtedness reached 140 per cent, British indebtedness grew to 169 per cent of disposable income – every £1 coming into the average home had to service £1.69 of debt.

In August 2007, Britain passed a grim landmark. Consumer debts in the form of mortgages, loans and credit card bills totalled £1.35 trillion and overtook the entire gross domestic product of the country, which stood at £1.33 trillion. To put it another way, the British owed more than the value of the output of every office, factory, farm, quarry, mine and fishery in the land – and that was before economists included the immense debts of the public sector and business, which took the sum of Britain's borrowings to three times annual economic output.

We were a bankrupt nation.

Don't fret, said conventional economists, most personal debt is secured against homes whose prices are heading heavenwards. It is not folly to borrow to secure a piece of the action. Nor were existing 'homeowners' adding to their burdens if they went back into the debt market by remortgaging to pay for holidays or cars or their children's stay at university. They were 'releasing equity' in their property, as the jargon of the day had it: receiving a share of profits that were rightfully theirs.

You can understand why heads were turned. By the peak of the bubble, the price of the average home was six times the average wage. Britain had never seen the like before. Even at the top of the last housing boom in 1989, average prices peaked at 4.8 times average salaries.

If they already had a halfway reasonable job, or were university students who looked to the bank as if they would have one soon, the British were flooded with offers of loans, credit cards and store cards. The managers of Northern Rock, whose roots lay in the mutual and self-help values of the building society movement of the Victorian North-East, abandoned prudential principles and hosed their customers with money.

Those who did not have the £250,000 income they needed to be truly wealthy in 2007 had no need to feel hard done by. They could still take a mortgage of up to five, six, seven, eight times their income, add in credit card and bank loans and live as if they were wealthy in executive homes with Porsche Cayennes in their drives.

Lending at this level was fantastically reckless behaviour for creditor and debtor alike when the few building societies, which had not taken advantage of Margaret Thatcher's offer to turn themselves into banks, stipulated that three times salary was the safe upper limit. Like other lenders, Northern Rock also gave mortgages on 125 per cent of the value of a property. The banks' generosity had the advantage of allowing borrowers to pay off credit card bills and have money left over to kit out their homes. It had the disadvantage of immediately placing debtors in negative equity.

Few cared. Houses had provided a phenomenal rate of return for a phenomenally long time. The Halifax bank estimated that between 1996 and 2006 the average house price rose by 10.6 per cent per annum (from £62,453 to £179,425). Investing in homes was more lucrative than investing in the stock market, which grew at 4.6 per cent per annum, and the returns outstripped the 2.6 per cent rise in retail price inflation fourfold.

Acquiring the capital to lever yourself on to the escalator seemed the wise option. And without doubt it is always wise to jump in and out of a bubble market, as long as buyers get the timing right and remember the cynical investor's advice to sell on to 'the greater fool' before it is too late. It was not only the rich who benefited, many ordinary families made large profits that transformed their lives and status by playing the property market and cashing in before the crash came.

The media trumpeted their good fortune, but paid less attention to the casualties, whose number was growing long before the markets turned. Journalists, entertainers and artists were hopeless at dramatising their suffering, and many revelled in it.

By the twenty-first century, the politically correct had placed racism and homophobia off limits. The culture industries compensated by turning on underprivileged whites with all the suspicion and condescension they displayed towards the old upper class. Wealthy media executives commissioned shows such as *Little Britain* and *Shameless* in which the white poor were white trash: stupid teenage girls who got pregnant without a thought for how they would care for their babies; alcoholic fathers with delinquent children who wallowed in the illicit pleasures of drugs and sex, which the taxpaying viewers could enjoy only in moderation because they had to go to work in the morning. The poor were the grasping inhabitants of a parasite paradise, scrounging off the cozened middle classes in television comedy, or freaks to be mocked on the British versions of the *Jerry Springer Show*.

There was truth in the stereotype – for there is truth in all stereotypes. Television comedy producers could point to estates with families that had not worked for generations, living at other people's expense on the edge of the law. The producers of the reality shows could say that they did not force their freaks to go on air. Contestants and guests willingly played their parts, hamming up their performances for all they were worth to secure a fleeting moment of fame. The failure of the BBC and Channel 4 was not their abandonment of residual notions of pity for the victims of an increasingly harsh financial system, but their lack of imagination. They did not have the intelligence to realise the fragility of their own and their scoffing viewers' lives. They never said, 'Don't laugh too loud because *one day you may be poor too*.' In the broadcasters' version of the make-believe world, the gap between living in the house with the Northern Rock mortgage and being on the council house waiting list was unbridgeable. Brute economic forces did not push people into poverty. The poor were poor because of their own depravity and weakness. They had chosen to be the way they were.

The idea that there would soon come a time when hundreds of thousands would face penury through no fault of their own was beyond them.

The high arts occasionally played the same games with race and class. In the 2007 film adaptation of Monica Ali's *Brick Lane*, cast and crew successfully conveyed the novel's sensitive portrayal of the struggles of a young Bangladeshi wife in London's East End, but could show her white neighbours only as neo-Nazis or obese and tattooed grotesques. In general, though, literary writers and film-makers had little interest in deprivation and wealth, and failed to see the connections between the two. Raised in public sector families, educated in universities and on creative writing courses, and working in day jobs in academia, they were the artistic equivalents of Westminster's political class: narrow professionals with few outside interests and fewer experiences of life beyond their trade. The only part most of them played in the debates of the day was to mouth the standard liberal platitudes and applaud when actors at agitprop theatres told them that Tony Blair and George W. Bush were very bad men.

No writer is obliged to write a state-of-England novel, but so few wanted to that the critic D. J. Taylor complained in 2007 of 'the fatal detachment of the modern "literary" writer from the society that he or she presumes to reflect'.

The markets were on the longest run in history, creating greed, envy, barely disguised sexual competition, riches and ruin. The decisions made in Canary Wharf and Wall Street affected everyone, high and low. But Taylor concluded that when it came to talking about 'globalisation, the rise of the international money markets, the creation of a virtual economic world stratospherically removed from the processes of ordinary life – the number of contemporary writers capable of understanding their complexity, much less rendering them into fictional form, could be accommodated behind a very small table'.

In short, there was no Dickens for the twenty-first century to bring to life the stunted aspirations and stultifying fears of the leveraged economy. Indebtedness became an everyday misery, quietly endured by stragglers the circus that had briefly enchanted, then left behind. You found them lamenting their folly and cursing the banks on radio phone-ins or in Internet chat rooms rather than on the Booker Prize shortlist or television schedules.

'Being young, naive and overwhelmed with the opportunity of all this cash, I took up almost every offer that was thrown my way – much to my deepest regret,' wrote a young woman from Liverpool on a BBC Net forum. 'I see now that I was extremely stupid, yet the way the interest-free overdrafts and "don't pay anything for 12 months" was sold to me, it was hard to resist. I finished university this year and I now have extreme amounts of debt. I let my overdrafts get overdrawn, and the charges have amounted to thousands. At the same time, my credit card charges have amounted to hundreds. And these are just a small example of the problem I am in. I am 22 and have been advised to declare bankruptcy.'

Others told how they had lost their homes, or how they were trying and failing to repay hundreds of pounds a month while living on benefits. A woman from Southampton gave a little sketch of the giddy world of banking when she said, 'I'm only 21 years old and already in more than £10,000 worth of debt. I even work for a bank! I just kept increasing my loans and over-drafts thinking that I could pay it back in the future, but now it has got to the point that I can't afford to have a social life. I'm on anti-depressants now to help me with the stress. Anyone out there that is just turning 18 and can now get loans and credit cards – don't! If you haven't got it, don't spend it!'

EVERY BUBBLE PRODUCES a self-serving ideology. In 1999, financial analysts who proclaimed that the Net was creating a 'New Economy' pumped up dotcom shares. The boom that led to the Great Crash of 1929 was cheered on by economists who reassured investors that they were living in a 'New Era' dominated by highly trained and ruthlessly efficient 'scientific managers'.

Equally fanciful dreams preceded the Great Crash of 2008. The most popular came from the American journalist James Surowiecki. In his 2004 *The Wisdom of Crowds* he claimed that diverse groups of individuals independently reaching their own decisions were more likely to find the right answers than experts, however well qualified. His democratic argument fitted neatly with the explosion of user-generated sites on the Internet, which had the potential to allow anyone to publish their thoughts on anything to an audience, which in theory extended to everyone in the world with access to a computer. All users were equal on the Net. Politicians, academics, journalists and specialists could no longer monopolise media news, as they had done in the days when a few publishers controlled the outlets. Everyman could be his own expert. Everywoman could be her own publisher. Jimmy Wales echoed Surowiecki when he declared that he had no more faith in the knowledge of a Harvard professor than in a high-school kid. On Wales's Wikipedia site both the professor and the kid had the same intellectual authority, which, as the critic of techno-utopianism, Andrew Keen, pointed out, was 'really the same as saying that neither had any authority at all'. Wales was also a true believer in the free market and a disciple of the ultra-capitalist Ayn Rand. The theory of wise crowds not only chimed with the flightiness of the Web 2.0 boosters, but also provided ideological support to the bubble market.

Surowiecki recognised that bubbles posed problems for his belief in collective wisdom – as did, he might have added, mass panics, teen crazes, religious hysterias, superstitious fears, tribal loyalties and outbreaks of belligerent nationalism – and tried to adjust his theory. His refined version boiled down to 'crowds are wise – except when they're not'.

Unsurprisingly, no one took any notice. Popular capitalism was the spirit of the age. Politicians and central bankers bowed before the market's judgements. If tens of millions of people independently decided to take out loans, if tens of thousands of bank managers and mortgage brokers calculated that there was no risk in lending to them, and if thousands of dealers in finance houses packaged their debts and offered them as lucrative mortgage-backed securities, what right did they have to gainsay them?

The market was not mad. It was the wisdom of the masses in motion.

Believers is wise crowds and rational investors forgot that the human race can be pushed into speculative frenzies by emotions that are far from wise: the herd instinct, the appeal of acquisitiveness, the fear of missing out, the envious desire to keep up with friends and neighbours and the seductive temptation to gamble and win.

I learned how far crowd psychology had taken over in 2007 when I talked to Capital Economics, a hitherto sceptical London consultancy. In 2005, it had warned that house prices were unsustainable. First-time buyers could no longer afford to buy. Developers were throwing up blocks of flimsy flats on brownfield sites, not as homes for people to live in but as casino chips for investors who had taken out 1 million buy-to-let mortgages. The folly had to stop, Capital Economics declared. But the folly did not stop.

Instead of reaching the conclusion that the fall would be all the harder when it came, they recanted. When I asked whether prices could keep on rising, the reply came, 'You're going to think I'm utterly insane, but they can.' Immigrants were still heading for a booming Britain. In the City, 4000 bankers and traders had received bonuses of £1 million or more. The law of supply and demand, low interest rates and the City's special place in the global market guaranteed a prosperous future. The profits from property had overwhelmed the prophets of doom.

In June 2007, Professor Stephen Nickell, the chairman of the government's Housing and Planning Advice Unit, predicted that the price of the average home would rise to £300,000 and that the average first-time buyer would have to obtain a mortgage ten times the size of their annual income.

Three months later, Northern Rock crashed and panicking depositors queued outside a British bank for the first time since Overend, Gurney & Company went under in 1866.

Those rogue economists, who have never believed that crowds are wise, have a name for the emotion that surges through investors as the market reaches its zenith: *euphoria*. It builds gradually. After a long period without a recession, speculation grows. Belief in free markets or corruption stops politicians intervening while the damage can be contained. Allegedly elitist financial experts do not stand aloof from the crowd, as Wales and Surowiecki imagined, but prove their democratic credentials by joining the mob and egging it on. Finally, as everyone who can piles in to take a share of leveraged profits, swindles proliferate, eye-watering debts become normal and, in the words of the economic historian Edward Chancellor, a carnival atmosphere descends. 'The spirit of speculation is anarchic, irreverent and anti-hierarchical,' he wrote in 1999.

It loves freedom, detests cant and abhors restrictions. From the tulip colleges of the 17th century through to the Internet investment clubs of the late 20th century, speculation has established itself as the most demotic of economic activities. Although profoundly secular, speculation is not simply about greed. The essence of speculation remains a Utopian yearning for freedom and equality which counterbalances the drab rationalistic materialism of the modern economic system with its many inequalities of wealth. Throughout its many manifestations the speculative mania has always been, and remains to this day, the Carnival of Capitalism, a Feast of Fools.

No one who saw the roaring boys of the City in the early twenty-first century, or watched the gurgling presenters of the 'property porn' shows, could doubt him.*

On this reading, all bubble markets are the same. The bust of 2008 was no different to the South Sea Bubble of 1720, which ruined early Georgian London, or the railway share mania of 1845, or the Great Crash of 1929, or the slower unwinding of the Japanese market in the nineties. 'Progress is cumulative in science, but cyclical in finance,' wrote the economic analyst James Grant in 1993, and there is a strong temptation to respond to the crash of our day with banalities about there being nothing new under the sun.

The politicians, the speculators, the bankers and the crowds of mad investors did not see the crash coming, but then their predecessors did not realise that the South Sea Bubble was about to burst. What's new?

---

* When her world fell apart, Kirstie Allsopp, who hosted *Location, Location, Location*, the most boosterish of all the property programmes, could not accept that her assumptions had been faulty but instead saw a conspiracy of doom-mongers. 'In recent weeks I've been described as a "property porn queen" in the *New Statesman*, sniped at on the pages of the *Guardian* and lambasted by *Panorama* for excessively inflating house prices. Some of the recent gloomy headlines make me suspect that all the journalists in the country have sold up and are doing everything in their power to cause a property house price crash so that they can buy at rock bottom.'

Not much sounds a fair answer, but it pays no attention to the nagging difference. This time around, a left-wing government ignored a monstrous bubble.

Its behaviour needs explaining because, contrary to cliché, 2007 saw something new under the sun.

LOOKING BACK AT the ruins, I can see faults in my writings from the bubble years. I have never been interested in consumerism, never seen shopping as anything other than a chore, and I suppose I underestimated the happiness the boom brought to many. In theory, I know that distress brings no good and poverty inspires no nobility. In practice, I find misery interesting and contentment dull. Like most writers, I instinctively believe Tolstoy's assertion that while 'all happy families are alike; each unhappy family is unhappy in its own way' – and do not want to remind myself that happiness comes in many forms while desolation in its final stages is grindingly uniform.

Therefore, and in fairness, I ought to balance what follows by acknowledging that the period this book covers was not all bad. The British were richer than they had ever been. Between 2003 and 2007, national income per head grew faster in Britain than in any other developed country. The formerly privileged complained of downward mobility, but the debt bubble, like every other bubble, created upward mobility and allowed City boys from humble homes to leap the fences of old England. I also accept that if money could not buy the British happiness, it at least allowed them to be miserable in greater comfort. We lived longer and enjoyed greater access to education and healthcare. We were free to read what we wanted, sleep with whom we wanted, think what we wanted and live where we wanted and how we wanted. Our Labour leaders had reason to be proud. They could walk into any town, see new schools and surgeries, and think 'we built those'. They did not damn the flood of wealth in London, but used it to revitalise Britain. The boom brought the best of modern urban architecture to once forlorn provincial cities. Manchester was a grim northern town when I grew up there in the seventies. Birmingham had had the life beaten out of it by the collapse of manufacturing industry when I took my first job there in the eighties. The Labour years transformed both for the better.

I make no further apologies for the tone of this book, however. Writing in 1931, Frederick Allen Lewis rightly feared that people would one day think of the Jazz Age of the twenties as the good old days and 'would forget, perhaps, the frustrated hopes that followed the [First World] War, the aching disillusionment of the hard-boiled era, its oily scandals, its spiritual paralysis, the harshness of its gaiety'.

I hope that no one will forget that the years before 2008 had oily scandals and aching disillusionments of their own. Even before the crash, it was obvious to me that for all its benefits globalisation was battering Britain. As the nation-state disintegrated, we did not know what to call ourselves, 'British', 'English', 'Scots', 'Welsh'.* The immigrants brought in by the boom changed the country, and neither the right nor the left understood how to think clearly about coping with the concomitant social tensions. Increased wealth and better health created citizens who seemed to believe that death was optional and the human condition escapable. They made impossibly authoritarian demands for the state to follow the precautionary principle and guarantee that they would never suffer accidents or harm.

Above all else towered the misery brought by asset-price inflation, as housing, one of life's necessities, became nonsensically dear.

* I get around the problem of deciding when to say 'English' and 'England' and when 'British' and 'Britain' by using whichever sounds best in the context of the sentence. I won't pretend that this is a solution which stands up to rigorous scrutiny.

London was as close to being the financial centre of globalisation as anywhere in the world could claim to be. With the City accounting for a fifth of the British economy, the political left cut a deal.

I don't want to accuse it of 'selling out'. However shamelessly Tony Blair and Peter Mandelson welcomed the super-rich into Downing Street and accepted invitations to their Mediterranean villas in return, however cravenly Gordon Brown capitulated to demands from billionaires to provide them with privileges, the paradox of the 1997 Labour government was that it was at once a left- and a right-wing administration. It wanted a huge public works programme. It aimed to redistribute enormous amounts of wealth. To achieve both these desirable goals, it made a bargain with the markets.

All right, the political left said, we will accept extremes of wealth we once denounced as obscene. We will embrace your speculators and not drive them overseas with tough regulation. If the authorities overseeing the Wall Street markets or the Frankfurt bourse become too inquisitive, capital will always be able to find a sanctuary from scrutiny here. Nor will we restrict the operations of financial services, even though they are entrapping our supporters in levels of debt that the puritan in us finds frightening. We will concede all this, if in return you will give us the tax revenues which will allow us to the build the new schools and hospitals, and increase the incomes of our struggling constituents.

For all its virtuous intentions, the political left was living off the proceeds of loose financial morals. Prostituting itself, to be blunt.

The brightest and the best graduates went to work for City firms. By 2007, politicians of all colours regarded them as their intellectual superiors, modern alchemists who could conjure gold out of lines of flickering figures on a screen. Ken Livingstone, the allegedly left-wing mayor of London, genuflected before the cardinals of the money market with as much reverence as any Tory. If he had had his way, London would have become a Shanghai-on-Thames, its skyline punctured by gleaming towers for the bankers and dealers he assumed would always be landing at Heathrow.

The anti-capitalist movement had nothing interesting to say about high finance, but spitefully concentrated on opposing free trade, the one neoliberal policy that raised the living standards of the world's poor. Everyone else was lulled into acquiescence by the success of globalisation. Young radicals from Gordon Brown's generation did not abandon socialism because they 'sold out', they abandoned it because they saw that socialist societies produced stagnant economies, along with some of the worst crimes in human history, while market economies not only worked but produced the revenues social democrats could use for leftish ends. The British economy had been growing since the collapse of the Soviet Union in the early nineties. Like so many others, Britain's social democratic leaders came to take growth for granted and forgot that no one can abolish the business cycle.

In his March 2007 budget, Gordon Brown described a happy land of 'rising employment and rising investment; continuing low inflation, and low interest and mortgage rates'. The 'longest period of economic stability and sustained growth in our country's history' was marching on, bringing 'prosperity and fairness for Britain's families ... We will never return to the old boom and bust!'

In the same month, the International Monetary Fund issued a prophetic warning. By encouraging the UK economy to become dependent on international financial markets, it said, Brown ran the risk of a global financial contagion infecting a country that was already drowning in debt and in no fit state to cope with hard times.

The government took no notice. As late as April 2008, Labour MPs fell about laughing when the Liberal Democrats presented a motion to the Commons warning of imminent disaster. 'The Liberal Democrat motion has been much commented on, possibly because it reads like the storyboard for *Apocalypse Now*, or perhaps even *Bleak House*,' guffawed Angela Eagle, a Treasury minister. 'According to the motion, we are facing an "extreme bubble in the housing market" and the "risk of recession", and we must "act to prevent mass home repossessions". Fortunately, for all of us, however, that colourful and lurid fiction has no real bearing on the macro-economic reality. Now that we have had *Apocalypse Now* and *Bleak House*, I am going to talk about *An Inconvenient Truth*, which is that the economy is strong and stable.'

The spivvery of the City afflicted the political left as severely as its blind optimism. Early on in the Labour government, I had an argument with one of Robin Cook's aides about a project I thought a waste of public money. I cannot remember the details but I cannot forget his incredulity at meeting an apparent leftist who worried about value for money for taxpayers. The left allowed its supporters to condemn businesses that exploited the vulnerable. In 2006, Farepak, a hamper company that collected monthly payments from humble families saving for a Christmas treat, collapsed. The left knew instinctively that it was wrong for its capitalists to run off with other people's money. They did not need to have it explained to them. They felt it in their bones. When employers underpaid their workers, the left again had no trouble in condemning them. But when the state took taxes on pain of imprisonment and then threw them away, the left treated other people's money as casually as a Lehman Brothers dealer. So accepting of profligacy and confident of future growth did Gordon Brown become, he saved nothing during the boom years to help Britain through a recession. When the crisis came, his country was naked before the storm.

And so in an unprecedented manner, and with not wholly bad intentions, the left in power went along with a lawless market, and only after it went down did it show the boldness of true social democrats by taking over much of the banking system. It left it too late because while the bubble lasted it did not want to think what would happen if the City fell apart. Failure was an unimaginable eventuality because, in truth, no one on the left or right had the faintest idea how else a country in which agriculture formed a tiny part of the economy and manufacturing industry had withered could make a living. The political left might have tightened the regulation of the banks and the City, but the financiers did not seem to be joking when they said that they would respond by emigrating and leaving the economy in the lurch. It might have given the Bank of England the authority to raise interest rates to stop the growth of debt and the rise in house price inflation, but the economic consequences would have seemed too severe to contemplate. By 2007, the only sectors of the economy that were booming were retail and leisure, funded by consumer debt, financial services, dedicated to getting consumers further into debt, housing, bought with yet more debt, and state spending, based on levels of government debt which made borrowers from Northern Rock seem like paragons of responsibility. If they brought down the debt economy, what else could they put in its place?

By the end, Labour politicians were boxed in. Even if they had realised the danger Britain was in – and there is no evidence that they did – the price of changing course would have struck them as unacceptably high. They couldn't challenge the status quo, until the status quo changed and challenged them.

Politicians and pundits are already providing many reasons for England's crash, and there is merit in blaming the Bush administration, Gordon Brown's catastrophic complacency and global financial forces beyond any government's control. Yet too few commentators could say why the British left's recession looked like being worse than recessions in comparable developed countries.

The best answer is also the simplest: England crashed because England did not have a Plan B.

THE LIBERAL INTELLIGENTSIA that dominated Britain's cultural life as completely as Labour politicians dominated its government, might have reminded the politicians of the need to stick to leftish principles. But, and here I come to the second theme of this book, liberal England's dereliction of duty surpassed that of its political leaders. The roots of its recklessness are to be found in another unprecedented feature of the 2008 crash.

Previous stock market crises occurred in times of peace. The South Sea Bubble began four years after the end of England's long war against Louis XIV's France in 1715. The railway and the canal manias flourished in the Pax Britannica after Waterloo. The destruction of Wall Street shares in 1929 came a decade after the end of the First World War, while the Japanese bubble peaked once the cold war was over.

Peace breeds booms. Politicians grow lazy and no longer feel the need to stop speculation before it imperils the national interest. Their citizens, meanwhile, have nothing to distract them from getting and spending.

The crash of 2008 broke the pattern. Britain and America were at war in Afghanistan and Iraq, and had been for years. For if the chaos in the markets represented the end of the liberal economic dreams of the era of globalisation, a dark shift in world politics had dashed liberal political hopes long before.

When the Berlin Wall fell in 1989, it was possible to believe that Immanuel Kant's dream of enlightened nations living in 'perpetual peace' was at last being realised. Liberalism in the form of democracy, open government, free markets, common security and respect for human rights seemed the best and only way for societies to grow and prosper. Francis Fukuyama proposed that history was over, and although his many critics mocked and misunderstood him, he was making what seemed an unanswerable argument. Certainly, if a gang of totalitarian fanatics in Afghanistan wanted to order their territory according to the barbaric principles of medieval religion, it could. Fukuyama was not saying that every society had to be liberal; simply that if societies wished to be successful, liberalism was the only model on offer.

Twenty years on, his confidence lay in tatters. The most rapidly advancing power was China, whose dictators combined repression with economic success. Individual dissidents protested, but there was little doubt that the majority of the Chinese went along with their rulers' mixture of nationalism, capitalism and authoritarianism. Russia, which had seemed likely to become a normal nation, turned its back on the Europe of human rights conferences and limited government, and embraced autocracy. Liberal Russians protested, but again only optimists could doubt that most were happy with Putin's plans to rebuild the empire of the tsars and commissars. Meanwhile radical Islam, the most psychopathically anti-liberal ideology since Nazism, was not confined to the mountains of Afghanistan, but swept the Muslim world. Although polite commentators maintained that only a 'tiny minority' of Muslims supported clerical fascism, it was embarrassingly obvious to honest reporters that a far wider section of the Muslim population was unwilling to oppose it.

The American strategic thinker Robert Kagan encapsulated the shift from the late twentieth to early twenty-first century by putting himself in the shoes of an aspiring dictator. In the nineties, a potential strongman would have thought autocracy a bad bet. Everyone believed that you could not combine dictatorship with economic growth, and if you did not have economic growth, your power as an autocrat would fade, leaving you at the mercy of your enemies. Twenty-years on, Kagan continued, well, the world was looking a *much* better place.

The Chinese and the Russians are demonstrating that economic growth and strong autocracy can coexist perfectly happily. Now in Russia's case it's mostly about oil, but it's not entirely about oil. In China's case, it's not at all about oil. China clearly is an increasingly market economy; it's an increasingly capitalist system but nevertheless with rigid political controls. And the bargain that's being offered to both of these peoples is a very old bargain. It is the bargain that says, 'you can live your life, you can have whatever private life you want, no one's going to come and in and tell you what to read or how to think (within certain limits), you can make money, you can prosper … just keep your nose out of politics. And if you get your nose involved in politics, we'll cut off your nose.' If the money is flowing, I think that's a bargain people will take for a very long time.

He might have added that Islamists and other apocalyptic sects did not even need a successful economy to hold the world in thrall. The growing availability of weapons of mass destruction meant that the twenty-first century would have to live with the nightmare of relatively small bands of psychopathic men obtaining and detonating armaments that had previously been the sole possession of superpowers.

No one could have expected liberal England to applaud the thundering market and its inequalities of wealth. But outsiders might have expected it to support the promise that human rights and democracy offered the world, and oppose the enemies of freedom when they attempted to roll them back. In their own countries, no one shouted louder against real or actual diminutions of personal liberty, yet when confronted with ultra-reactionary movements and dictatorial regimes, liberals recommended surrender.

The first years of the twenty-first century were a second 'low, dishonest decade': a time when the BBC was more likely to indulge supporters of oppression than Fox News; when embattled feminists from the Muslim world were more likely to be belittled by writers from the *New York Review of Books* than the editor of the *Daily Mail*; when you were more likely to find anti-Semitism by looking to the left rather than the right; and when the general secretary of Amnesty International was more likely to denigrate human rights as white, middle-class indulgences than the general secretary of the Communist Party of China.

Few progressive movements worthy of the name could survive in such a poisonous environment, and few did.

Although liberal England liked nothing better than condemning left-wing politicians for being cowards, it was no braver than its leaders. Labour in power failed to deal with the thundering market because it could not bring itself to face the economic consequences of a necessary confrontation. Liberal England stayed silent as tyranny swept by because it too wanted the quiet life.

Normally, left-wing eras end because the left loses itself in ideological excess and careers off into the margins of politics. The left of the early twenty-first century was an exception. It failed not because it was left-wing but because in crucial respects it was not left-wing enough. It forgot the lessons of the Great Depression and failed to regulate runaway markets. It forgot the best of its achievements of the twentieth century and failed to defend them from the assault of the twenty-first.

As economies crash and governments make colossal interventions to save them, it might seem reasonable to predict a revival of the better side of the left-wing tradition. I hope to see it come, not least because social democrats have the best answers to today's financial and environmental crises. But I won't pretend that many obstacles remain in the way of a return to reputable politics. Liberal opinion went wilder in Britain than in any other European country. Although some liberals will 'recover their senses slowly, and one by one', as Charles Mackay predicted, others will be stuck in their ideological prisons for the rest of their lives. Meanwhile, although Labour responded well to the crash, it cannot escape responsibility for failing to see the crisis coming and may well pay the political price for its failure.

I cannot think of a more revealing measure of that failure than the transformation of the English aristocracy from pantomime villains and chinless wonders into viable leaders of the nation. At the end of the longest period of left-wing government in British history, the Etonians were back for the first time since the fall of the Empire. A battered public seemed willing to embrace its old ruling class with something approaching relief.

A NOTE ON THE TEXT

To paraphrase Norma Desmond in *Sunset Boulevard*, 'the newspapers got small' during my career in journalism. In selecting works for this book, I have not only tidied up ugly sentences, but also added material I could not fit into the original articles at the time of writing. Since my last collection of essays, I have published two full-length books – *Pretty Straight Guys* and *What's Left?* I have tried to avoid overlap, and the only large repetition I have allowed is in 'Vänster Om, Höger Om!', the second half of which appeared in the postscript to the paperback edition of *What's Left?*

Everyone is in debt now and I am no exception. I must thank Robin Harvie of 4th Estate for suggesting this book and being a model editor and Natasha Fairweather of the A. P. Watt literary agency for making everything possible. No writer can work without editors who will publish him and I am also indebted to John Mulholland of the *Observer*, Jason Cowley of the *New Statesman*, Daniel Johnson of *Standpoint*, Veronica Wadley of the *Evening Standard*, Mat Smith formerly of *Arena*, Johan Lundberg of *Axess* and Kenneth Baer of *Democracy*. 'The Reasonableness of Ranters' originally appeared in *Time Out*'s

1000 Books to Change Your Life. The quotes from Max Frisch's *Arsonists* come from the new English translation by Alistair Beaton, which Ramin Gray directed at London's Royal Court in November 2007. The lyrics by Joe Strummer come from 'White Man in Hammersmith Palais', written by The Clash. Francis Wheen talked me through problems with the text.

As ever, all errors of taste and judgement remain the sole responsibility of the author.

PART 1

The Classless Society

'Fortunately in England, at any rate, education produces no effect whatsoever. If it did, it would prove a serious threat to the upper classes, and probably lead to acts of violence in Grosvenor Square.'

OSCAR WILDE,
The Importance of Being Earnest, 1895

Holding on to Nurse

NINETEEN SEVENTY-TWO was a good year for Jonathan Gathorne-Hardy to publish *The Rise and Fall of the British Nanny*. At the time it seemed reasonable to predict that the institution was dying, and with it relationships that readers living in the nuclear households of the day found unnatural. They could join him in looking back with amusement and a little revulsion at aristocrats in the mould of Winston Churchill, who had greater feelings of tenderness for his Nanny Everest than for his parents. She adored him and called him 'my lamb'. When she died, Churchill said she 'had been my dearest and most intimate friend during the whole of the 20 years I had lived'. He was not an exception. Gathorne-Hardy said that 'the annals of nanny literature are filled with desperate and brutal partings' as carer and child were pulled apart by market forces or parental whims.

The nannies who shouted, 'there are three sorts of sin: little sins, bigger sins and *taking off your shoes without undoing the laces*' at the children of the upper-middle classes looked as if they were going the way of the Empire. In 1972, the second wave of feminism had yet to roar in, and most women brought up their own children. The high rates of taxation of the post-war social-democratic settlement meant that only the rich could afford to contract out childcare.

Even if lower taxes had allowed a greater demand for nannies, there was not the supply to meet it. Few working-class

English women wanted to lose their independence and become live-in servants. They would not have taken nannying jobs even if they had been on offer. A glimpse of a nanny pushing a pram was as rare a sight in the seventies as a beggar on the streets. Outside central London, with its extremes of wealth and poverty, you rarely saw either.

Today it is the economically egalitarian but sexist past which seems a lost world. In 'How Serfdom Saved the Women's Movement', the American writer Caitlin Flanagan described how she saw it changing in 1978, when at the age of fifteen she was sent to her first psychotherapist. 'I can't remember a thing I talked about on all those darkening afternoons,' Flanagan said.

> But I do remember very clearly a day on which she suddenly sat up straight in her chair and began discussing, for reasons I could not fathom and in the most heated terms imaginable, not the vagaries of my sullen adolescence but, rather, marriage – specifically, her own. 'I mean, who's going to do the shit work?' she asked angrily. 'Who's going to make the pancakes?'
>
> I stared at her uncomprehendingly. The only wife I knew intimately was my mother, who certainly had her discontents, but whom I couldn't even imagine using the term 'shit work,' let alone using it to characterize the making of pancakes – something she did regularly, competently, and, as far as I could tell, happily (she liked pancakes; so did the rest of us). But in 1978 shit work was becoming a real problem. Shit work, in fact, was threatening to put the brakes on the women's movement.

The question feminism raised was, if middle-class women were to realise their potential and carry on with their careers after childbirth, who was going to look after their children? Who was going to take them to the doctor, wash their dishes, change their nappies, or pack the lunch boxes? The only solution the idealist feminists of the time imagined was binding marriage contracts or some other form of persuasion that would oblige men to do their fair share of chores. It was idealistic because few feminists believed that more than a handful of men were prepared to do their fair share of chores. Even if there were, an upper-middle-class couple determined to pursue interesting, rewarding and lucrative careers would still not have the time for childcare and running a home, however scrupulously they shared out the shit work.

The second wave of feminism was breaking on the rock of domestic necessity.

Until, like magic, says Flanagan, 'as though the fairy godmother of women's liberation had waved a starry wand', globalisation came to the rescue.

> With the arrival of a cheap, easily exploited army of poor and luckless women – fleeing famine, war, the worst kind of poverty, leaving behind their children to do it, facing the possibility of rape or death on the expensive and secret journey – one of the noblest tenets of second-wave feminism collapsed like a house of cards. The new immigrants were met at the docks not by a highly organized and politically powerful group of American women intent on bettering the lot of their sex but, rather, by an equally large army of educated professional-class women with booming careers who needed their children looked after and their houses cleaned. Any supposed equivocations about the moral justness of white women employing dark-skinned women to do their shit work simply evaporated.

Financial liberation for the fortunate followed. The engine that drives household income inequality is the professional couple who can draw high salaries throughout their working lives by contracting out the childcare that once forced women to stop working (and earning). The high-flying woman, and by extension her partner, relies on equality between the sexes enforced by equal pay acts and anti-discrimination legislation. Yet the results of sex equality are profoundly unequal. As sexual inequality declined, inequalities of wealth shot up, indeed had to shoot up, so that nannies could keep the professional marriage in business – and, although no one realised it for a while, the peeping Toms of the media too.

From Charles Stewart Parnell on, newspaper sex scandals have destroyed public careers. Men tempted from hearth and home faced the consequences when the betrayals of their private life became public. Now that the upper-middle class has privatised its private life, scandals come from inside as well as outside the home. When American activists want to stop their president from giving a plum job to a political opponent, they know the best place to start digging for dirt is in his or her child-care arrangements. If they scrutinise the nannies, housekeepers and cooks, there is a fair chance they will find illegal immigrants paid in cash to keep the costs down and away from the prying eyes of the tax authorities.

Unlike Parnell, David Blunkett* did not fall because he had an affair with a married woman. In our liberated age, Tony Blair saw no objection to Blunkett pursuing his former lover in the courts to ascertain paternity of her unborn child. Blair had to fire him only when the friends of Kimberley Fortier leaked to the press that Blunkett (or his staff at the Home Office) had

---

* While Home Secretary, David Blunkett had a three-year affair with Fortier, the American-born publisher of the Conservative *Spectator*. It ended in a spectacular public row in 2004 when Fortier decided to stick with her husband, Stephen Quinn, another publisher. The rival camps gave daily updates to a grateful press. The war between the rancorous ex-lovers culminated when Blunkett went to court to demand the right to know whether the pregnant Fortier was carrying his child rather than Quinn's. The besotted Blunkett did not realise that his ex-mistress's friends had information that might destroy him and, sure enough, the story of how Home Office rules had been broken to speed up the nanny's visa application duly appeared.

helped Fortier by speeding up a visa application for her nanny, Leoncia 'Luz' Casalme.

The nanny was at the centre of the affair, and the cause of the downfall of a public figure, yet she was barely discussed. Like many another servant, she was at once essential and invisible. Her superiors talked through her as if she weren't in the room.

The first thing to notice was that Fortier and Quinn had hired a Filipina rather than a local girl. It was not as if there weren't English women who might have filled the vacancy. After the collapse of full employment in the seventies, jobs as servants were often the only jobs available for women, while Gordon Brown's employment and benefit policies had the perverse consequence of forcing mothers from humble backgrounds to leave their own children to look after other people's. The habitual meanness of the rich may explain why Fortier and Quinn went for poor world labour – Fortier did not want Blunkett to arrange a new visa to make her nanny's life better, but so that Casalme could look after her children when the family travelled to its Irish holiday home. Stinginess may not be the whole story, however. In an interview with the *Mail*, the nanny described Fortier as 'the only person I have ever worked for who has made me cry. She is a loving mother but also a very pushy woman. What she wants she has to get, and if she doesn't get it she starts yelling and shouting.'

You cannot reduce an English nanny to tears too often and expect to hold on to her. As a friend from one of the better London postal districts put it to me: 'There are lots of things English women won't do. They won't cook and clean, if they're not paid to cook and clean, and they won't be bullied.'

Vulnerable foreigners are another matter: a trade union organiser's nightmare. They are cheaper and more pliable and unlikely to know how to ask for the protection of the law. Because they live under their employer's roof, it is all but impossible for outsiders to hear their grievances and help remedy them. The illegals among them are outside the rule of law because the fear of deportation stops them going to the authorities.

Occasionally, charities manage to break sensational accounts of rape and violence. More typical are the stories like that of another Filipina nanny I have encountered, whose life is close to Flanagan's serfdom. She worked for a Middle Eastern family in London. They locked her in her bedroom at night and searched her when she left the house to make sure she was not stealing the spoons. She escaped and found employment with what she took to be a progressive young English woman in Chelsea. The civilised appearance was an illusion. Her new mistress harried and abused her. A drop of water left on a ludicrously impractical teak kitchen surface produced a tantrum; a failure to obey the most trivial command produced a screaming fit.

The nanny was close to a nervous breakdown. When she said she wanted to leave, her mistress said she would shop her to the Home Office as an illegal immigrant if she dared defy her. (She fled anyway, and has not been picked up yet.)

Hers was a small tale of human misery from a potentially vast pool. Half the world's migrants are women. They look after the children, the sick and the old of the rich countries while the children, the sick and the old of their own countries fend for themselves. In 2006, the American journalist Barbara Ehrenreich edited *Nannies, Maids and Sex Workers in the New Economy*, which contained many a heartbreaking account of modern Nanny Everests. Such uncomfortable reading drew an indignant response. Critics complained that maids and nannies were often well paid and well treated, which I'm sure is true. Others said that society made women feel guilty whatever they did, and that is undeniable as well. (In the fifties, when middle-class women stayed at home, psychiatrists accused them of lavishing 'smother love' on their sons and turning them into schizophrenics, psychopaths or – worse – homosexuals. Now, concerned outsiders condemn mothers for not staying in the home long enough *to* smother their children.) But the strongest reaction was amused condescension. Ehrenreich and her quixotic colleagues were raging against an economic order that couldn't be changed.

They forgot that, just as the sexist, social democratic order of thirty years ago seemed natural to Jonathan Gathorne-Hardy, so our assumptions will one day seem bizarre. In the meantime, wealthy couples would seem a little less selfish if they complemented their constant demands for tax breaks on the money they spend on caring for their children, with equally enthusiastic demands for better protection for the Leoncia Casalmes who actually care for their children.

Observer, March 2006

Class Hatred: A Defence

IN *VERY GOOD, JEEVES,* Bertie Wooster's behaviour is so distracted his Aunt Dahlia has no choice but to suspect him of being in love, a fact he confirms.

'I do indeed love.'

'Who is she?'

'A Miss Pendlebury. Christian name, Gladys. She spells it with a "w".'

'With a "g", you mean.'

'With a "w" and a "g".'

'Not Gwladys?'

'That's it.'

The relative uttered a yowl.

'You sit there and tell me you haven't got enough sense to steer clear of a girl who calls herself Gwladys? Listen, Bertie,' said Aunt Dahlia earnestly, 'I'm an older woman than you are – well you know what I mean – and I can tell you a thing or two. And one of them is that no good can come of association with anything labelled Gwladys.'

She was right, as aunts invariably are. Life is short and there is not time to ignore collective wisdom. Bertie should have remembered what had happened to other men who had fallen in love with girls called Gwladys. He should have seen the

'Stop!' sign and jammed on the brakes. His aunt could not prove in advance that associating with this particular Gwladys would bring certain ruin, just as you or I cannot prove in advance that our prejudices are always justified. But put it like this: if you resolve never to be judgemental, and to treat everyone as innocent until they prove themselves guilty beyond reasonable doubt, the odds are that your savings will vanish into a Nigerian bank account.

Class hatred once provided the 'Stop!' signs of the left. If you were invited to entrust your money or your heart to someone who was rich, you would instinctively know to make an excuse and leave because leftish custom held that no good could come of the relationship. The gut reaction against the wealthy was based on three reflexes.

1. *Economic.* Excessive wealth leads its holders to expect to get their own way whatever the rules say and whatever damage is done to others.
2. *Political.* No just country can be created while extremes of wealth persist.
3. *Aesthetic.* The wealthy are vulgar. They waste their money on the art of the Chapman brothers or the fashions of John Galliano and use their domination of taste to silence the little boy who says the emperor has no clothes, or, rather, has gauche and ill-fitting clothes.

Today, class hatred has fallen into disrepute, along with race hatred, homophobia and all other forms of prejudice. It is easy to see why. If my employers were to send me on a class-hatred awareness course, I would have to admit that there was no logic to my bigotry.

Recently we spent the night at a country house hotel. It was a mistake – we were way out of our league. Leaving behind menus announcing that a pot of tea with cake was the price of the weekly shop, I took my son to the swimming pool, where I met a challenge faced by generations of parents. Changing rooms are potential death traps. The wet, tiled floors all but invite red-blooded toddlers to crack their skulls. But at some point you must put them down and get changed. Fortunately, mine ignored the enticing opportunities for self-harm and contented himself by playing with the locker keys.

A kindly American looked on. 'What is it with boys and keys?' the old man asked. 'My grandson's just got to have the keys. Mind you, they've got to be the right keys or he throws a tantrum. The keys to the Merc, the keys to the yacht, the keys to the plane ...'

I should have said, 'You know, mine's just the same!' I glared at him instead. Why? Whom did I expect to meet in a hotel for the super-rich? Postmen? The American was friendly and may have made his money with a product that had done nothing but good for the human race. What sense was there behind my scowl?

Some of my friends from university have dedicated themselves to a life of poorly rewarded public service. They're no better or worse than they ever were. Others went into the City and made a fortune. They're still the same people and still friends. By the standards of most people in this country and the overwhelming majority of people on the planet, I am rich. But I would be shocked to be hated as a result.

Class prejudice appears thoroughly discredited. It is now commonly deployed *de haut en bas* by the powerful against the powerless. I've lost count of the number of times that big business or the BBC or New Labour have condemned their critics as 'elitists' who arrogantly want to overrule the democratic decisions of the marketplace. This line of reasoning reached its nadir when Tessa Jowell denounced opponents of her plans to let casino operators fleece gullible punters as 'snobs'. When the wife of Silvio Berlusconi's lawyer can use the language of class struggle to defend the favourite business venture of the Mob, I think it is fair to say that socialism is dead.*

Even before it came to power, I realised New Labour had a reckless streak when newspaper diarists reported that Lady Carla Powell had befriended Peter Mandelson. Not only was she a society hostess and the wife of Charles Powell, Margaret Thatcher's foreign policy adviser, but her husband asserted that 'Powell, should be pronounced 'Pole''. This was as glaring a warning as a girl called Gwladys. Anthony Powell might have been a greater novelist if he had not wasted so much time correcting people who called him 'Powell' instead of 'Pole'. Sir Charles's brother, Jonathan Powell, was Tony Blair's chief of staff. He pronounces Powell 'Powell', thank God. On the day he switches to 'Pole', the merger of old Tory and New Labour will be complete.†

Ever since the party stepped out with the wealthy, it has been beset with scandals. After every one of them, I wondered what

* Tessa Jowell was the Labour minister who pushed through the deregulation of gambling. Her husband, David Mills, set up offshore trusts for Silvio Berlusconi in the early nineties. Italian magistrates investigating tax fraud and money laundering tried to prosecute him. They were suspicious because one woman was a director or company secretary of nineteen of the companies. It is hard enough for the most qualified woman to manage nineteen companies; harder still when the woman in question was a single mother from an East End council estate.

† After this piece appeared, Charles Powell wrote to me to explain that although his pronunciation of 'Powell' could sound like 'Pole' to the careless listener he in fact called himself 'Pohwell'. He was perfectly entitled to do so. His family was from Wales and his paternal grandfather pronounced 'Powell' as 'Pohwell', as many in Wales do to this day. Far from being a snob, his grandfather was a clergyman who despised the vanities of this world. Jonathan Powell began life by pronouncing 'Powell' as 'Pohwell' but slipped into 'Powell' as his career advanced. On this reading, the affectation lies with Jonathan for adopting the blokey pronunciation 'Powell' the better to fit in with the compulsory informality of the new establishment. But maybe not. It is easy to get lost in this country's class system.

Labour politicians thought they were doing when they accepted donations from and invitations to dinner with Bernie Ecclestone, the Hinduja brothers, partners in Arthur Andersen, Enron executives and Lakshmi Mittal. Did they truly believe that predatory capitalists wanted to talk about the politics of the progressive coalition? Did no alarms ring?

To be fair, a folk memory of socialist propriety occasionally troubled them. During the Hinduja affair,* Peter Mandelson told the head of the New Millennium Experience Company: 'I agree that they [the Hinduja brothers] are an above-average risk, but without firm evidence of wrongdoing how could we bar them from involvement in sponsorship?'

Mandelson was right, strictly speaking, but he missed the wider point. The billionaires strongly denied accusations that they had been involved in corrupt arms sales to India and no court had found them guilty beyond reasonable doubt of any offence. But if you see billionaires facing accusations of playing a part in an arms scandal, you are under no obligation to start worrying about the burden of proof any more than you are obliged to hire a plumber your neighbours have warned you is dodgy. Why not just smile politely and cross the street?

* The Hinduja brothers – Srichand, Gopichand and Prakash – were Indian billionaires, who, like so many other rich men, based themselves in London because of the tax breaks Gordon Brown gave the wealthy. They sponsored the Faith Zone in the Millennium Dome and announced that they believed in 'multicultural and interfaith understanding, tolerance and respect between the different people and their faith'. As the cynical would expect, the promoters of understanding, tolerance and respect were also involved in the supply of military vehicles. While New Labour was trying to raise funds for the Dome in 1999, the Indian authorities were accusing them of being involved in a corrupt arms deal. They claimed the charges were politically motivated, and an Indian court threw them out in 2005. Tony Blair sacked Peter Mandelson from his government in 2001 after press claims that Mandelson lobbied on behalf of Srichand Hinduja, who was seeking British citizenship.

The same question haunts David Blunkett's infatuation with a woman who appears to have been the result of a union between a diamond mine and a hotel chain. If the name 'Kimberley Fortier' wasn't warning enough, then her job as publisher of the conservative *Spectator* ought to have told a Labour minister that the fling could not end well.

The fault may have been with Blunkett's civil servants, who perhaps skipped the fashion pages when they read the morning newspapers to their blind master. They may have thought that the Home Secretary had more pressing matters to concern him, and missed the piece in which Fortier described how she used the pull of her husband, the publisher of *Vogue*, to jump a nine-month waiting list for an £11,000 Birkin bag. He 'moved heaven and earth to get her a Birkin within two months,' reported the *Observer*, 'sneaking her into the shop one night after closing to allow her to examine the bag, only to have her say: "It's the wrong one. It's light brown. I want the dark brown one."'

If it is bigoted to pass on the pleasure of such company, then good taste is bigotry

In years to come historians will conclude that New Labour had a fatal weakness. It lacked a wise aunt to save it from itself. There was no one to collar ministers and bellow, 'David, you sit there and tell me you haven't got enough sense to run a mile from a girl who calls herself Kimberley Fortier?'

New Statesman, December 2004

The Cool Rich and the Dumb Poor

TO SAY THAT today's Britain is a class-ridden country dominated by hereditary elites is to invite incredulous ridicule. No
one in a position of power supports privilege any more. John
Major announced his determination to achieve a 'classless
society' more than a decade ago. Tony Blair declared in 1997
that 'the Britain of the elite is over'. In the 2005 election
campaign, New Labour announced that it was on the side of
'hard-working families' while the old Tories claimed to be the
voice of 'the forgotten majority'. Both agreed that the old
notions of hierarchy were dead.

Once the newspapers the British read and the television
programmes they watched were social markers. Today the old
gap between middle and upmarket newspapers is vanishing,
and if it were not for the ads, no one would be able to tell the
difference between the BBC and commercial television. When
what we once called 'society' drops its aitches and affects an
estuary accent, it is possible to imagine a future when the queen
will be the last person left speaking the Queen's English.

All social and cultural institutions are emphatic in their
commitment to egalitarianism.* The BBC's Diversity Unit

---

* And I mean all. In 2005 the Lake District National Park threatened to cancel
its guided treks up the fells because too many ramblers were 'middle-aged,
middle-class and white'. 'Ethnic minorities and people with disabilities' were

promises not only to tackle colour prejudice, but an apparently exhaustive list of other bigotries about 'age, gender, race, ethnic origin, religion, disability, marital status, sexual orientation and number of dependants'. In Whitehall, the Civil Service says it will end the under-representation of women and members of ethnic minorities among its upper ranks. The NHS announces that its ambitions are not limited to the petty task of providing care for the sick, free at the point of delivery. It intends to go farther and create 'a fairer society in which everyone has the opportunity to fulfil their potential'.

A foreigner who hears the declarations of solidarity with the masses would assume this country was in the grip of red revolution, so thoroughly does the egalitarian style dominate public life. Radical human-resources managers and anti-elitist mandarins make good money out of a career in leftism, as long as they never talk about the old left's central concern: class. For embarrassingly good reasons it has become unmentionable.

In the late fifties, Harold Macmillan found ministerial jobs for the duke of Devonshire and the noble Lords Carrington, Dundee, Gosford, Home, Lansdowne and Munster. In 2004 Cherie Blair said, 'Whoever's calling the shots in this country, it isn't the people on the grouse moor.' Indeed it is not; the aristocratic order and the old class system are gone. But here's what is odd: a child born in 1958 into the Britain of Harold Macmillan and his dukes and lords was far more likely to break away from his class and pursue a career that reflected his talents than a child born in 1970. As John Major's classless society dawned, class divisions were hardening. The more Tony Blair insisted that elitism was over, the prouder elites became.

Far from being a meritocracy, Britain has become a country of castes, and the divisions between them are widening with each

not willing (or able, I guess, in the case of the disabled) to take to the hills, and so the walks must stop.

decade. The children of the rich remain rich when they grow up. The children of graduates graduate themselves; meanwhile the children of the working and lower-middle classes sink ever farther into financial and intellectual impoverishment.

A series of studies for the Sutton Trust looked at the fate of newborn children through schooling to adulthood. On average, a boy born to a well-to-do family in 1958 earned 17.5 per cent more than a boy born to a family on half the income. If the equivalent Mr and Mrs Moneybags produced a son in 1970, he would grow up to earn 25 per cent more than his contemporary from the wrong side of the tracks. In other words, far from decreasing, the class advantage of those born to wealth grew as the second half of the twentieth century progressed.

However they measure class, statisticians have found that the huge university expansion of the past twenty years has dispro-portionately benefited the children of the already well off. The gap between the higher-education participation rates of the working and middle classes is now wider than ever.

The effort that New Labour has put into increasing the chances of the poor – all Gordon Brown's Sure Start schemes and measures to redistribute wealth – has merely slowed the march of inequality.*

There are few signs that it is slowing in the twenty-first century. I suppose it is possible that upper-middle-class parents working full time to maximise their income, and contracting out their childcare to east European nannies, will be handicapping the prospects of the next generation of rich kids. Babies raised by Bulgarians may not have the linguistic and cultural advantages of

---

* In 2008 a grateful government seized on a report that showed family back-ground seemed to have become less significant in determining children's GCSE performance, prompting a minister to claim there were 'signs of good news'. Well, maybe. As the report's authors said, the clutch of policies Labour introduced may have a lasting impact on social mobility for children born after 2000. But, 'it is a bit premature to claim a big success'.

their parents. Even if that risk arises, I am sure that private tutors and private schools will fill the gaps in their early education.

The economic reasons for our sclerotic society are easy to grasp – money begets money. The rich pass on their wealth and its rewards to their children. The explosion of wealth at the top of society has left social mobility far more constricted in 'classless' Britain than in the more egalitarian economies of Germany, Canada and Scandinavia. The greatest myth of the free-market right is that its policies allow the poorest child to go from rags to riches. Healthy societies have few citizens in either rags or riches.

Economics alone cannot explain why the children of the poor are finding it ever more difficult to move on, however. As the saying goes, the right won the economic war and the left won the cultural war; and it is in the confusions of liberal-dominated cultural life that the second set of explanations for middle-class dominance can be found.

I have written as if it were obvious that social mobility was worth having, but in the twentieth century, the left was far from sure that it was. Michael Young in his *Rise of the Meritocracy* of 1958 put the case against. He was nervous about a future where the rich believed they had earned the right to be rich because of their inherent merits and the poor believed that their poverty was their own fault. Better to have an aristocracy that feels guilty about its luck in being born to wealth and power than a world where winners and losers believe they have received their just deserts. The poor would still be poor but they could find consolation in the thought that they were the victims of an unjust social order rather than their own failings.

Young's ideas helped pushed Labour to abolish grammar schools. Many Tories took up the cause. They grasped that if you combine a comprehensive state system with a selective private system – as Britain and America do – you have the rich parents' dream. If their children are bright, they go to a good private school. Competition for places is fierce, but the field is limited by the parents' ability to pay. If their children are clots, their wealth can still be decisive because it allows them to move into the expensive catchment areas of the best comprehensives. Either way, money talks, and poor but talented children are confined to the worst schools. For all his erudition, Young was a fool not to realise that, in the name of equality, the wealthy could exploit the education system.

The unintended consequences of egalitarianism in education would not have mattered so much if they did not coincide with wider cultural changes that were profoundly hostile to the working class. At the end of his *Intellectual Life of the British Working Classes*, Jonathan Rose asked why 200 years of self-improvement through libraries, lectures, schools and newspapers organised by and for the working class stopped in the sixties. His conclusion was that the supposedly egalitarian assault on the 'dead white men' of the classics served only to increase middle-class privilege. When there was agreement on the canon, when society accepted that, for example, you could not be educated without knowing Shakespeare, there was a clear path for the self-taught to follow if they wanted to catch up. Since the sixties, however, the canon has been careering around the deck. Cultural trends have had 'as brief a shelf-life as stock-exchange trends, and they depreciate rapidly if one fails to catch the latest wave in architecture or literary theory,' Rose noted. The eruptions of faddism – avant-garde, progressive, *le dernier cri*, new wave, modernist, postmodernist – 'reflect the Anxiety of Cool, the relentless struggle to get out in front and control the production of new cultural information'.

Each new wave carries fashionable 'high' culture farther away from the working class. Once, the middle-class left saw the workers as the very vanguard of history; now it dismisses them as sexist, racist and conservative. Rose searched a database of academic books published between 1991 and 2000. He got

13,820 hits for 'women', 4539 for 'gender', 1826 for 'race', 710 for 'post-colonial' and a piddling 136 for 'working class'.

It should not be a surprise that the lower orders do not care about education, when the educated care so little for them.

New Statesman, March 2005

The Moneyed Young Beasts

MIDDLE-CLASS HATRED of the upper class used to erupt regularly in Britain. From 1815 to 1914, it inspired the campaigns against rotten boroughs, the Corn Laws and the House of Lords. It rages in novels from the eighteenth to the mid-twentieth centuries, sometimes as a dominant theme, as in *Nicholas Nickleby*, for example, more often in the background, as in *Keep the Aspidistra Flying*. Today, the old anger seems dead. People talk with passion about the gap between the top and the bottom – between rich and poor – but not the gap between the top and the middle. The only modern writer I can think of who uses middle-class fury at the privileges of the rich in most of his plots is James Hawes. His typical character realises that working hard and playing by the rules will never get him the family home in a nice area the middle-class children of the seventies took to be their due.

To join the ranks of the respectable he has to stop being respectable. He must rob a bank, cut a deal with the Russian mafia or humiliate himself on a reality TV show. The system is stacked against him, as the graduate hero of his 1996 *A White Merc with Fins* explains, after learning that the children of the rich he thought of as friends at university are from a world whose admission price he cannot afford.

You have slept about and hitched around and your body-clock is locked into the chimes of midnight and the long, slow summers, and now that you have just about realised who you actually are, or might be, you have to go and be an accountant or a schoolteacher or work for ICI developing brave new deodorants.

Fair enough?

What?

Suddenly, the brief yoof-socialist near-equality of college is gone: the nice guy who had the crap old funny GTi is off to see America, the nice girl who subbed your drug experiments has gone to Mum's spare flat in South Ken to look up some pals in publishing, and little you are left high and dry, wilting towards teacher-training, accountancy or the dole office.

Mum, Dad!

The Imperfectly Launched Young Adults swarm home for more money.

Except Mum and Dad have no money.

A decade on, his angry young man is as likely to be an angry young woman. She hears that nearly everyone is middle class now, but experience shows her there is middle class and then there is Middle-Class. Her parents have modest savings, and helped a little with tuition fees – but that was it. She still left university with a pile of debt and a degree that was next to worthless because so many of her contemporaries had one too. Like the nurse I met who spat tacks at how the children of editors and celebrity columnists had an entrée to careers that weren't open to the likes of her, our heroine had ambitions to go into the glamorous world of media London. She found that to gain admission she needed to fund not only a first degree but a postgraduate degree as well. After she had paid for her training, editors told her they still would not give her a job that would allow her to pay the bills and repay her debts. She would first have to endure what they quaintly described as 'work experience', a refined version of slavery. She would work for nothing for six months, a year or however long it took an editor to condescend to hire her. Unsurprisingly our heroine cannot think of taking the media up on its generous offer because she does not have a private income and cannot afford to live without a wage.

She realises that in the culture industries – publishing, theatre, TV, radio, film-making, the fine arts and the serious newspapers – it helps to have a mummy with a spare flat in South Ken, and if Mummy's friends are also your prospective employers, all the better. In 1936, George Orwell complained about 'snooty, refined books on safe painters and safe poets by those moneyed young beasts who glide so gracefully from Eton to Cambridge and from Cambridge to the literary reviews'. The beasts are gliding again. I'm not saying it is impossible to get a job in the arts or the media without family money and connections, but when I meet a graduate with a familiar name at a party, I no longer bother to ask if they are X's daughter or Y's son. The question is superfluous.

When the BBC exploded into one of the world's most interesting arts institutions in the sixties, innovation came from grammar-school-educated producers and writers from modest backgrounds. At first glance, modern British institutions still seem determined to foster egalitarianism. Diversity is king at the BBC and elsewhere. To be accused of racism, sexism or homophobia is a career-breaking charge. Yet look closer at the men and women who make the decisions. The working-class boys are long gone and the managers' diverse appearance conceals a uniform background in the moneyed class. In the name of diversity, everyone is the same. They will argue for positive discrimination to compensate for sex or race or sexual orientation or disability … but for class, never.

The striking difference with Orwell's day is that the Cambridge graduates produce *Big Brother* and *Ant and Dec.** I can't say that's an advance, although obviously there is more money in it for the beasts. From a class point of view, churning out pap that keeps ordinary children stupid can also help the beasts' own children beat them in the competition for jobs a generation down the line. A TV producer, who once believed the media was honourable, told me how his child's sixth birthday party opened his eyes. He had hired an entertainer for the sons and daughters of other television executives. The act flopped. 'Don't worry,' the entertainer told him, 'I'll get them to guess TV theme tunes. That always makes them happy.' For once, his sure-fire hit failed. The children stared blankly at the wretched man as he played the jingles for *Hollyoaks* and *Emmerdale.* My friend learned then what he ought to have guessed years before: television executives do not allow their children to watch the programmes they push at the masses.

Despairing of ever working for Channel 4 or Tate Modern, our young woman decides on an ordinary middle-class career. Maybe she joins the public sector as a teacher, or becomes an administrative officer for a private firm. She is bright and competent and is soon earning £35,000 – well above the average salary. Yet she does not feel remotely well off because the gap between what she earns and what her bosses earn is enormous. Local authority chief executives are making £150,000. The average salary of a corporate chief executive is £550,000, even though neither our young woman nor any reputable economist can find a correlation between their pay and performance. The gap between £35,000 and £550,000 is

---

* The man behind *Big Brother*, Peter Bazalgette (Dulwich College and Fitzwilliam College, Cambridge), was the great-grandson of Sir Joseph Bazalgette, who designed the London sewers. 'He's undoing all his great-grandfather's work by pumping shit back into our homes,' said Stephen Fry.

not a difference within the middle class; it is an unbridgeable gulf between classes.

Part of her grievance is due, no doubt, to the greed of the consumer society that writers for the liberal press denounce with such gusto. The British Market Research Bureau agrees and says that the middle classes are in the grip of what it calls 'luxury fever'. Nearly half of those earning more than £35,000 a year, and 40 per cent earning over £50,000, told its researchers they felt 'deprived' because they couldn't afford 'essential' purchases such as Jaguars, cosmetic surgery and kitchens with enormous cookers and bigger fridges. The Bureau blamed the media, as everyone does, for spreading decadent tastes and giving the middle classes ideas above their station. In the past, they 'set their aspirations for their standard of living by their own social class, and the people around them'. Now they want it all.

Such jeremiads contain a portion of truth – you have only to look at the debt burden to know that – but blaming greed and the media misses the crucial change in British middle-class life of the late twentieth century.

Sociologists would have classified many of today's rich as middle class thirty years ago. Then the council's chief officer did not earn five times as much as the teacher; the chief executive did not earn sixteen times as much as the bright graduate in personnel. Thatcherism made them wealthy for no better reason than they happened to be sitting behind a manager's desk when their industry was privatised or public service commercialised. Conspicuous consumption with so little economic justification was bound to turn middle-class heads.

Nor do lamentations about selfishness take account of the greatest cause of class tension between the top and the middle: the unselfish act of having and rearing children.

For some time now, women writers across Fleet Street have been repeating the same anecdote in angry columns. City dealers with six- or seven-figure bonuses are flaunting their wealth by having four or more children. A large family shows that the hedge-fund manager or venture capitalist makes enough for his wife to stay at home – with ample support staff – and for him to educate his brood privately. The story is popping up everywhere because it hits the most sensitive of nerves. In the twenty-first century, having children comes as naturally to the rich and to the poor as it always has, but our middle-class woman is likely to get in all kinds of trouble if she wants to follow suit.

First, she will have difficulties with men, which other women don't have to lose sleep over. The brute economic fact is that a single mother on a council estate does not have to worry about the financial cost of a father abandoning his children because the state will pay for them. Equally, the wife of the hedge-fund manager may not be happy if her husband runs off with a girl from Lloyd's, but her lawyers will make her feel better by taking a fortune from him in alimony. By contrast, a middle-class woman does not want to raise children alone on a council estate, but she cannot be sure of having the money to raise children in comfort if her partner leaves. Alimony from her ex will not be enough to adequately support her and her children. Even if she is confident that her partner will stay with her, they will still have to find a decent home, and if she lives in London, the South-East, Edinburgh and, increasingly, Leeds and Manchester, decent homes are beyond her means.

This combination of social and financial pressures has produced one of the most familiar figures of our time: the middle-aged, middle-class woman being prodded by fertility doctors because finding a home she can raise children in and a man she can raise them with has taken her such a long time – perhaps too long a time. She may not be starving in Darfur or living in a Glasgow slum, but suffering is not a competition and her misery remains real.

If the test results come in positive and she is still lucky enough to be able to have children, she will confront an education system that, despite stiff competition, remains the crowning glory of English hypocrisy. The best schools are likely to be in the private system, and she cannot afford to send her children there. If she stays in the state system – as she must – she will find it is nowhere near as egalitarian as it pretends to be. If she cannot afford to meet the inflated price of a house in the catchment area of a good comprehensive, her children will be disadvantaged for life.

What will she make of her country by the time she has experienced university, work and motherhood? She may well have found that wealth determines what job she can get, where she can live, when and if she can have children and whether her children will receive a good education. Ever since the eighties, the voices of the consensus have told us that the 'politics of envy' is dead. Margaret Thatcher's triumph was to make people admire the wealthy and wish to emulate them. But the achievement of Thatcherism was double-edged. In the seventies, union militancy pushed large sections of the middle class, and many in the working class, to the right. Now the main threat to middle-class interests is from the rich.

It is not a conspiracy. Employers are not consciously excluding young people on modest means, just taking advantage of the mismatch between supply and demand. The media grandees who pump out trash they would never allow their own children to watch are not plotting to keep people stupid, just giving the market what it wants. Supporters of comprehensives believe in equality and never ask why, in eighteen years of power, Tories never insisted on a return to selection by ability in state schools.

When he was young, Tony Blair knew how the system frustrated middle-class hopes. The snag for Labour is that his behaviour is now an affront to middle-class values. He made it clear that he wanted to join the super-rich for whom taxes are what the little people pay. His party sold them peerages, his ministers' spouses advised them on how to shift their fortune from tax haven to tax haven. So accustomed has New Labour become to the world of the wealthy that it mistakes it for the whole world. A mistake I suspect the middle classes will make it pay for one day.

New Statesman, March 2006

In Search of the Normal

JULIAN BAGGINI SEEMS a standard member of the liberal intelligentsia. The books he reads, the clothes he wears and the food he eats match those of tens of thousands of others. He stands out because he has done what very few of his contemporaries are prepared to do and confronted England. Not by denouncing its government or letting out long sighs about its lack of sophistication, but by living among people he would not ordinarily notice in an attempt to understand the core beliefs of the England which doesn't listen to the *Today* programme.

It is a simple idea, and I'm surprised no one has thought of it before. Polly Toynbee and Fran Abrams have written tender accounts of life on the poverty line, while the *Sunday Times* was not exaggerating when it described Michael Collins's *The Likes of Us* as an 'absolutely essential' guide to London's white working class. There are also thousands of academic studies of the national character – from the British Social Attitudes Survey to Kate Fox's *Watching the English*.

But Baggini wasn't interested in the poor, but the average. Nor did he follow Collins by staying in London, which is a separate country, as everyone says. He determined instead to concentrate on the mainstream English who cannot be found on the minimum wage or living in the capital, but among the homeowners of the provinces. The piles of academic research and opinion poll findings helped him, but they could not give him the feel of England. For that, he had to uproot himself mentally and physically.

He asked the computer analysts who compile demographic profiles for marketing companies to give him the postcode of the English district that was closest to the national average. They consulted their databases and told him to head to S66 on the outskirts of Rotherham. Its working-men's clubs, eat-as-much-food-as-you-can-cram-on-to-your-plate restaurants, out-of-town shopping centres and local radio stations are indeed typical, but they are also about as far away from Baggini's England as it is possible to get.

'Three of the last four constituencies I lived in went Liberal Democrat at the last election,' he said, as he tucked into an un-English vegetarian breakfast. 'And the Lib Dems only lost the fourth by a few hundred votes. I have been in a parallel country for most of my adult life.'

Baggini expected to find sexism, racism, homophobia, celebrity worship, small-mindedness and superstitious fears. What makes his *Welcome to Everytown* a thought-provoking book is not that he didn't discover illiberal prejudices in Rotherham, but that he managed to come to terms with them.

Baggini is not quite the standard middle-class liberal he appears. His mother is from the Kent working class and his father grew up in an Italian farming family before emigrating to Britain. His Italian side meant that he 'never really felt entirely at home in this country', while his working-class background distanced him from the public-school boys of the London intelligentsia. More important, I think, is his membership of a group of freelance intellectuals who gather round the *Philosophers' Magazine* and live by their pens. None has the security of a university job, and all are suspicious of intellectual orthodoxy. (Ophelia Benson and Jeremy Stangroom, two of Baggini's colleagues, produced an attack on postmodernism, whose title, *The Dictionary of Fashionable Nonsense*, encapsulates the group's disdain.)

His background and philosophical training gave him the intellectual honesty to be as critical of the biases he and his friends
shared as of the biases of others. Even before he went to Rotherham, he was wary of the thoughtless anti-patriotism that lay
behind David Hare's cry that 'most of us look with longing to the
republican countries across the Channel. We associate English-
ness with everything that is most backward in this country.'

Baggini noticed that when his friends went overseas 'they
always found something to delight in. They would tell me how
wonderful it was to share a glass of wine with the old boys in a
rural French bar, and not realise that if those old boys were
speaking English they would probably be saying, "That Jean-
Marie Le Pen, he's got the right idea."'

He moved to Rotherham, rented a modern house by a main
road, and read the newspapers and watched the television
programmes that his neighbours read and watched. He
encountered many prejudices he disliked, but gradually his
views on popular attitudes and culture softened. He learned to
tolerate the *Sun* and the radio phone-ins. Only the *Daily Mail*
remained too much for him.

The regulars of Rotherham pubs and clubs deserve credit for
his softening. They did not allow the strange, bookish South-
erner to sit by himself for long. But Baggini also realised that
what he had taken to be idiotic views came from a comprehen-
sible working-class philosophy.

Although the polls that report that six out of ten people still
regard themselves as working class always produce middle class
incredulity, Baggini says you only have to listen to the radio
programmes he heard and go to the bars he drank in to realise
that working-class culture dominates England. People may have
more money than their parents had and holiday in Florida
rather than Blackpool, but that does not mean that working
class attitudes have changed. Central to them is the importance
of place.

The majority of the English still live within five miles of where they were born, and the attachment to locality keeps England a country where a sense of being a member of a community underpins national values. The English want 'local jobs for local people', local radio, local papers and raffles for local good causes. Complementing local pride is the strong notion that you cannot enjoy England's benefits without belonging. Baggini got into endless arguments about the Human Rights Act, but his attempts to persuade his new friends that foreign terror suspects should never be deported if they could face torture always got nowhere. The New Labour slogan 'you can't have rights without responsibilities' summed up the English mainstream. 'It's an illiberal thought,' he told me. 'Liberals believe that you have rights on the basis of your membership of the human race. But most of the English aren't liberal. They believe that you only have rights if you are a fully paid-up member of this society. That is why they will be very illiberal about Muslim preachers of hate and say, "We don't care about their rights." What about ours?'

Although he met a few real racists, Baggini does not see such beliefs as racist in themselves. Instead, he draws on the image of the 'hefted' sheep of northern fells, whose instinctive knowledge of where they can graze means they never stray from their patch of land.

People who have lived in an area all their lives are uncomfortable if the character changes because of a large influx of immigrants. But that doesn't make them racist. They just want their locality to stay the way it was. No one calls families racist when they object to large numbers of students moving into their street or says that the residents of Hampstead were racist for wanting to live in an area without McDonald's.

Frankly, I didn't believe it when people in Rotherham said they wanted immigrants to fit in. That's not quite right. If you

go to Manchester or London, there are Chinatowns that adver-
tise their differences, but no one ever says, 'the problem with
these bloody Chinese is that they don't fit in', because there's no
threat or no perceived threat. The multicultural agenda is that
everyone must respect each other, but I don't think that's possible. We need to be far tougher with the minimal demands that
people don't threaten each other.

Interestingly given the current preoccupation of his class, he left
Rotherham far more concerned about sexism than racism.
Watching the way women tried to please men in Rotherham
clubs and reading semi-pornographic lads' mags didn't make
him think that the reassertion of traditional stereotypes after
the retreat of feminism was 'harmless' fun. There is, he says,
nothing fun about a country where most women say that they
are deeply unhappy with their appearance.

Baggini refuses to adopt the declamatory style of the polemicist, and his writing is refreshingly self-deprecatory. At one
point in *Welcome to Everytown* he says he had to leave Rotherham to visit London. Once back in Islington, he could not resist
the lure of 'proper food'. He went to an Italian restaurant,
ordered pasta, olives and a glass of wine, and then buried his
head in a book. Minutes later, he looked up to see another man
of his age and class come in and order pasta, olives and a glass
of wine, and then bury his head in a book.

In Rotherham, I lost a certain sense of superiority I had about
food, holidays and the things I did to enjoy myself. I now find it
hard to say that liberal middle-class culture is better than
looking after your garden, going fishing and watching ice
hockey. There is nothing intrinsically worse in that than in
listening to opera. Some of the world's worst people have been
opera buffs.

I was glad to find that he had not overreacted and become an inverted snob. He does not pretend that he would like to spend the rest of his life in S66. He's got his world and the mainstream has theirs. But he has relaxed.

I asked whether he felt more comfortable with his country. 'I think I've learned that most people here are fine with you as long as you treat them fairly. I am very pleased that my book has gone down well in Rotherham, even though I was unsentimental and didn't hide my disagreements. That speaks well of the people I wrote about, and so, yes, I feel more at peace with England.'

New Statesman, April 2007

PART 2

Who is England? What is She?

'For every professional woman who is able to go out to work because she has a Polish nanny, there is a young mother who watches her child struggle in a classroom where a harassed teacher faces too many children with too many languages between them. Wanting a better deal for her child doesn't make her anti-immigrant. But if we can't find a better answer to her despair then she soon will be.'

TREVOR PHILLIPS,
2008

Celebrity Chefs and
Invisible Immigrants

WHEN I APPEARED IN MY HAIRNET and apron in the kitchen of the Gay Hussar, the cooks were less shocked by the sight of a customer choosing to roll up his sleeves by than by my nationality.

'I'm Nick,' I said cheerily.

'Your name is Ick?' asked one.

'No, Nick.'

'Nick?'

'That's it. N-I-C-K. Nick.'

'Nick. You're saying you're English?'

'Er, yes.'

He looked bewildered. Everyone else looked at me as if I were lying.

Zoltan from Hungary tried to clear up the matter. 'Are your parents English?' he asked, as if trying to make an inexplicable phenomenon understandable.

'Yes, they're English, too, from Manchester. You know: Bobby Charlton, Alex Ferguson, Wayne Rooney …'

I mumbled myself to a halt, as baffled at my reception as my new colleagues were by me. Only later in the morning did I understand the reason for their surprise. Most had never met an Englishman or woman in a London kitchen. One old hand said he remembered an English cook at the Gay Hussar, but he had left some time in the nineties. Since then, they had talked about how to prepare food and handle fussy customers in a pidgin English used across London kitchens by every nationality, except the English.

Maybe, I thought, Conservatives had a point when they laughed at Gordon Brown's pretence to believe in the Protestant work ethic, and decried his BNP-ish slogan of 'British jobs for British people' as so much flam. Perhaps Brown had created a welfare system so riddled with poverty traps that jobs went to foreigners while the natives drew benefits and stewed at home.

The Gay Hussar was not the best place for such Tory thoughts. If you've never been, you've missed an old Labour institution. Of course, not only the left eat at this remnant of Mitteleuropa in the middle of London. All kinds of people who have never argued about the reasons for the Russian Revolution's descent into tyranny come: actors from the nearby theatres, Soho admen plotting campaigns and tourists looking for a good night out are attracted by the echoes of the Austro-Hungarian Empire. The faded red wallpaper, book-lined dining room, wood panelling and framed pictures of long-dead politicians are not only for the politically committed.

Nor do you have to be left-wing. John Wrobel, the Polish maître d', won't ask you to leave if he overhears you carelessly saying to your companion, 'Let's face it, entrepreneurs are the real wealth creators', while tasting the wild-cherry soup. Upstairs from the main restaurant are private rooms in which politicians of all parties have conspired. The Conservative 'Wets' met in one in the early eighties to discuss their doomed conspiracy against Margaret Thatcher. The Eurosceptic 'bastards' followed in the nineties to conspire against John Major. Tory, Labour, right, left, wet, dry ... everyone is welcome.

Yet when all the caveats have been made, the restaurant still belongs to the vanishing world of the twentieth-century left. Martin Rowson has covered one wall with cartoons of the regulars, and they are overwhelmingly Labour politicians, or Labour journalists – nearly all old, nearly all men. This is the closest they have to a Pall Mall club: a mixture of a drinking den and canteen.

Victor Sassie, a Hungarian refugee, opened the Gay Hussar in the fifties, but there was a leftish restaurant on the site long before then. Michael Foot remembers taking the Soviet ambassador to its predecessor in 1939 and begging him to tell Stalin not to form an alliance with Hitler. Somewhat naively, the future Labour leader did not understand that if the Soviet ambassador had whispered a word out of place, Stalin would have murdered him and everyone associated with him.

John becomes melancholy as he repeats the story, and for good reason. The Hitler–Stalin pact that the young Michael Foot had tried to stop carved up his native Poland and started the Second World War. His father's parents had to flee advancing German troops who burned down their home, and his mother's parents had to flee advancing Soviet troops who burned down their home.

The catastrophe of European totalitarianism as well as the quieter history of the British Labour movement caught up many who worked here. When I knew I was coming for the day, I dug through political biographies and found stories of the energetically homosexual Labour MP Tom Driberg organising a lunch in the late 1960s during which W. H. Auden leaned across to Marianne Faithfull to ask whether she hid her drugs 'up her arse'.

There are plenty more rib-ticklers where that came from, but I suspect that the appetite for tales from old Bohemia and old Labour is a specialist taste these days. If people went to the Gay Hussar only because it is a relic of a lost London, the restaurant would be all but empty. It's packed most days, and not only by nostalgics who can still remember Nye Bevan in his prime but by customers looking for a virtue that restaurants with far higher profiles and prices can't supply: conviviality.

In my experience, if restaurant critics have a fault it is that they overestimate the importance of food. I have been to two Michelin-starred restaurants. The first, Juniper in Altrincham, was like a laboratory. I felt as if I should have put on a white coat before entering, and could not wait to leave. In the second, a Gordon Ramsay joint, the atmosphere was not as clinical but it was no less stifling. Diners sat in devotional silence, as if they were praying in a cathedral rather than enjoying a meal. If anyone had roared with laughter or raised their voice, it would have seemed a blasphemy.

Even though its Hungarian cuisine is fantastically unfashionable, the Gay Hussar prospers because there have been too many drunken lunches over the decades for it to succumb to prudery or chef worship. Even the hearty Hungarian food – the salamis, pâtés, pickled herrings, roast geese and ducks, Wiener schnitzels, dumplings, stuffed cabbages and strudels – is only unfashionable to the minority who take food faddery and dieting seriously. Most would consider it a feast.

'In French restaurants, the plates look like a work of art, but an hour after you've eaten, you're hungry again,' Carlos, the head chef, explained as he sighed about man's infinite capacity for folly. 'What's the point of that? Eat here, and you know you've eaten.'

Well said, I thought, as I followed him down to the kitchen.

IT HADN'T OCCURRED TO ME until I got there that, at 6ft 1in and with a paunch, I was too big for the job. Space is tight in most restaurant kitchens for the brute economic reason that the owner needs to pack in as many tables as possible for paying customers. In the Gay Hussar, it is not only profit maximisation but also the demands of Georgian builders which cramp the cooks. Land has always been expensive in central London, and eighteenth-century developers cut costs by building tall, narrow houses. There wouldn't be much room to cook whatever floor the kitchen was on. As the only plausible floor for it is the base-ment, a low ceiling intensifies the claustrophobic atmosphere.

If you imagine a narrow rectangular space packed with appliances, you will get an idea of the design. An oven with hotplates fills most of one side and a large sink fills much of the other. Down the middle is a kind of extended butcher's block, a run of surfaces for chopping and preparing. It forms two narrow corridors down the length of the kitchen. Storage cupboards that have been hammered into every available space overhang the aisles. When hot pans are moving and sharp knives whizzing, the last thing a head chef wants is a lumbering innocent waving his arms about.

Carlos put up with my intrusion with good grace. I offered to wash up, but he was happy for me to experiment with a sweet-pepper salad. I did not think I'd have any difficulty. I have cooked for twenty-five years. Not lunch and dinner every day, but four times a week, often more. I halved a pepper and took a knife to the seeds and pith with what seemed to me to be the delicacy of a brain surgeon. After three, perhaps four, seconds, Carlos intervened and showed me how to chop peppers properly. He halved ten and put them in the sink. I was to run water over each half, stick my hand in, yank out the innards in one movement, flip over the pepper and slice it horizontally into perfect pencil-thin strips that would melt into the dressing.

'Like this … see … easy.'

The kitchen knife, which I had handled with nervous respect, flashed up and down half an inch away from his fingers. I couldn't do it. After forty minutes of chopping, I was faster than when I started but still ten times slower than Carlos. Also my strips were – er – not quite *comme il faut*. Put it like this – if, during a recent visit to the Gay Hussar, you found the sweet-pepper salad to be on the clunky side, then that was one of mine. It was the same story with the onions. Again, I had several decades' worth of what I assumed to be hands-on dicing experience. Again, I could not match the speed or the consistency of a proper cook. As for trimming veal, by the time I'd finished with it the fatted calf looked anorexic, so much meat had I thrown away with the gristle.

All around me, the kitchen went through its daily rhythm. Preparation and cleaning begin at 8 a.m. and carry on until midnight. The peaks are between 12.45 p.m. and 1.30 p.m., and 7.30 p.m. and 8.15 p.m., when nearly all the meal orders come one on top of the other. The kitchen goes quiet and everyone concentrates.

For all their resistance to nouvelle cuisine and nouvelle labour, the customers are not without their eccentricities. 'Number two wants to know where our veal is from,' shouts a waitress. 'It's all right. It's from Holland,' Carlos tells her, and turns to me and says, 'They're worried about foot-and-mouth. We get asked all the time.'

'But humans can't catch foot-and-mouth,' I mutter.

I checked with the waitress. They were worried about foot-and-mouth. And blue tongue.

When the pressure was on, I got out of the way and watched from a corner of the kitchen. 'Never work for a liberal newspaper, they'll sack you on Christmas Eve,' runs the old Fleet Street maxim. But observing the cooks and waitresses at the Gay Hussar, I could see that working in a left-wing restaurant was about as good as it gets in the drone's trade of catering.

I don't want to romanticise it. Just before the lunchtime rush, the cooks and waitresses put their pounds in for the Wednesday lottery. Like low-paid workers everywhere, they were clutching at a fourteen-million-to-one chance of escape. They asked me whether I wanted to join the syndicate. I didn't think I could. I've dismissed the National Lottery as a tax on the stupid and the desperate so often that I could recite my stock piece in my sleep. But Nick, they said, there was a cook here who won. Not the big prize, but £67,000 – enough for him to retire. The story of his good fortune kept the others going, and inspired me. This was a lucky kitchen!

I duly put my pound in, and we duly lost.

However gratefully its staff would seize the chance to escape the grind, the Gay Hussar remains a happy workplace. Everyone has known everyone else for years. John Wrobel confessed to occasionally shouting at the waitresses, but, he said, 'they just shout back at me'.

They're lucky that they can. I recommend that anyone who eats regularly in restaurants should spend time in a kitchen. Obviously, every decent person already knows that you should never be rude to waiters and always leave a tip. (The tip should be bigger, incidentally, if you are not happy with your treatment: bad service is a sign of an understaffed and therefore overstressed kitchen.) But it is only when you see catering from the other side that you realise that the media's celebration of the chef as a bully is sickening in its cowardice.

While I was working, I heard the story of an acclaimed chef who branded a young member of staff with a hot knife. He had to lie low for a couple of years, but he's back running a celebrated restaurant and no one mentions his past. People in the business told me that in his kitchens Gordon Ramsay is not the foul-mouthed thug of his TV appearances. He just plays the bully for the cameras to please the watching mob. Whatever their behaviour in private, chefs such as Ramsay and Marco Pierre White have fostered the idea that, in order to be a culinary genius, you must abuse your staff. So successfully has the hounding of subordinates been marketed in various 'reality' documentaries, the leader of one of the teaching unions said her members were finding it hard to convince children that bullying was wrong, when the television told them that 'celebrity status and money can be acquired on the basis of shouting at and swearing at and humiliating others'.

At least in a school, factory or office, there are places to hide. The kitchen, by contrast, is a perfect environment for the sadist because there is nowhere to run to until a temper tantrum passes. Managers do not allow cooks into the restaurant. If they're in a basement, there isn't even a back door on to the street.

Appreciate too that the workforce is overwhelmingly poor and foreign, with little English and low union membership, and you will understand how kitchens become hells.

Last year the TGWU and GMB unions issued reports on conditions in the catering industry. Along with the normal stories of poor pay and long hours, there were accounts from cooks of incessant abuse. One worker at a five-star London hotel said harassment and racism were an everyday experience. 'You fuckers!' his manager would scream. 'Don't be stupid like the Poles!' He had come to Britain for a new life but found that the hotel was a state within a state: a closed society where the writ of the outside world didn't run.

The old left that used to dine and drink in the Gay Hussar can be criticised on many grounds but it would never have put up with today's giggling approval of culinary tyrants; it would never have said that the price of a good meal should include the degradation of underlings who can't answer back. It would have protested, and so should we.

Observer Food Magazine, October 2007

Black on Brown/Brown on Black

WHEN I WAS a reporter on the *Birmingham Post & Mail*, I could guess readers' politics by how they described the looting and murder that overwhelmed Handsworth in September 1985. If they talked about the 'Handsworth riots', I knew they were conservatives who had seen criminals go berserk. When they said 'riot' they meant that the two days of violence were a thugs' orgy open to all regardless of colour or creed. Its 'root cause' was unbridled criminality. Drug dealers and gangsters were fighting a legitimate police attempt to uphold the law in what had been a no-go area. As I ducked and dived to escape machete-wielding rioters, I took their point. When a pair of men cornered me and demanded my money, I was saved only by the honest conviction of my junior reporter's cry: 'But, but ... I don't *have* any money!'

Equally, I knew without needing to ask that those who talked of the 'Handsworth uprising' or 'rebellion' were on the left. Dick Knowles, the old Labour leader of Birmingham City Council, muttered that real revolutionaries would not have burned their neighbours' homes but headed for Sutton Coldfield, in Birmingham's stockbroker belt. But his younger comrades did not listen. They did not see dangerous fools destroying what little their community had, but insurgents rising up against the poverty and racism of Margaret Thatcher's Britain.

Before they became respectable, Herman Ouseley and Keith Vaz were fire-spouting radicals who announced in a report for the old West Midlands County Council that the word 'riot' didn't begin to describe what had happened in Handsworth. 'The never-employed black under-class, interned in the workless gulags of Britain', had risen up against their oppressors, they insisted. Birmingham was seeing 'violent resistance' by blacks who believed they were being forced to live under 'a form of apartheid'.

Fire crews found the charred bodies of two Asian shopkeepers in the wreckage of the Lozells Road post office, but Vaz and his colleagues warned that you were falling for the ruling class's old 'divide and rule tactic' if you said there were tensions between ethnic minorities. In 'Handsworth Revolution', the reggae band Steel Pulse sang, 'We once beggars are now choosers/No intention to be losers' – and black Birmingham, the young and the university-educated left of the eighties agreed that the dispossessed were fighting back.

For all the hyperbole, I had sympathy with the leftists as well. In Brixton, Tottenham and Handsworth, riots began after a real or rumoured assault on a black woman by the police. The rioters were poor young men without a future. To say the violence had nothing to do with racism and the mass destruction of manufacturing jobs in Margaret Thatcher's first recession was wishful thinking or Tory propaganda. No one rioted in Maidenhead, after all.

Twenty years on, I am back on the Lozells Road after another riot. Nothing has changed, but everything is different. The red-brick terraced houses are as poky and dilapidated as ever. Handsworth remains a place where you can smell the disappointment of people who must live in a slum because they have nowhere better to go.

Little else was familiar. The arguments of the eighties about why young men took to the streets felt antique and irrelevant. Beyond repeating the platitude that workers with good jobs tend to be law-abiding, you could not pretend the 2005 riot was an uprising against unemployment. The economic and law enforcement policies of official society – 'white society', to stretch a point – had nothing to do with the violence. Racism was on display, but not between blacks and whites. So were religious tensions, to which I had never given a second's thought in 1985.

The 2005 riot did not start with a bungled police round-up of drug dealers, but a racist rumour that swept black Birmingham. Everyone knew someone who could swear that an Asian shopkeeper had locked up a fourteen-year-old black girl he had caught shoplifting and then raped her with the help of his friends. Detectives have been investigating for a week. They have not found the girl, the crime scene or the rapists. Unless that changes,* and it probably won't, the rumour will be a grotesque libel that painted Asian shopkeepers as the bestial abusers of female innocence.

Warren G spread it on his show on a pirate station. Mr G is not a standard DJ. He is a religious man who worships at the New Testament Church of God, which glares across the Lozells Road at Handsworth's mosque. The congregation met to discuss the 'rape'. Rumour fed on rumour. The radio stations and Net got to work and the fighting began. Gangs hit each other and passers-by with petrol bombs and guns. One police officer and thirty-five civilians were injured. An Asian gang murdered Isaiah Young-Sam, a twenty-three-year-old black man who, by a stroke of capricious fortune, was a school friend of Warren G.

Ligali, a black African pressure group, called for a boycott of Asian shops. Not of the shop where the crime took place – no one knew where it was or if, indeed, it existed – but of all Asian shops. When I knew Handsworth, there were black traders. But while Hindu, Sikh and Muslim families have followed the

* It didn't, of course.

classic immigrant path of sticking together and building on the success of a well-run business, many blacks have fallen behind. The postings in chat rooms blamed an Asian conspiracy. They succeeded in taking over black hairdressing salons, which once dotted Handsworth, by undercutting their rates and forcing black owners to buckle under the 'unreasonable' competition. 'Black people need to realise that they are being shitted on by Indians who now supply them with the very food they eat, their cosmetics and health care.'

Theodore Dalrymple, the pseudonym of a Birmingham doctor and writer, noted recently in the *Telegraph* that the shop-keepers were facing a modern variant of anti-Semitism. Once, white Christians accused Jewish traders of kidnapping their children and draining their blood; now, black Christians accuse Asian traders of kidnapping their girls and raping them.

These prejudices are incredibly powerful because they combine race hatred of the alien, class hatred of the prosperous and religious hatred of the infidel.

In *World on Fire*, published in 2004, Amy Chua argued that globalisation had created an explosion of racism in the anti-Semitic mould. The new wave of capitalism had raised the living standards of ordinary people by a little and of the rich by a lot. The supporters of free markets and democracy thought everyone was benefiting and had not noticed that their ideas helped fuel resentments in those countries where ethnic minorities dominated business.

Sectarian leaders were exploiting the antipathies of race and class. Across the planet, you heard the same demonic accusations of bloodsucking, corruption and secret influence, whether about the Chinese business class in South-East Asia, the white farmers in Zimbabwe and South Africa, the Spanish 'whites' in Latin America, the Jews in Russia, the Ibo in Nigeria, the Croats in the last days of Yugoslavia and the Americans everywhere. The markets of economic globalisation made minorities richer.

The democracy of political globalisation allowed demagogues to whip up the resentments of the majority.

I said earlier that unlike its predecessor the 2005 Handsworth riot had nothing to do with the official world of local and national government. That was true in all respects but one. With unforgivable recklessness, our leaders are not diminishing the importance of race and religion, but fuelling sectarianism.

The untutored might think it the job of government to promote common citizenship. Yet in Birmingham, you see projects for the black unemployed, not all the unemployed, for disadvantaged Asians or Indians or Muslims, not all the disadvantaged. Across the country, wherever the BNP makes gains, you can guarantee it has been the beneficiary of white anger at grants and services dispensed on communalist lines.

State-sponsored sectarianism is about to take off. We are to have religions redefined as races, which they are not, and opposition to religion redefined as race hatred, which it is not. Meanwhile, Labour promises more faith schools that will segregate children and their parents by religion and race and, indeed, class in the case of top-end church schools.

I can see no more urgent task than taking the fight to those on the right and the left who are busily piling bricks on ghetto walls. If they are not stopped, I do not like to think what Handsworth or the rest of the country will be like in another twenty years.

Observer, October 2005

Ryanair Migrants

IF THE BNP had a camera crew, it could not have produced a more revolting depiction of immigrant life in London than David Cronenberg's film *Eastern Promises*. It starts as it means to go on with a Kurdish barber forcing his son to cut a customer's throat. A pregnant Russian child prostitute then dies having a Caesarean. Anna, a naive midwife at the hospital, resolves to find the newborn child's father. The trail leads to a Russian restaurant. The apparently avuncular proprietor does not only bring exotic foods to grateful Londoners, he is also a people trafficker, who holds girls in sex slavery – and has a psychopath for a son, for good measure.

The British barely feature in their own capital. Apart from Anna, a second-generation Russian, they are minor characters: police officers who examine mutilated corpses or passers-by who run for cover when Chechen assassins storm a public baths. Whether as victims or victimisers, Cronenberg's London is a city of foreigners. All right, all right, I know a storyteller is under no obligation to accept the constraints of a documentary maker. I would not have mentioned *Eastern Promises* if the critics had not treated Cronenberg's fantasy as fact. 'This is the kerb-crawling reality. This is London,' declared the man from *The Times*. Cronenberg shows London as a 'magnet for hucksters, desperadoes and fortune-seekers; a militarised, relentlessly surveillanced police state in the making,' said the

Telegraph. Philip French was more restrained, but still told *Observer* readers that this was a picture 'about the dark under-side of globalisation and multiculturalism'.

It is easy to feel like that living here. Ken Livingstone will be remembered for authorising the building of jagged skyscrapers that celebrate the global power of money while diminishing the little people on the pavements far below. The old English rich complain that they cannot compete against the new men from Russia and India. Crime is not as bad as you would guess from the papers – but our police force struggles to cope and the reas-suring bonds of community have broken down in suburbs where fifty different languages are spoken. The middle class, which was once delighted to have cheap Polish plumbers, can see it will not be too long before foreigners will be competing for its jobs. The working class – white, black and brown – has never liked new immigrants, and is as suspicious as ever. Every-one is frightened about Islamist attacks, including those who say they are not.

This darkening mood explains why liberal-minded critics do not respond to a picture of London as a city terrorised by foreign mobsters by recalling the tolerance of normal life. Why should they when a Labour prime minister comes out with a BNP slogan of 'British jobs for British people'* that would provoke a police investigation if an employer put it on a recruit-ment ad? David Cameron talks of 'unsustainable demographic change', safe in the knowledge that the old charge that the Tories had 'lurched to the right' would no longer stick. For voters from the middle and working classes, left and right, immigration is now their chief concern.

Superficially, it is hard to understand why. If I had said in 1997 that Britain would experience the largest influx of

---

* The prime minister was Gordon Brown engaging in the first of his many attempts to make himself popular.

migrants in history and not have a wave of racial violence, most readers would have regarded me as a cheerful innocent.

But there's the rub: no one did predict that Britain would see the largest wave of immigration in her history, not least the government. It is almost funny to go back to its assertions that only 15,000 migrants would come when Poland and seven other East European countries joined the EU. True, forecasting is a perilous business, but for 600,000 to arrive and for the forecasters to be out by a factor of 40 is quite an achievement. Ministers now admit that the official estimate that there were 800,000 foreign workers in Britain was wrong, too. The figure should have been 1.5 million – maybe more. Damian Green, the Conservative immigration spokesman, has a collection of parliamentary questions about immigration the Home Office can't answer. A full catalogue of government ignorance would fill a book, but as a taster: Home Office ministers have been unable to tell him how many convicted murderers, drug dealers and racists have been granted British citizenship; how many deported foreign offenders turned round and flew straight back again; and how many times the police and ambulance services were called to riots at immigration detention centres.

A feeling that the system cannot cope pervades those who work in it as well as the opposition benches. A judge told me he felt he was wasting his time with immigration cases. Even if he ordered a deportation, the immigrant was free to leave the courtroom and disappear into the slums. Officials from the PCS union, which represents immigration officers, are just as exasperated. Ever-changing Home Office targets drive their members' work. Depending on the morning's headlines, their superiors tell them to go after asylum seekers one day, foreign prisoners the next.

The confusion at the top is a sign of how old policies and old attitudes no longer fit the modern world. Both the racism and the anti-racism of the twentieth century developed in response to the migration of large blocs of people from a few specific locations – black immigrants coming from the West Indies, Asians fleeing from the terror of Idi Amin's Uganda. They faced culturally specific forms of racism: the young black man as a mugger; the Asian shopkeeper as interloper and legitimate target for native yobs. The left was willing to meet popular fears – the Wilson government of the sixties passed anti-immigration legislation that was just as tough as the Blair government's laws against asylum seekers – but because most immigrants came in blocs from specific cultures, the left could also develop an anti-racist strategy to bring them into national life. It co-opted 'community leaders' of doubtful democratic legitimacy to represent each bloc on to the boards of quangos and public bodies and bent over backwards to announce its respect for diversity.

We are now living with the consequences. Parts of the ignored white working class have realised that they, too, can play the identity politics game and rebrand themselves as 'the whites', but it isn't only the rise of the BNP which is doing for multiculturalism.

Twentieth-century racism and anti-racism are out of date because today's migrants are not from a few parts of the world but from dozens of countries. Modern racists do not shout about black criminals or scheming Pakistani traders but have to content themselves with more generalised complaints about 'immigrants'. Their real diversity also cripples the ability of the left to carry on with the old anti-racist tactics. How can quangos and public bodies co-opt new immigrants on to their boards when in Britain 'ethnic minority' no longer means people descended from West Africans, Indians, Bangladeshis and Pakistanis, but also Hungarians, Poles, Bosnians, Albanians, Lithuanians, Latvians, Ethiopians, Somalians, South Africans, Kurds, Iraqis, Peruvians ... to name but a few? A public body that tried to find a seat for every minority would be crushed by the bureaucratic effort. Respecting the diversity of dozens of cultures is beyond the mental capacity of the most broad-minded liberal.

Unlike their predecessors, new migrants do not always settle. There is less need to integrate, which should calm those who wonder how much integration one society can take, but equally their transient presence makes Britain feel more fragmented, less solid. They send money home, and then go home themselves – 'immigrants for the age of Ryanair', as Trevor Phillips calls them.

'Stay away from people like me,' warns one of the many villains in Cronenberg's blood-drenched movie, and many of today's immigrants will stay apart. The trouble is the government does not know who they are, where they are, how long they will stay or when they will go. As seriously, wider liberal society does not yet grasp that the only way to cope with real diversity is to stop feeding communalism, religious sectarianism and neo-fascism by emphasising difference and return to the classic liberal determination to treat people equally and to hell with their colours and creeds.

Observer, November 2007

Neo-Fascists at the Village Hall

NOTHING HAPPENS IN UPPER BEEDING, David Coldwell, the editor of the village newsletter, used to complain. The 'mooted bus shelter in the high street' had been delayed by the planning process, along with the refurbishment of the village playground. As for his proposal to put up signs directing visitors to the shops in Hyde Square, West Sussex County Council was so shocked by his radicalism it threw it out.

Until now, the most newsworthy event was the annual boat race in which well-lubricated contestants paddled down the River Adur to Shoreham-by-Sea in adapted baths, while being pelted from the banks with flour bombs, eggs and anything else that came to hand. Although it occasionally got out of hand, the jolly competition only reinforced Upper Beeding's charming image.

'The wheels turn slowly, but they do turn!' Coldwell cried as he explained the sluggish pace of progress, but I wonder whether he believed it. Upper Beeding seemed to fit a sentimental ideal of an English village where nothing changes.

Supplies of charm ran out just before Christmas when twenty-three villagers marched from the pub to the parish buildings to demand that local worthies put a member of a neo-fascist party on the council.

'I never realised the speed with which neighbours can turn,' Simon Birnstingl, a gardener who sits on the council, told me.

'One minute, we were discussing how to get the swings fixed, the next a crowd burst in calling for me to be barred from the meeting. I've learnt to toughen up. I look at politicians when they're in trouble and feel sympathy now. Gordon Brown must go through the struggle I'm going through every day, so I am determined to see it through.'

However strange it sounds to talk about an anti-fascist struggle in Upper Beeding, that is what he has been facing.

It began when Birnstingl was talking to his wife about villagers who wanted to be co-opted into empty seats on the parish council. The name Donna Bailey sounded familiar. She checked and found that Bailey had run twice for the British National Party in district elections.

Birnstingl assumed that once he told the rest of the council their task was to improve Upper Beeding, not divide it on racial lines, that would be the end of Bailey's candidacy. Not so. Or, rather, not entirely. After Bailey's friends heard that Birnstingl was planning to veto her appointment, they stormed into the parish meeting room. Undeterred, the council twice voted not to co-opt Bailey as a member, but only by a majority of one on both occasions. She forced a by-election and although two candidates stood against her, she had many supporters in the village.

Townies will say that they have always known that the countryside is full of dangerous fanatics. But it's clear that not all Bailey's friends think they are fanatics. They are otherwise ordinary men and women who cannot see what is wrong with a member of the BNP participating in village life.

When I tracked Bailey down, she was all outraged innocence. She had helped raise funds for the local school for four years, she said. When the Round Table decided to stop supporting the Bath Tub Race because of the ubiquitous worries about health and safety legislation, she intervened and saved it. The parish council did not make political decisions, but dealt with street lights and playgrounds. Why shouldn't a citizen who has worked hard for local causes join it?

Many in Upper Beeding agree that being a member of the BNP is like being a member of the Liberal Democrats, a choice that has no effect on personal standing or moral worth. If she is a help at the village school, her politics don't matter.

The same view can be found across the country, although how deeply it is held is impossible to determine. As I have said before, the notion that the mass of people are racists, programmed by our imperial past to despise outsiders, has been shattered by the population movements of the past decade. The largest wave of immigration in British history was not accompanied by riots, just grumbles.

Nevertheless, there has been a small but palpable electoral effect. Sean Fear of the politicalbetting.com website says that the BNP won an average 14.4 per cent of the vote in thirty-eight council by-elections it fought in 2008 and polled higher than 20 per cent in ten. This was a far better performance than the National Front managed in the seventies and way above the average vote the Greens win today. Like most other analysts, he expects that proportional representation will bring the BNP seats on the London Assembly in May.*

The far right is as crippled by sectarian hatreds as the far left. The back-stabbing of its leaders and rank incompetence of its councillors would make all but the most committed neo-Nazi despair. Nevertheless, significant minorities are prepared to vote BNP, even in districts with few or no immigrants. Like

---

* Just one candidate won a place in the end, Richard Barnbrook, who had hung around the fringes of the subsidised arts where so many totalitarian ideas are treated with indulgence. Barnbrook had an affair with a ballerina from the English National Ballet, even though she had previously had a child with a Cuban dancer. 'I'm not opposed to mixed marriages,' he explained, 'but their children are washing out the identity of this country's indigenous people.'

Donna Bailey's neighbours, they think there is nothing wrong with BNP activists.

Gerry Gable, of the anti-fascist magazine *Searchlight*, told me that theirs was a hard attitude to confront. The press and the BNP's rivals like to seize on the criminal convictions of BNP leaders or chronicle its splits and purges. Less easy to document is what happens when far-right views become normal in a pub or social club. Are there more racial attacks by whites and blacks and Asians? Do blacks and Asians attack whites? No one can say for sure.

In Upper Beeding, Joyce Shaw, a former stalwart of the parish council, who's come out of retirement, and Becki Davoudi, who has an Iranian father, and, like the Asian family who have revived the village shop, had good reason to oppose the far right, are standing against Bailey. What they're fighting is nothing as concrete as a political programme or the certainty of violence, but something vaguer: a chilling of the atmosphere; a potential for disgrace.

'When I take my children to school, there are people who used to smile and say "hello", who now give me hostile looks,' said Simon Birnstingl. 'They don't realise that we're trying to stop this village falling into disrepute.'*

Observer, January 2008

---

* A few weeks later I received a note saying,

Dear Nick,
We got the result, despite the split vote. Nearly 500 voted against Ms Bailey.
Thanks for all your help.
Regards, Simon Birnstingl

Shooting the Foxes

ABOUT THREE HUNDRED hunts were roaming the countryside on the first anniversary of the ban on the hunting of foxes with dogs. Parliament thought it had erased this traditional scene from the English landscape, but there the hunters were, carrying on as their predecessors had done for centuries, and treating all the debates in the Commons as so much wasted breath. If you had inspected one, everything might have looked as it had always looked. Bellowing riders would still have been tearing across fields. Yelping hounds would still have been chasing after foxes and killing them when they caught them. Only if you had looked closely would you have noticed small departures from tradition. A few of the hunters may have set off early to lay a trail and one of them could have been carrying a falcon.

Depending on your point of view, God or the Devil would have dwelt in these details. They may seem tiny, but they have killed the anti-hunting law whose passing was greeted with such triumphal whoops by Labour MPs and animal rights activists. Those of us who were not moved by the passions of either side are seeing the obvious flaws in a doomed attempt to criminalise a rural tradition.

For all their protestations to the contrary, the opponents of hunting were not trying to save the lives of foxes but punish a specific type of hunter: the caricature Tory toff with a red coat and redder face. As foxes have flourished in both town and country, they could not ask Parliament to declare them an endangered species. As they are predators which go for lambs and chickens, MPs couldn't have declared them a protected species either. Very quietly, so that their urban supporters did not notice, Parliament accepted that foxes had to be culled, and riddled its apparently authoritarian prohibition with loopholes large enough to run a pack of hounds through.

A farmer can still shoot or snare a fox that is threatening his animals – it would be outrageous if he could not. He might wound it and leave it to endure a long slow death, but such apparent cruelty remained legal. The farmer can still use one or two dogs to chase a fox and flush it out of its hiding place, and then shoot it. According to the law, he is guilty only if he goes after it with more than two dogs and allows them to kill it. Cross that line and his Chief Constable would have to send snatch squads to the fields of Devon or the fells of Cumbria to arrest him. If the legal theory sounds an exercise in hypocrisy, posturing, hair-splitting, special pleading and pointless vindictiveness, the practice is worse.

Lord knows, I find the class hatred behind the hunting of the hunters easy to understand. Britain is the only rich country not to have had a modern revolution. In France, America, even Ireland, hunting arouses no great opposition because the aristocracy's estates were broken up in the eighteenth and nineteenth centuries, or were never there in the first place, in the case of the free-soil states of America.

The typical Continental smallholding, with a few acres on which the owner can do as he or she pleases, is a rarity here. This land is not our land but the property of the great families, Forestry Commission and National Trust. Naturally, its owners are resented. I also understand how after eighteen years of Conservative rule, Labour MPs wanted to get their own back on the Tories and, indeed, on Tony Blair, who had made them give up so much they had held dear. Nevertheless, their vengeance is looking not only dictatorial but also vacuous: a sham that allows the Parliamentary Labour Party to pretend it can still fight a war which Margaret Thatcher and Tony Blair won. The MPs who forced through the ban are starting to resemble an old drunk flailing his fists and succeeding only in punching the air.

They were too consumed with hatred to care that no measure that stopped short of giving predators a protected status could be enforceable. Because their legislation would not and could not protect foxes per se, hunters are exploiting its exemptions. As Labour MPs have nothing against falconry – perhaps because *Kes* moved them to tears when they were young – Parliament allowed falconers to set off with an unlimited number of dogs to flush out mammals for birds of prey to swoop on. All right, said the fox hunters, we will take a falcon with us.

The law says the police have to prove that hunters intended to set their dogs on a fox; otherwise, they would have to prosecute a pet owner whose dogs bolted in a country field and chased a fox, as dogs are prone to do. All right, said the hunts, we will lay a trail for the hounds to follow and if they run off after a fox, we can say our intention was to have a drag hunt, not a fox hunt.

The current issue of *Horse & Hound* contains an interview with one Graham Sirl, who blames the League Against Cruel Sports and the Royal Society for the Prevention of Cruelty to Animals for running a lavish lobbying campaign that has produced nothing but gesture politics. 'I despise the people who put the Hunting Bill forward,' he says. 'I despise those organisations that threw money at that campaign for an end that was absolutely zero. They had the opportunity, it was given to them on a plate and they blew it.'

No surprise that *Horse & Hound* should condemn the ban as an absurd waste of Parliament's time, you might think. And it would be unremarkable if Graham Sirl were not a former chief officer of the League Against Cruel Sports. He is not alone in giving up on the cause he once championed. In the past decade, the league has lost two chief executives, two chairmen, one treasurer and one regional head. All of them concluded that an effective ban would lead to the slaughter of foxes by farmers with guns who no longer had to keep them alive to give their local hunts a quarry to chase. I cannot think of another protest group that has seen so many of its officers go over to the other side. It is as if senior officers of Greenpeace were resigning to join the board of Texaco.

The people who are at the league, for the time being at any rate, told me they expected the police to collect evidence that the hunts are intentionally breaking the law and bring prosecutions soon. If hunters carry on without the police prosecuting them, the ban will join Margaret Thatcher's prohibition of the promotion of homosexuality and Jack Straw's curfews for children in that list of fatuous legislation politicians designed to make vocal minorities feel good which succeeded only in bringing the law into disrepute.*

Observer, February 2006

---

* The police sensibly steered clear of a law that was close to unenforceable. The League Against Cruel Sports brought a private prosecution and managed to secure a conviction against a Devon hunt whose hounds, it claimed, were killing foxes on Exmoor rather than flushing them out so a hunter could shoot them. The anomalies and contradictions in the animal rights campaigners' legislation couldn't be gainsaid for long, however, and the conviction was overturned on appeal. The hunt saboteur groups, that had once been able to mobilise thousands of supporters to harass hunts, realised the futility of their cause and dispersed. Charles Frampton, master of the Portman Hunt in Dorset, declared the phoney war over when he said, 'We are pretty much left alone. We haven't seen any hunt saboteurs for a long time. It's business as usual, within the confines of the Act of course.'

Law without Order

I LIVE IN AN AREA which is no longer a real network of streets in north-east London but a joke or an insult or a synonym for the folly of the bleeding-heart middle class. I live in Islington, which according to national legend is the home of air-kissing, cocaine-snorting, gym-going, *Guardian*-reading, latte-slurping, organic, fair-trade, GM-free-munching fashionistas. If literary critics and conceptual artists enjoying the newest and hottest Byelorussian eatery packed the borough, I would have no right to complain. But the reality is worse than that. City bonuses have priced Islington's few bourgeois streets beyond the reach of young intellectuals, while the overwhelming majority of its households are wretchedly poor.

The remnants of the intelligentsia, the foreign exchange dealers, the shop girls and the asylum seekers appeared to have nothing in common, until traffic wardens united the drivers among them in a common cause. Ever since the council privatised the service, they have experienced zero-tolerance policing, and tales of the wardens' rapacity have supplanted the weather or the fortunes of Arsenal as the conversation opener guaranteed to break the ice. You may not care about the fate of the capital's motorists, but local government's voracious appetite for ready cash and Gordon Brown's efficiency drives, all but guarantee that what is happening in central London will be coming soon to your neighbourhood.

On the face of it, the strict application of parking regulations is a policy everyone should applaud. Making driving harder and more expensive benefits the environment and saves children's lives. Who but a sociopath could object to that?

But parking restrictions are still the law, and the example of Islington shows that when private companies are put in charge of law enforcement the law is pushed to its limit and beyond.

The wardens' discretion went first. There was no place for it. Mourners at funerals and witnesses pulling over to tell the police about crimes have had wardens slap tickets on their windows. Contractors doing up the borough's rotting council estates have had to add the costs of recovering their vehicles from the car pound to the price of the job. 'We are being deliberately targeted,' said one to the *Highbury and Islington Express*. 'In the last two weeks alone, I have paid £719 on the company credit card for vehicles that were either clamped or towed away. It is ludicrous.'

They even dared to clamp Kate Winslet after she left her car for a moment to go into an Islington shop. In the past, her car could have stood for hours or days with a ticket on the windscreen before the pick-up truck hauled it away. Now they can be gone within minutes, as I found when I thought mine had been stolen while my back was turned, only to be directed by the weary officer at my local station to the car pound. Inside, furious people, stunned at having to pay £250 fines, surrounded me. The staff worked behind toughened-glass screens, which looked as if they could stop a bullet. Their days were spent listening to screaming rages and pleas for mercy, and their dead eyes and expressionless faces had the look of men and women who had trained themselves to be completely detached from their surroundings.

There is no slack in the privatised system. And if you believe in the 'broken windows' theory, the right's favourite piece of cod criminology, no quarter should be expected or given. If you leave broken windows in a building, the theory runs, vandals will realise no one wants to protect it and will destroy the rest of the house. Allow them to do that, and drug dealers will move in, decent citizens will move out and before you know it, a once respectable neighbourhood will be a crime ghetto. For windows, read illegally parked cars.

A woman who stops on a yellow line merely so she can help an elderly relative up a steep flight of steps must be punished to prevent a greater evil.

Like so many modern politicians, Steve Hitchins, Islington's leader, had to wrestle with the problem of how to promote efficiency in the public sector. The London *Evening Standard* regularly carried stories about publicly employed wardens knocking off after an hour and going to cafés or the cinema for the rest of the day. Their unions thought they had a guaranteed monopoly and, somewhat unwisely in the light of subsequent events, decided to demonstrate their power by calling the wardens out on strike. A private company offered to send in its wardens as strike-breakers. The revenue shot up, and Hitchins learned that his council could earn more if he contracted out parking.

He dismisses the complaints that fill the local papers as middle-class whinging, and talks about joining with other councils across Britain to bulk-buy private warden services, in line with the Treasury's plans to promote economies of scale in public spending. The prospect may not sound so terrible. Offenders replenish the public purse and the affluent learn that zero tolerance includes intolerance for their petty crimes as well as the crimes of the poor. And yet anyone who has seen London's parking privatisation in action knows that the price mechanism is an incentive for miscarriages of justice. A contractor is obliged to deliver so many thousand tickets a year. If it exceeds its target, it receives a cut of the additional income. Poor wardens, most of them immigrants, are pushed to hit the target and make the profit. They have to get by on £6.75 an hour. They make extra money not by enforcing the law conscientiously but by issuing more tickets. Private wardens, or 'parking attendants', as they have been fatuously renamed, receive a £50 monthly bonus if they issue two tickets on average an hour, which rises to £215 if their hit rate rises to three an hour.

One worker in Westminster told the *Standard* that 'Wardens feel under massive pressure. Some end up issuing dodgy tickets to meet the targets.' Everywhere you go, you hear stories like my neighbour's. He lives in a council flat but drives a Bentley (we don't ask where he got the money from in case he mistakes us for grasses). One morning at 8 a.m., he caught a warden crawling along the pavement. The parking restrictions don't come into effect until 8.30 a.m. According to the tickets he was surreptitiously slapping on cars, it was 9 a.m. My neighbour is a big man and had to be restrained from beating the warden up.

A few streets away, a warden stabbed a nineteen-year-old in disputed circumstances. (Witnesses claimed it was because the boy had warned drivers that they were about to get a ticket.) The atmosphere has become so nasty that the police have to go on joint patrols with wardens to protect them from the public. No one, from the leader of the council downwards, would be surprised if someone was killed.

In its small way, what has happened in Islington shows why 'broken windows' theory should never be put into practice. English policing used to be as much about order as law. Officers used their common sense, and intervened to calm potentially violent confrontations and move people on. There were quiet words rather than arrests, and extenuating circumstances were considered.

Zero-tolerance policing destroys the social balance because it allows no discretion. The system rewards officers for making arrests or issuing penalties, not for keeping the peace. Relatively law-abiding citizens become violently intolerant of the law – and of the luckless men and women who have to enforce it – a cost no accountant is prepared to measure.

New Statesman, August 2004

Svengali at the Church School

OF ALL THE RELIGIOUS SLOGANS that pushed European liberals into anti-clericalism, the Jesuit boast 'Give me the child until the age of seven and I will give you the man' was the most provocative. The impressionable were to be brainwashed. Superstitions were to be embedded so deeply in their minds that they would be beyond the reach of reason when they grew up.

It feels like dragging up ancient history to speak of intellectual child abuse today. The wars between militant Christianity and militant atheism died in the early twentieth century. They fought each other in France, Spain and other strange countries, not dear old Blighty with its traditions of tolerance and rubbing along. They had ideological wars; we had the Church of England, whose muddled moderation offended no one but Richard Dawkins.

Secular middle-class parents go to extraordinary lengths to get their children into C of E schools. They know that church schools offer the next best thing to a private education because they can select, albeit covertly. No mother dragging herself to church every Sunday to feign an interest in a god she doesn't believe in thinks for a moment that her child will grown up into a burning-eyed zealot.

When extremism is sweeping the world's religions, the past may no longer be a reliable guide. The same reason why a majority of the British reject established beliefs – that the Bible, the Torah or the Koran, or whatever, can no longer seriously claim to be a source of authority – is turning faith into the extremism of the defeated. Like nations, religions are at their most dangerous when they feel their power diminishing. The need for evangelical piety is all the greater as the foundations of their faith become more fragile. In its own small way, the Church of England is no exception.

According to documents collected by the National Secular Society, if parents send their five-year-old children to C of E schools in the diocese of Canterbury, their teacher will subject them to what sounds very like hypnosis.

It is a far cry from *The Vicar of Dibley*. First, the diocese tells the teacher how to arrange her charges. 'The legs are uncrossed. Feet are flat on the floor. Hands are resting on the lap and, most importantly, the back is straight.' Then the teacher begins controlling the children's 'ability to imagine'.

She lights a candle, closes the curtain, and tells the children to shut their eyes. Using a 'calm soothing voice' she begins her 'unhurried narration'.

Anyone who has tried hypnotherapy will be familiar with the attempt to create a suggestible, dreamlike state. The Church does not call what it is doing hypnosis, but 'guided meditations'. It accepts that they can 'produce deep emotions', and the diocesan schools adviser says it is important to make the exercise voluntary. She does not explain, however, how a five-year-old at a C of E primary school is any more capable of voluntarily understanding the risks of 'deep emotions' than a seven-year-old at an old Jesuit college.

She goes on to list the thoughts the teacher can implant. Snippets from her guidance do not convey their hypnotic force, so I will go through one exercise in full.

You are a child again. You are sitting, eyes closed, back straight, hands in your lap, in a darkened room. A calm, soothing voice begins.

Imagine you find yourself in a kitchen, a very old-fashioned kitchen, no modern cookers or refrigerators. Food is hanging in sacks from the ceiling ... There is a fire burning ... There is a large table in the middle ... and an open fire on which are cooking pots ... You gaze around. What sort of kitchen is it? Is it small or large? Can you smell all the food? As you are looking around, there is a tap on your shoulder. 'Come on, stop daydreaming, take the food in. The Master will be here soon.'

You pick up a big bowl from in front of you full of delicious-smelling stew ... You carry it through the door and into the next room where people are gathering ... They're all dressed in long robes, men and women ... All standing around talking ... Peter, one of the disciples, comes across ... What does he look like? ... 'Here, I'll take that,' he says. You pick up some bread from the side table and put it on the main table ... You feel very shy in the room full of adults ... but everyone is very friendly ... You stand and look around the room. What is it like? ... walls ... ceiling ... floor ... Can you see anything out of the windows?

Then the cook comes and speaks to you: 'Come and sit down with me. The Master will be here any minute.' You go and take your place at the end of the table with the cook ... Everybody else begins to sit down. The door opens and in comes Jesus. Can you see him? ... What does he look like? ... Is he clean-shaven or bearded? ... Young or old? Happy or sad? Everybody greets him, including you ... He goes and takes his place in the middle ... Jesus takes the bread that you set out and breaks it in half and says: 'Take this and eat, because this is my body,' and he passes the bread along ... How does he look? ... The bread comes along and everybody breaks off a piece and eats it ... What does it taste like? ...

Now nobody is talking and everyone looks very serious ... Then you see Jesus take the jug of wine and pour into two goblets. He lifts them up and says, 'This is my blood which will be poured out for many.' And he passes the cups along and everybody in turn takes a drink ... You turn and whisper to the cook, 'What does it mean?' Watch the scene in your mind. Does the cook explain? ... What is he saying? ... What happens next?

Like any good hypnotist, the Diocesan Board of Education recognises that it needs to manage the moment of coming out of a trance carefully. When the calm voice has finished its gentle pleading, the board advises, 'It is probably wise after guided meditations and guided imagery to bring children back to reality, e.g., get them to say their names. Always disengage from meditations or guided visualisations slowly and peacefully so as not to break the mood.'

Follow-up questions to the children reinforce the message once the spell is broken. An impressionable five-year-old going through the above evocation of the Last Supper is not likely to have had scepticism banged into his or her mind. But just to make sure that the lesson has hit home, the teacher is instructed to ask, 'What were your thoughts and feelings as you watched the disciples and Jesus? How did you feel about Jesus?' The correct answer is not 'This is gross' and no child would say so.

Terry Sanderson of the National Secular Society says the Church is engaged in brainwashing, and the determination to indoctrinate is part of a pattern, which those who attack Christian fundamentalism in British schools have missed. Most critics have gone for the teaching of creationism in the handful of city academies run by Sir Peter Vardy, the second-hand-car dealer New Labour has allowed to buy his way into the education system.

It's an outrage, to be sure, but concentrating on the sheer weirdness of Vardy misses the wider point that the Anglican Church isn't the quasi-agnostic institution it once was. As pews empty, controlling children's education is the Church's last best hope. In its 2001 report *The Way Ahead: Church of England Schools in the New Millennium*, the Church criticised C of E schools that were indistinguishable from ordinary state schools. Their heads must stop offering a good education with a bit of God thrown in and 'demonstrate that educational "effectiveness" is concerned with the development of the whole person as a child of God'.

The Church was going to be saved by capturing the young early. 'Our work over the past 18 months has confirmed the crucial importance of the Church schools to the whole mission of the Church to children and young people, and indeed to the long-term well-being of the Church of England.'

The hypnotic classes in Canterbury are not a one-off. Readers might object that children are subject to all kinds of brainwashing, delivered by everyone from advertisers to PlayStation manufacturers, and that most manage to survive. But advertising and PlayStations aren't funded by the taxpayer, and parents can control what their children watch. They cannot control what happens in Church schools, yet the Church expects everyone to fund them through their taxes. If a desperate Church feels the need to start playing mind games with children, shouldn't it at least do so in its own time and at its own expense?

New Statesman, August 2004

Blowing Britishness Away

THE PARIS COMMUNE horrified the crowned heads of Europe. Monarchs and emperors responded to the world's first socialist revolution by ordering their officials to round up the incendiary thinkers who inspired rebellion. The German ambassador to London demanded that Lord Granville, Home Secretary in 1871, arrest the most dangerous of the lot: a shabby-genteel scholar who was living in exile in London.

The rulers of Spain, France and the Austro-Hungarian Empire agreed with the Kaiser that Karl Marx was a menace to life and property. After consulting with the queen, Granville dismissed them with the magnificent disdain of a high-Victorian liberal. There would be no coalition of the willing against terror, he declared. Foreigners living in England were entitled to enjoy the freedoms of this country. As for Marx's inflammatory doctrines, the police had informed him that British trade unionists had the good sense to ignore them. 'Extreme socialist opinions are not believed to have gained any hold upon the working men of this country,' he said, and sent the ambassadors away.

Underlying his insouciance were three assumptions about Britain and the British:

1. Britain had freedom of speech and conscience. There was no place here for a thought police.

2. A British citizen, or an immigrant to Britain, was not obliged to swear loyalty to any idea or constitution. Nor could the state order him to appear before some Commons Un-British Activities Committee if he failed to subscribe to the nation's principles. There were no ideological obligations in Britishness.
3. Because the British were a level-headed lot who ignored dangerous ideas from the Continent, these liberties did not endanger security.

The Islamist atrocities in London wounded, perhaps fatally, all three propositions.

Until 7 July 2005, history had vindicated Lord Granville's confidence. According to Marx's doctrines, Britain was the most advanced capitalist society and therefore should have been among the first to experience a socialist revolution. His Lordship understood the working class better than the radical dialectician did, and British Marxism remained a tiny force; an ideology which appealed more to intellectuals than workers, stronger in the senior common room than among the common people. You might say that Bin Ladenism has as little appeal. Estimates of the number of British Muslims who have trained in Afghanistan and Pakistan are obviously imprecise, but every analyst says the numbers involved are in the hundreds or thousands rather than the hundreds of thousands.

As with the communists, we are dealing with tiny groups of men, but it as this point that the comparison breaks down. There were communists who were spies, such as Kim Philby, and fellow-travelling Labour MPs who represented the interests of Stalin better than those of their constituents, such as D. N. Pritt.* Yet, however many tens of millions were murdered in

---

* Denis Nowell Pritt, KC, MP (1887–1972), is one of ugliest figures in Labour history. After graduating from Winchester and joining the Bar he became a

Marx's name in the twentieth century, British communists never slaughtered their neighbours. Most were committed to peaceful protest and could not have changed Britain without the democratic support of millions of people. Islamism shares the totalitarianism of British communism but not its commitment to non-violence. As it takes only a handful of psychopaths to take thousands of lives, the difference between the present and the past ought to be clear. The trouble with Islamism is that it does not need to recruit many fanatics to transform Britain.

The government is pressing on with its woefully unwise plans to outlaw incitement to religious hatred – a measure which will strengthen the very fruitcakes who want to kill us – and is planning to introduce the odd crime of 'indirect incitement to terrorism'. Granville's belief that refugees could come to Britain and speak their minds is already under assault and the attacks may soon become fiercer.

Ever since the attack on the Tube, critics have been laying into the intelligence services for allowing the creation of Beirut-on-Thames in London. It was true that in the early nineties, there seemed to be no limit to the number of Islamists who could find a home here. But the authorities long ago gave up their hope that they wouldn't attack the country that had given them sanctuary. The government's difficulty is that it cannot persuade the courts to take a harder line. Tony Blair's frustration was evident long before 9/11. We know precisely what he was thinking as early as 1999, because court orders made his private thoughts on the case of Hani Youssef public. Youssef was allegedly a member of Islamic Jihad, which, in addition to

Labour activist. In 1932 he visited the Soviet Union. According to Margaret Cole, the Fabian who organised the trip, the eminent KC 'swallowed it *all*'. Far from condemning mass murder, his introduction to a defence of Stalin's show trials published by the Left Book Club in 1937 suggested the tyrant's secret policemen had had not gone far enough.

organising atrocities, had declared that it was the duty of Muslims to kill Jews, Americans and their military and civilian allies – including, presumably, British troops and civilians. The security services said he shouldn't be granted asylum. As those they judge to be a threat to national security have never had rights to asylum under British or international law, his deportation to Egypt seemed inevitable.

His lawyers said the Home Office must grant him sanctuary, nevertheless, because of the possibility that he could be tortured when he returned home. The Foreign Office tried to get an undertaking from the Egyptians that they would not torture him, and guarantees of access to lawyers and to a fair trial. As the list of conditions needed to remove him grew, Blair scrawled in the margins of the official papers, 'This is a bit much. Why do we need all these things?' As the diplomats negotiated, the Red Cross intervened and fluttering lawyers inserted ever more caveats, his bemusement turned to rage. 'This is crazy,' he wrote. 'Why can't we press on?' The courts would not let him because the government could not prove a negative and show that Youssef would not be mistreated in Egypt. They allowed him to enjoy the same freedom to live in Britain unmolested that Marx had enjoyed and compensated him for the injustice he had suffered.

Whether they will carry on being as accommodating if the violence escalates is another matter. Judicial independence is a bit of a myth, as the judiciary tends to move with public opinion. In a time of peace, it will impose all kinds of conditions. My guess is that, if London comes under further attack, the judges will be a little less fussy. Even if they do not, Britain is, in the end, a democracy, not a judgocracy. If Parliament votes to override the courts, then overridden they will be.

Youssef was fighting extradition to face criminal charges, but what about Islamists, who, like the early Marxists, only express an opinion. As far as we know, the secret case that sent Abu Qatada to Belmarsh prison after 9/11 was not that he organised terrorist outrages or was likely to do so. Rather, he was imprisoned because his preaching inspired suicidal killers including the 9/11 hijackers. A large part of the liberal left is so anxious not to appear judgemental, that it won't condemn. It meets Robert Frost's definition of a liberal as 'a man too broad-minded to take his own side in a quarrel'. Yet even the part of the left which is prepared to stick up for itself and stand by its comrades in Iraq, Iran and elsewhere, has to accept that interning Abu Qatada is as much a suppression of free expression in our age as interning Karl Marx would have been in the Victorian era.

For Islamist asylum seekers, residence in Britain is becoming dependent on belief: on what they say and what they do not. This restriction ought to be opposed. But there is a real difference between silencing those who inspired communists, who killed no one in Britain, and those who inspire Islamists, who do and will. This distinction changes everything. It is all very well saying you're for freedom of speech, even freedom of speech for fascists ... but for fascists who inspire *suicide bombers*? Defend that freedom and you may have blood on your hands, maybe your own blood.

Whether any of the government's restrictions will stop the bombers is another matter. New Labour cannot ban visits to the training camps of Pakistan, nor can it ban access to the websites and bookshops of the religious right.

Yet New Labour can change the country. You see it changing in the citizenship classes for schoolchildren and for immigrants, which insist that being British requires the learning of British values; in the near-universal acceptance of armed police on the streets and security cameras on every corner; and in the sad feeling that our world is closer to the deranged religious fanaticism of the Middle Ages than to Lord Granville's liberal self-confidence.

New Statesman, July 2005

PART 3

Oh, Comrades!

'By virtue of a new ruse, but one not unprecedented in the history of ideas, the most singular characteristic of this second temptation is that it no longer takes its inspiration from the left but from the right. A right-wing left indeed. Literally, from the Right, in fact. An oxymoronic left, a left that makes your head spin – a left that, if words have any meaning at all, is sometimes more right wing than the right wing itself.'

BERNARD-HENRI LEVY,
Left in Dark Times, 2008

Pacifists and the Bomb

BEFORE YOU GO TO a left-wing meeting, prepare yourself for the likelihood that everyone you meet will be standing on their heads. Do not be surprised to see communists supporting fascists, feminists throwing their arms around misogynists and liberals apologising for tyranny. It has been like this since 9/11 turned the world upside down, and the temptation for a journalist is to play the cynical reporter and pretend to be unshockable. I try my best to be a hard man, but the shocks keep on coming. Take the fates of two venerable left-wing institutions, the Campaign for Nuclear Disarmament and *Searchlight*.

For eighteen months, I had CND workers telling me how the same people who disgraced the anti-war movement had forced them out. I could not see how to write about their treatment. How could I prove that they were victims of a political purge rather than second-rate workers fired for poor performance? In any case, the peace movement was always a tense alliance between Christians and communists. Feuds were inevitable, but the bitterness they produced did not mean that CND's ideas were inevitably wrong. Certainly, when enthusiasm for unilateral disarmament swept Labour in the thirties, fifties and eighties, it destroyed the party's electoral chances. Pacifism so clearly favoured the interests of first Nazi Germany and then the Soviet Union, the public could never support it. Even when the agents of the old Eastern Bloc infiltrated CND, however, the peace movement had a more general critique of the nuclear age which remained pertinent after the fall of the Berlin Wall. Nuclear power breeds nuclear weapons and nuclear weapons breed more nuclear weapons, CND argued. Unless proliferation stops, they will fall into the hands of men who are prepared to use them, with unimaginable consequences.

Or so it once said. Anyone who now believes CND is as much against nuclear proliferation as for the unilateral abolition of Britain's nuclear weapons should have gone to its annual conference. Among the guests was the startling figure of Dr Seyed Mohammad Hossein Adeli, the Iranian ambassador. Iran is building the nuclear power stations CND once protested against – an anomalous project for a country with one of the largest reserves of oil in the world. Not only the US government but also the United Nations and the European Union suspect the Islamic Republic wants the bomb. The clear course for those who are sincere about nuclear disarmament is to oppose Tehran as vigorously as they oppose a replacement for Trident.

But there's the rub: standing by its principles would have put CND members on the same side as George W. Bush and Tony Blair, if only for a moment, and that was unthinkable. It was psychologically easier for CND to betray, and pretend it was being principled while it betrayed.

Betrayal and the hypocrisy that accompanies it have defined the liberal left since Iraq, because anti-Americans find their comrades in the Kurdish socialist movement or the Iraqi Communist Party or Arab liberal parties an embarrassment and cannot stick by them or pay them the common courtesy of acknowledging their existence. Given that record, I guess it was inevitable that CND, whose governing council is stuffed with activists who call themselves 'socialists', 'workers' and 'communists', would take the next step and betray the Iranian left.

The Islamists murdered tens of thousands of leftists, perhaps up to 100,000, after the 1979 Iranian revolution. Trade unionists, atheists and women's rights activists can now expect flog-gings and jail sentences. Members of the Worker-Communist Party of Iran exiled in London therefore gazed with astonishment on CND's dalliance with a 'fascistic' state. The invitation to the ambassador was an 'outrage', the party said. CND was insulting 'the people of Iran who are struggling to get rid of this brutal regime', and the countless thousands who have died in the attempt.

Iranians went to the conference to protest. CND stewards threw them out when they heckled the ambassador, just as Labour Party conference stewards had thrown out CND's Walter Wolfgang when he heckled Jack Straw the previous month.

CND's Kate Hudson told me she opposed the Iranian nuclear programme. She was not shouting 'rah-rah Iran', and had invited the ambassador merely to hear what he had to say. In her small way, I'm sure she's sincere. But if CND does not invite speakers from the Ministry of Defence or the American embassy to hear what they have to say – and it does not – and never issues a press release condemning the Iranian regime – ditto – outsiders are entitled to look at the burden of the evidence Hudson is presenting and consider her opposition to Iran to be little more than throat-clearing.

The conference over, Iran's new president, Mahmoud Ahmadinejad, gave every indication that if he had the bomb he would press the button. His threat to 'wipe Israel off the map' got the headlines, but as interesting to anyone who knows the history of totalitarianism was his apocalyptic conception of history as a Manichaean fight to the death stretching back over the centuries.

'We are in the process of a historical war between the World of Arrogance [the West] and the Islamic world, and this war has been going on for hundreds of years. The situation at the fronts has changed many times. During some periods, the Muslims were the victors and were very active and the World of Arrogance was in retreat. During the period of the past 100 years, the walls of the world of Islam were destroyed and the World of Arrogance turned the regime occupying Jerusalem into a bridge for its dominance over the Islamic world ...'

This is the messianic ideology of religious fascism, and the truest friend of British anti-fascists over the past twenty-five years has been *Searchlight* magazine. The police use it and centre-left political parties rely on it. If you read a story about the violent criminal record of a BNP candidate, or how Combat 18 is recruiting football hooligans, the chances are it will have come from *Searchlight*. Dealing with neo-Nazis is dangerous work, and its journalists need physical courage as well as detective skills. They have displayed both magnificently and I cannot think of another left-wing campaign that has been so consistently brave and effective. Now its staff are wondering what has happened to the left they served so well. *Searchlight* has had to pull out of Unite against Fascism – a supposedly 'broad-based' campaign, in fact run by the usual crowd – because of a whispering campaign against it. The Trotskyists are accusing the magazine of 'Zionism' because it stands up for universal principles by condemning Holocaust denial and attacks on Jews, regardless of whether the deniers and attackers have white or brown skins.

The turmoil in small groups may seem trivial, but it reflects the fracturing of the wider liberal left. In classic socialist terminology, we are witnessing an argument between 'anti-imperialists' and 'anti-fascists'. The anti-imperialists see US power as the greatest threat of our day. The reckless brutality of the Bush administration appalled them, as did Tony Blair's willingness to go along with it. This view so dominates the mainstream liberal press and parts of the BBC that it often seems like the only left-wing view it is possible to have. The danger for the anti-imperialists is that they will end up excusing or endorsing the far right.

A few have reached the logical terminus of their politics already, and many more will follow.

The anti-fascists see totalitarianism as the greatest threat of our day and say that in the struggle against it any democracy is better than every dictatorship. Our voice dominates only the left-of-centre weblogs. The danger for anti-fascists is that we are stuck with George W. Bush, who is not a general any soldier should want to follow into battle. They call us neoconservatives, armchair generals and Zionists. We call them the pseudo-left, the red–brown alliance and empty-headed liberals on an ultra-rightist binge. You can see the argument going on in the splits in the Stop the War Coalition when it abandoned the Iraqi democrats, or the slow realisation by CND activists and *Searchlight* journalists that they can no longer take the goodwill of the people around them for granted.

Although we are in a minority, we believe we will win in the end. As democratic socialists, we are optimists. Despite all the evidence to the contrary, we believe there is only so much rubbish the human race can swallow.

New Statesman, December 2005

Communists and Fascists

IN 1935, IN LONDON'S EAST END, Sir Oswald Mosley, a former Labour MP and moustachioed loudmouth, addressed members of the British Union of Fascists, the cult he had founded to worship his personality. 'The yelling mob of socialists and communists are paid by the Jews,' he yelled at his mob. 'The big Jew finances and controls the old parties, both Conservative and socialists; the little Jew sweats you in the sweatshop.' Writers on British fascism vary from the soft-hearted Lord Skidelsky to tough-minded researchers from the East End. On one point, they agree: Mosley's decision to play the race card was entirely cynical. He may have bent the knee to Hitler and Mussolini, but he was not more or less racist than other members of the aristocracy were. He embraced anti-Semitism as it was the best way to appeal to the East End voters he thought would propel him back to power.

Ranged against Mosley was what we used to call 'the left' back in the twentieth century. The Labour movement and the communists declared that religion, race and skin colour did not matter. Immigrants and natives alike were members of the working class or the brotherhood of man. Their common interests were more important than their superficial differences. It was a wildly romantic view. George Lansbury, the saintly leader of the Labour Party, who was as adored by activists in the thirties as Michael Foot was in the eighties, fell for it so badly he couldn't bring himself to admit that there was racism in his beloved East End.

A fantasy, then, but a useful fantasy, and for much of the century immigrants were helped by a left which told them that what native and foreigner had in common was more important than what set them apart. They were as much a part of the struggle against the boss class as any other worker.

In 2005, in London's East End, George Galloway, a former Labour MP and another moustachioed loudmouth, urged supporters of Respect to propel him back to power. Just as Mosley bent the knee to the fascist leaders of his day, so Galloway bent the knee to Saddam Hussein when he flew to Baghdad and declared, 'Sir, I salute your courage, strength and indefatigability.'

I have no doubt that Saddam was from the classic fascist tradition, but it is difficult to make the argument, not only because, in his purges of his Baath Party colleagues, Saddam followed Stalin rather than Hitler, but also because of the common assumption that fascism died in the forties. Fascism today means a father who tells his son to take the stud out of his nose or George W. Bush when a drunk is losing the plot in a pub argument.

But fascism – that is, an extreme nationalism which wages genocidal campaigns against 'impure' ethnic minorities and restless wars of aggression against its neighbours – survived and flourished in Iraq. The Baath Party's ideologues were as inspired by Nazi Germany as Sir Oswald. When Hitler planned the extermination of European Jews, he let out a contemptuous: 'Who remembers the Armenians?' When Saddam's cousin, Ali Hassan al-Majid – 'Chemical Ali' – began the extermination of the Kurds, he let out a contemptuous: 'Who will say anything? The international community? Fuck them!'

Galloway's kissing of the ring of a tyrant with the blood of 1.5 million people on his hands was not a one-off. Iraqi left-wingers loathe him because he denounced Iraqi trade unionists as 'quislings'. The fact that their comrades are still being tortured and murdered by a Baathist and Islamist 'insurgency' which retains all of the far-right's hatred of unions hasn't helped cool their tempers.

Undeterred, Galloway continued to propagandise on behalf of the old regime when he insisted that Tariq Aziz, Saddam's foreign minister, was a 'political prisoner' who should be freed. For Galloway to say that he should not stand trial is to top Mosley. I can find no reference to Sir Oswald calling for the Nuremberg defendants to be released without charge.

To add to the foul atmosphere, there was a whiff of old hatreds in the air. Oona King, the Labour candidate, became sick of Respect supporters bringing up her Jewish mother, although she said it made a change from the British National Party bringing up her black father. King and a group of mainly Jewish pensioners gathered for a sixtieth-anniversary memorial service for the 132 people who died in the last V2 rocket attack on London in 1945. Muslim thugs spat and threw eggs at the mourners and shouted: 'You fucking Jews.'

In a letter to the *Guardian*, members of Respect said there was 'no evidence that this egg-throwing was anti-semitic'. Although it didn't condone them, 'such episodes do occur', and Galloway, John Major, Tony Blair and John Prescott had all had eggs thrown at them.

What can you say to that? Either it is slyly trying to avoid alienating potential supporters, or Respect is so morally shrivelled it cannot tell the difference between disrupting a political speech and attacking a service for the victims of fascism.

King is a strong woman who can look after herself. The worst work Respect is doing is to its Bengali and Somali supporters. I was tempted to write that the party was as much a cult of the personality for Galloway as the British Union of Fascists was for Mosley, but that's not right. The media never tell you but Respect is not a new organisation but is dominated by the old

Socialist Workers Party, which ran the anti-war movement. After the great demonstration of February 2003, it hoped for electoral gains. In the May 2003 council elections, it flopped. The only seat it won was in Preston, where local clerics ordered Muslims to vote for their candidate.

The SWP has learned the lesson and made its own entirely cynical switch. It hopes to ride the religious tiger by persuading devout Muslims to follow the lead of godless communists. To facilitate the marriage, it has dropped boring old causes. 'I'm in favour of defending gay rights,' declared Lindsey German, the SWP leader. 'But I am not prepared to have it as a shibboleth, [created by] people who won't defend George Galloway and regard the state of Israel as somehow a viable presence.'

As the line changed, the party's paper tried to reconcile anti-capitalism and religious fanaticism by calling on the comrades to protest against Spearmint Rhino lap-dancing clubs.

Galloway's propaganda follows the same pattern. It featured a picture of Oona King with a cheesy smile and a low-cut dress. The headline does not say 'Decadent Western Bitch', but then it does not need to.

The sight of Trots in burkas would be hilarious if it was not a symbol of the shambles on the left. From the seventies, the number of people who believed in working-class solidarity fell by the year, to the immense detriment of immigrants. Instead of being met by a left which emphasised what they had in common with the native population, they were met by cultural relativists who emphasised the separateness of their race and religion. Notoriously, the process had the unintended consequence of keeping immigrants poor and isolated from the mainstream.

Respect is the dead end of this failed idea. It's as if the left of the thirties had decided to fight Mosley by creating a party which emphasised Jewish separateness and then wondered why anti-Semitism persisted.

Many of my colleagues think that Galloway could beat King. He's a ruthless operator, she voted for the war against Saddam. I'm not so sure. I went to speak at a King rally on the strange histories of the far left and far right. I expected it to be like most meetings I address: all but empty. Instead, it was packed and the audience was up for a fight.

The Labour movement, Iraqi refugees and people with no great history of political activism are uniting behind King. The East End left may just manage to win one last battle.*

Observer, April 2005

---

* Alas, we lost and one of the poorest constituencies in Britain was stuck with an MP with one of the worst attendance records in the House of Commons.

Pseudo-Leftists and Real Rightists

THE USEFUL LABEL 'the pseudo-left' has been knocking around the Internet sites since 11 September, and it is high time it was brought into the mainstream media. It is a shorthand description of the spectacle of the left moving to the right, often to the far right, and embracing theocrats and, in the case of Saddam Hussein's Iraq and the Baathist 'insurgents' who appeared after the fall of Baghdad, fascists.

The pseudo-leftists are still on the left because they believe in leftish policies of tolerance and social justice at home. They are pseuds because their principles flip as soon as they leave Heathrow. All that the left has opposed since the Enlightenment becomes acceptable, as long as the obscurantists, theocrats and fascists are anti-Americans and as long as their victims aren't Western liberals.

For months Ken Livingstone, the greatest pseud in left-wing politics, was challenged by a rainbow coalition of gays, lesbians, feminists, Sikhs, Hindus, Jews and genuine leftists over his dogged support for the Egyptian theologian Yusuf al-Qaradawi. When today's middle-aged leftists were young, we hummed along to the Clash as Joe Strummer sang about political betrayal. He predicted that if Adolf Hitler came back from the dead and arrived at Heathrow, the authorities would 'send a limousine anyway.'

If the mayor ever heard the lyrics, he has long forgotten them. The sheikh flew to London, and the mayor welcomed him to City Hall and treated him as an honoured guest. 'On behalf of the people of London, I want to apologise to the sheikh for the outbreak of xenophobia and hysteria in some sections of the tabloid press which demonstrated an underlying ignorance of Islam,' intoned the mayor, who cannot apologise for his own behaviour, only for other people's.*

Er, not in our name, mate, muttered gays and feminists. They had checked out the reports of the 'xenophobic and hysterical' press, and found them to be entirely accurate. Livingstone would not reply to their letters but instead produced a propagandistic dossier. At public expense, his officials puffed up Qaradawi as the 'leader of a great world religion'. He was a moderate and a progressive enemy of violence, they told Londoners, 'one of the Muslim scholars who has done most to combat socially regressive interpretations of Islam on issues like women's rights and relations with other religions'. Alastair Campbell on his worst day never issued a piece of flummery so easy to pull apart. All Livingstone's former supporters had to do was look at what Qaradawi said on his 'Islam online' site and contrast his public pronouncements with the flattering picture Livingstone presented.

In June 2003, Qaradawi pondered the question of how a Muslim who decided of his own free will to convert to another religion, or abandon all religion and become an atheist, should

---

* At around the same time, Oliver Finegold, a reporter for the London *Evening Standard*, had stopped Livingstone as he left an official reception and politely asked how the evening had gone. 'What did you do before?' replied Livingstone. 'Were you a German war criminal?' Finegold: 'No, I'm Jewish, I wasn't a German war criminal and I'm actually quite offended by that. So, how did tonight go?' Livingstone: 'Ah right, well you might be [Jewish], but actually you are just like a concentration camp guard, you are just doing it because you are paid to, aren't you?' Livingstone refused to apologise to a courteous Jew for comparing him to a Nazi and when Jewish organisations said that he ought to say sorry, he accused them of assaulting democracy.

be treated. Instead of saying that what adults chose to believe was none of his business, Qaradawi replied, 'He is no more than a traitor to his religion and his people and thus deserves killing.'

Female genital mutilation was fine by him – 'whoever finds it serving the interest of his daughters should do it, and I personally support this under the current circumstances in the modern world'. A little light wife-beating could also be excused – 'if the husband senses that feelings of disobedience and rebelliousness are rising against him in his wife, he should try his best to rectify her attitude by kind words, gentle persuasion, and reasoning with her ... If this approach fails, it is permissible for him to admonish her lightly with his hands, avoiding her face and other sensitive areas.'

Livingstone claimed that Qaradawi was an enemy of terrorism. Yet when a genuinely moderate Egyptian cleric, Mohammad Sayed Tantawi, condemned the murders of Israeli children by suicide bombers, Qaradawi was furious. 'Has fighting colonisers become a criminal and terrorist act for some sheikhs?' he roared.

It seemed that gays had to die too. 'Muslim jurists hold different opinions concerning the punishment for this abominable practice,' Qaradawi said. 'Should it be the same as the punishment for fornication, or should both the active and passive participants be put to death? While such punishments may seem cruel, they have been suggested to maintain the purity of Islamic society and to keep it clean of perverted elements.'

These were not the ravings of one extremist cleric, nor were Livingstone's warm words a blunder by one eccentric politician. Qaradawi is a theologian for the Muslim Brotherhood, whose first ideologue, Sayeed Qutb, was the father of Islamism. If the left's new friends are hung up about sex, then they are honouring Qutb, who in 1949 experienced the modern world's most calamitous attack of sexual disgust in the unlikely setting of a church hall in Greeley, Colorado. The virginal Sayeed was studying the American school system on behalf of his employers at the Egyptian education ministry. He went to the party, and did not find innocent Americans enjoying a church social, but the temptations of Satan. 'The dance is inflamed by the notes of the gramophone. The dance-hall becomes a whirl of heels and thighs, arms enfold hips, lips and breasts meet, and the air is full of lust.' That Greeley was a teetotal town at the time in no way prevented him from seeing it as the new Sodom.

Qutb returned home to develop the ideas that so plague us today. The essentials of Islamism begin in his thought.

1. A world dominated by America is in a state of *jahiliyya*, the animalistic paganism of Arabia before Mohammed revealed God's will and created a paradise on earth.
2. A conspiracy of Jews controls America and, through it, all America's clients.
3. Paganism is cunning and seductive – 'a whirl of heels and thighs' – and will destroy Islam unless it is resisted.
4. True Muslims can use any means to fight back for their reward will be the recreation of God's empire on earth.

Much though the Muslim Brotherhood may hate the comparison, there has always been something of the American city boss about Livingstone. He pays the necessary pieties to ethnic and sexual blocs and banks their votes. For the sake of argument, let us assume that he's not just a grubby machine politician but is sincere when he declares that he is defending Qaradawi to the hilt because, as he said, 'I have a responsibility to support the rights of all of London's diverse communities and to maintain a dialogue with their political and religious leaders.'*

---

* Not all religions. Atma Singh, Livingstone's adviser on Asian affairs, later described how he had 'objected to Livingstone saying we must work with al-

Livingstone does not seem to realise that this bland formulation masks a deeply reactionary manoeuvre which is being practised across the Western left. First, leftists define 'communities' by their religion. Then they assume that misogynist and anti-democratic practitioners of that religion are the true leaders of their communities. Finally, and more deliberately than outsiders may realise, they drive away the liberals.

In 2004 Iraqi, Jordanian and Tunisian writers organised a petition to the United Nations by 2500 Arab intellectuals which condemned 'individuals in the Muslim world who pose as clerics and issue death sentences against those they disagree with. These individuals give Islam a bad name and foster hatred among civilisations.' Prominent in their list of the 'sheikhs of death' was one Yusuf al-Qaradawi. Just as the British anti-war movement chose to turn its back on the 8 million Iraqis who defied the murderers and voted in the last election, so Livingstone has chosen to ignore the Arab left and to offer comfort to its enemies.

As inevitable as the betrayal is the award-winning hypocrisy. In the name of anti-racism, Livingstone perpetuates the stereo-

Qaradawi and others who were soft on suicide attacks on Israelis. We had a good relationship with London's Jews and the Board of Deputies of British Jews worked with us in the National Assembly against Racism. But Livingstone's Trotskyist aides went on and on about the Board of Deputies of British Jews. They said they represented the "Zionist lobby" and that "we must smash the Zionists". I thought we should treat London's religious communities equally. Livingstone was more interested in the Muslim vote and thought that by pandering to al-Qaradawi he could get it. He began to say things he would never have said before, calling a Jewish reporter a concentration camp guard and telling Jewish businessmen to leave the country.'

As soon as Singh spoke out, Livingstone and his aides blackballed him. 'They took control of faith matters away from me. I was completely isolated. They didn't tell me about meetings or anything the mayor was doing and banned me from the official trips.' Singh had a nervous breakdown and resigned.

type of the Muslim as a death-obsessed, woman-hating, queer-bashing justifier of suicide bombers. In the name of multiculturalism, he talks as if something in the water supply of the Islamic world means that 1 billion people *want* to be ruled by clerics.

The joke of it all is that if the British leaders or a European or North American leader were to recommend the execution of homosexuals or the enforcement of Christian belief by death sentences on apostates, Livingstone would be sending letters of protest. But when the same policies are proposed by Muslim leaders, he changes his tune and sends the limousine anyway.*

Observer, February 2005

---

* Livingstone lost the 2008 mayoral election to Boris Johnson, a buffoonish Conservative political commentators said did not stand a hope in hell of becoming mayor of the most liberal city in Britain. They reckoned without the revulsion Livingstone's racial politics provoked. The traditionally Labour white working class deserted the party in droves because it realised – correctly – that the pseudo-left's version of multiculturalism no more included their culture than it included Jewish culture.

Eco-tourists and Islamo-terrorists

REPORTS FROM FRANCE say the Islamists could hit Paris next. French intelligence agents found a message on an Arabic website from the Salafist Group for Preaching and Combat, a demented Algerian outfit which is close to al-Qaeda. France was 'our first enemy', the terrorists said. The 'only way to discipline France is jihad, martyrdom and Islam'.

In the autumn of 2005, French police arrested nine alleged Islamists in a suburb of Paris and claimed they were planning to bomb the Metro. Nicolas Sarkozy, then the French interior minister, said the risk of an attack was currently 'at a very high level'. Marc Hecker, from the French Institute for International Relations, said it was 'a real error' to believe that France would be left in peace because President Chirac opposed the Iraq War.

Indeed it is. But as it is impossible to blame Iraq, what or who will liberals hold responsible if rucksacks explode at the Gare du Nord? Will they look Islamism in the face and see a cult of slaughter and self-slaughter powered by messianic faith? I live in hope, but the record suggests they will hold everyone except the perpetrators responsible.

If the French can't be blamed for their part in the downfall of Chirac's old friend Saddam Hussein, then maybe their rulers' support for the Algerian government will be used to explain the killings. No? How about the ban of headscarves in French schools? My money is on the headscarves but, frankly, the favoured 'root cause' could just as well be the effect of the Common Agricultural Policy on poor world farmers, or the provocation given by bikini-wearing holidaymakers at Club Med resorts in North Africa.

If you think I am exaggerating, consider the attempts to show that the latest slaughter in Bali was the fault of the liberal democracies. The *Independent on Sunday* declared, 'There can be little doubt that the bombs in Bali are linked to issues surrounding the war. It is no coincidence that Australia, whose citizens are likely to be the majority of the victims, is fully committed in Iraq.'

Actually, there could be a great deal of doubt, not least because the majority of the dead were Indonesian Hindus, whom I assume the Islamists were happy to designate as pagans before murdering them.

Pamela Nowicka of Tourism Concern, which campaigns for eco-friendly holidays, had doubts of her own. She decided that what mattered was that the dead Australian tourists were tourists rather than Australians. 'Many in the global south regard tourism as a new form of colonialism and cultural imperialism,' she wrote in the *Guardian*. 'While that may be hard for the suntanned holidaymaker to take on board, for the millions of ordinary people servicing their needs – the waiting staff, room cleaners, receptionists, shop workers, guides, massage ladies and taxi drivers – the linkage is clearer.'

Except that the bombers weren't disgruntled room cleaners and taxi drivers. They were members of a totalitarian movement which is against every principle Ms Nowicka professes to support. The first economic consequence of their killings will be to put cleaners and taxi drivers out of work.

I could go on – Mark Curtis, a historian from the Noam Chomsky school, blamed the bombs on the Wilson government's support for General Suharto's *coup d'état* in Indonesia a mere forty years ago. But what needs saying is that no mainstream commentator mentioned that Indonesian Islamists have put their grievance on the record. It had nothing to do with Harold Wilson's foreign policy in the sixties or stingy tipping in Bali's restaurants. After the 2002 explosions in Bali killed 200, Osama bin Laden declared, 'Australia is the one that we have warned before not to participate in Afghanistan, not to mention its continued awful chapter in East Timor. They ignored our warning and they woke up to the sound of explosions in Bali.'

Liberals do not want to look at al-Qaeda's condemnations of Australia's role in saving (largely Catholic) East Timor from destruction by the militias of (largely Muslim) Indonesia. For that route would take them into the darkness and force them to confront Islamism's impossible and therefore unappeasable demand for a caliphate that would dominate Muslims and subjugate all others.

Avoidance of what al-Qaeda stands for began in 9/11. It has become endemic since. My favourite piece of victim blaming was after the Madrid bombings. For a few hours, there was a rumour that they were the work of ETA and Eddie Mair, the presenter of Radio 4's *PM* news show, duly had a go at a representative of the Spanish government, alleging that Madrid's refusal to talk to Basque nationalists was the root cause of the atrocity. By the next day, it was clear that Islamists, not Basques, had attacked Madrid. Without pausing for breath, Mair duly demanded of Spanish officials whether the presence of Spanish troops in Iraq was the root cause of the atrocity. The identity of the bombers was irrelevant. The Spanish had to be the cause of their own suffering.

Perhaps it is too easy to mock. When confronted with an ideology that mandates indiscriminate killing on an industrial scale, it is natural to seek rational explanations of the irrational; to pretend that Islamism is merely a reasonable, if bloody, response to legitimate concerns which could be remedied if we elected wiser leaders.

Yet the masochism – 'Kill us, we deserve it!' – the subliminal dislike of democracy and the willingness to turn al-Qaeda into the armed wing of every fashionable campaign from sustainable tourism to the anti-war movement will in the end disgrace the liberals by making them ridiculous.

Observer, October 2005

Multiculturalists and Monomaniacs

DAILY MAIL READERS appear to believe that we are in a politically correct tyranny in which freeborn Englishmen face arrest whenever a busybody exposes them for letting slip a sexist joke or racist remark. They should look at what the police did to Channel 4 when it exposed the far deeper bigotries of well-funded, Saudi-backed clerics.

Its undercover journalists infiltrated radical mosques. They recorded assorted preachers calling for women to be subordinated to men, homosexuals to be murdered and for the faithful to reject the man-made laws of a democracy. The condemnations of religious extremism Channel 4 aired in reply did not come from white liberals – white liberals tend to stay silent about such awkward subjects – but from Muslims worried about the malign influence of a foreign power on British Islam. Haras Rafiq of the Sufi Muslim Council said, 'Wahhabis and their offshoots are teaching Muslim youngsters that America and Britain are against them and therefore they need to get up and fight with them. The radicalising power of this ideology is extremely dangerous.' Abdal-Hakim Murad of Cambridge University described Saudi influence as 'potentially lethal for the future of the community'. He got to the heart of the continuity between the Nazism and communism of the twentieth century and the Islamism of the twenty-first when, in the film's crucial passage, he continued, 'Its principle is totalitarian, it's highly judgemental, it has no track record of dealing with other sorts of Islam, or with unbelievers, with any kind of respect. If you are outside the small circle of the true believers you're going to hell and therefore you should be treated with contempt.'

The station took great care to ensure the accuracy of the programme. I speak from miserable experience when I say that being edited by Channel 4's commissioning editors is like having a team of revenue inspectors going through your accounts. Its lawyers swarmed over the script of *Undercover Mosque* to make sure it complied with the law and Ofcom's regulatory guidelines. Two weeks before transmission, they sent letters to every cleric criticised in the film explaining what Channel 4 had accused them of and offering them a chance to reply. The station showed its balanced and impeccably sourced documentary last year and the forces of law and order cracked down: not on demagogic preachers, but on the broadcasters who exposed them. Assistant Chief Constable Anil Patani from the West Midlands Police and Bethan David of the Crown Prosecution Service accused Channel 4 'of the splicing together of extracts from longer speeches'. The docu-fakers appeared 'to have completely distorted what the speakers were saying'. They referred Channel 4 to the broadcasting watchdog, Ofcom, an outlandish step for police and prosecutors to take, given that their job is to charge criminals, not moonlight as television critics.

The allegation was one of fraud. If authorities believed what they said, they must have meant that, for instance, Ijaz Mian, who preaches in Derby, was a good democrat. Only Channel 4's trick camerawork and sly editing had turned him into the man who appeared in the film raving: 'King, queen, House of Commons. If you accept it then you are a part of it. You don't accept it but you have to dismantle it. So you being a Muslim you have to fix a target, there will be no House of Commons.'

Similarly, when Abu Usamah of the Green Lane Mosque in Birmingham bellowed on air, 'Take that homosexual man and throw him off the mountain,' the police and Crown Prosecution Service must have believed that his apparently murderous homophobia was not a genuine expression of his prejudice, but a *Truman Show* illusion created by scheming editors.

Ofcom found no evidence that Channel 4 had misled the audience. The station offered the police and CPS the chance to apologise. They refused. So Channel 4 sued for libel and after wasting hundreds of thousands of pounds of taxpayers' money in a fruitless battle against the broadcaster, the authorities retracted, paid damages and issued a full and grovelling retraction.

The CPS and the West Midlands officers have not, however, condescended to explain their behaviour. The National Secular Society wants an inquiry to force them into the open. Until we get one, the best explanation lies in Patani's title: Assistant Chief Constable (Security and Cohesion).

Since 9/11, not only police officers, but New Labour ministers, the Home Office, Foreign Office and pseudo-left journalists and councils have sought to promote 'cohesion' by appeasing Islamist groups which aren't quite as extreme as al-Qaeda. They have turned them into the sole authentic representatives of British Islam and turned their backs on the Haras Rafiqs and Abdal-Hakim Murads. Among the many casualties of their betrayal of liberal principles and liberal Muslims is serious investigative journalism, which they now treat as a species of racism. To their minds, journalists cannot reveal or argue against the doctrines of religious extremists, for to admit their existence would destroy multicultural illusions. They want us to live in a pretend country where no challenges to liberal values exist and those who claim that they do are bigots inciting racial or religious hatred, or sensation-seeking producers looking for ratings.

The political calculation behind their denial was as transparent as it was delusional. Elements within the government thought that if they could co-opt supporters of the Muslim Brotherhood and Jamaat-i-Islami on to the Muslim Council of Britain and ignore their foul beliefs, they would isolate the terrorists to their right. Even Labour now admits that the policy has been a practical failure and a moral shambles. Elsewhere, however, a mushy feeling persists that it is somehow 'insensitive' to apply universal values.

Far more vulnerable people than journalists are suffering from the double standard. In 2008, Conservative researchers issued a report on honour killings and beatings. South Asian and Middle Eastern women's groups reported an increasingly widespread trend. Officials who should treat all women equally were deciding that where their community's religious and cultural practices conflicted with the law, the law had to give way.

Zalikha Ahmed, director of the Apna Haq refuge, told the report's researchers: 'We don't visit the station when certain Asian officers are on because some of them are perpetrators and one of them said that he would not arrest someone who used force on his wife.' A worker in a women's group in the north, who requested anonymity for fear of reprisals, added she had been 'appalled' by an Asian 'chief inspector who had offered to help a family track a girl down'.

The report's authors noticed that women's groups appeared to have problems with one force in particular. It was the West Midlands Police.

Observer, May 2008

Liberals and Murderers (Part One)

THINGS WILL HAVE reached a pretty pass when reporters from the *Daily Mail* can look down on liberal London from the moral high ground. But such was the result of the scandal about the treatment by *Index on Censorship* of the murder of Theo van Gogh in Amsterdam in 2004.

The idea that *Index* could have been at the centre of a scandal would once have been unthinkable. Stephen Spender founded it in the seventies to fight for the right of Soviet dissidents to speak freely. Vaclav Havel, Nadine Gordimer, Salman Rushdie, Doris Lessing, Arthur Miller, Aung San Suu Kyi and many another clear and true voice used its pages to denounce the suppression of opinion wherever it occurred. Yet when it contemplated the corpse of a film-maker, a fanatic ritually slaughtered by a fanatic for dramatising violence against Muslim women, its instinctive reaction was so loathsome it still has the power to sicken.

Index giggled.

Rohan Jayasekera, an associate editor, invited readers of its website to see van Gogh's murder as a smart business move – 'Applaud Theo van Gogh's death as the marvellous piece of street theatre it was,' he cried. 'What timing! Just as his long-awaited film of Pim Fortuyn's life is ready to screen. Bravo, Theo! Bravo!' Jayasekera slyly suggested van Gogh was suffering from an inherited strain of insanity because he was 'a descendant of the mad genius Dutch painter'. No one had the right to be surprised that the film had provoked a furious response, he declared. It had been 'furiously provocative' for van Gogh to 'feature actresses portraying battered Muslim women, naked under transparent Islamic-style shawls, their bodies marked with texts from the Koran that supposedly justify their repression'.

By now, you should be able to guess the rest. As has become routine, *Index* whisked the perpetrator away and piled the blame on the lifeless victim. The real censor was not the murderer, but the victim, who was guilty of roaring 'his Muslim critics into silence with his obscenities'. The real enemy of free speech was not the murderer who wished to silence it, but his victim, who was guilty of an 'abuse of his right to free speech'. The real fundamentalist was not the murderer but his victim, who was 'a free speech fundamentalist'. The real murderer was not the murderer who fired eight bullets into a defenceless man, sliced open his throat and stabbed him in the chest, but his victim who was on 'a martyrdom operation' and so, presumably, was responsible for his own death.

As repugnant was *Index*'s treatment of Ayaan Hirsi Ali, who worked with van Gogh on the film. I can remember a time when she would have been a liberal heroine. Ali is a Somali, whose family had her circumcised at five. She fled from an arranged marriage at twenty-two, and overcame her disadvantages to become a Dutch MP. As free men and women are entitled to do, she decided she did not believe in God. Needless to add, her atheism made her dangerous enemies, and the police had to protect her from Islamist assassins. The authorities increased the size of her guard when van Gogh's killer used his knife to stick a five-page letter which threatened her, along with Western governments and the Jews, into the director's carcass.

In the twentieth century, feminists had a little success in persuading men to treat women as independent creatures whose intelligence ought to be respected. But these small gains are abandoned when brown-skinned women contradict the party line that religious extremism is all the fault of poverty or racism or Bush or Israel and isn't an autonomous totalitarian ideology with a logic of its own. Jayasekera dismissed Ali as if she were a geisha girl. That her experience of mutilation and abuse as a child could be expected to inform her adult thinking did not occur to him. She was a silly little fool who had allowed a white man to manipulate her. As he explained to *Index* readers, 'Van Gogh's juvenile shock-horror art finally led him to build an exploitative working relationship with Somalia-born Dutch MP Ayaan Hirsi Ali, whose terrible personal experience of abuse has driven her to a traumatising loss of her Muslim faith.'

Consider *Index*'s casuistry: pious men have horribly abused an intelligent woman. *Index* accepts that the abuse was 'terrible' but insinuates that the abuse did not traumatise her. Her trauma in *Index*'s confident opinion was caused by her rational decision to abandon the religion in whose name her abusers assaulted her.

The ridicule and contempt were too much for many who once admired *Index*, and a ferocious row about basic principles brewed up nicely.

Frank Fisher, a former production editor, said *Index* was advocating 'Capitulation. Surrender. It says, "Come at us with a gun and we'll turn tail and run. Our defence of human rights is not so heartfelt that we're prepared to risk offending you."' Dame Ann Leslie, the *Mail*'s foreign correspondent, who had helped *Index* for years, was incandescent and refused to judge its cutely titled Freedom of Expression awards.

Index's editors and board said in a statement that no one was 'more distressed by the murder of an artist for his opinions' than they were. If this were true, they had a funny way of showing it. When I asked Jayasekera if he had any regrets, he said he had none. He told me that, like many other readers, I should not have made the mistake of believing that *Index on Censorship* was against censorship, even murderous censorship, on principle – in the same way as Amnesty International is opposed to torture, including murderous torture, on principle. It may have been so long ago in its idealistic youth when Spender was in the editor's chair, but now it was as concerned with fighting 'hate speech' as protecting free speech.

For all the sniggering malice of his writing, Jayasekera was right to say that van Gogh hated religion. He laid into Catholics, Protestants, Jews and Muslims in the most offensive manner he could muster. It's true, too, that attacks on religion can on occasion be a form of covert bigotry against Arabs, the Irish and, increasingly, evangelical Americans.

Why not go along with the new tough liberalism and, as the government is suggesting, make it a criminal offence to incite religious hatred? There are plenty of reasons why not and van Gogh's killer provided the best. When society decides that people's religion, rather than their class or gender, is the cultural fact that matters, power inevitably passes to religious fanatics who believe religion justifies any crime.

Observer, December 2004

Liberals and Murderers (Part Two)

I LOOKED AT THE HECKLER shouting at me from the floor at a Labour Party meeting, and thought I could imagine his life in an instant. As a militant from the 1968 generation, there must have been sit-ins and marches, along with vicarious thrills at the triumphs of communists from Cambodia to Cuba. I guessed that with communism dead he would have no difficulty in endorsing the new threat to the status quo from the radical right. I was not disappointed.

Only rich Iranians wanted democracy, he declared. Liberals, socialists and feminists in Iran were contaminated by their incorrect class origins. The true voice of the masses, the tribune of the people we must attend to and negotiate with, was Mahmoud Ahmadinejad.

Leftists defending reactionaries no longer surprise me, but my '68er displayed a form of bad faith I had never seen in the flesh before. Alongside me on the platform were liberals from Muslim backgrounds: Ed Husain, who renounced the jihadis of Hizb ut-Tahrir and joined the Labour Party, and Rokhsana Fiaz, whose Change Institute works to diminish cultural tensions. They shared the principles he claimed as his own. But he looked through them as if they weren't there. Whether liberal Muslims were in London or Tehran, he could not acknowledge the legitimacy of the concerns of the opponents of the radical religious right.

You might say that Fiaz and Husain are hardly marginalised figures. I agree, and would not waste time defending people who can look after themselves if their confrontation with a sixties radical did not echo a broader *trahison des clercs*.

In 2007, Ayaan Hirsi Ali published *Infidel*, an account of how she escaped from a world where genital mutilation and forced marriage were imposed on women, to find asylum and the free-thinking of the Enlightenment in Holland. She was attacked, as feminists always are, but the assault was not led by the traditional enemies of the emancipation of women in the churches and conservative press but by Timothy Garton Ash and Ian Buruma, men who see themselves as liberal thinkers and are seen as such by the liberal press of New York and London. There was an intellectual scandal in Europe, and the *New Republic* in Washington devoted most of an issue to what the controversy revealed about the contortions of liberal thought. Accusations of double standards weren't thrown about simply because sheltered academics who had known no terror in their lives had turned on a woman who could not step outside without body-guards to protect her – just because fanatics want to kill her doesn't make Hirsi Ali right – but because the liberals treated her with a superciliousness unthinkable in the late twentieth century.

Garton Ash wrote in the *New York Review of Books* that journalists were more interested in her beauty than her ideas. 'If she had been short, squat, and squinting, her story and views might not be so closely attended to.' She was an 'Enlightenment fundamentalist', he continued, as bigoted in her way as the Muslim Brotherhood she opposed. 'Fundamentalist' was an unintentionally revealing insult. It showed that Garton Ash saw no moral difference between those who believed in the extermination of all liberal ideals and those who did not. Liberal intellectuals had no obligation to make a choice between 'Enlightenment fundamentalists' and religious fundamentalists, he implied – or between the open society and its enemies, to use a phrase that once meant something to them – and could devote their energies to fighting the former rather than the latter.

Garton Ash met Hirsi Ali at an electric meeting in London. Unlike Buruma he had had the good sense and good grace to think again and he gave her a public apology. Nevertheless, he stuck to the argument that there was no point in liberals treating her as a heroine because her abandonment of Islam and embrace of atheism meant her arguments carried no weight with Muslims. Instead, he told us to engage with those Muslims who find Koranic arguments against killing women. Religious debates about whether the Prophet Muhammad really approved of stoning them to death may be 'gobbledegook', he cried, but 'we must support gobbledegook that is compatible with liberal democracy'.

I am not sure how he can be certain that Hirsi Ali has no influence. How does he know what seeds she may be planting in the minds of Muslim women? I know one former jihadi who thought again after reading Salman Rushdie, but I accept he is not typical. Ed Husain says that he and most men like him did not embrace democracy because liberal secularists had won them round, but because they had found alternative interpretations of the Koran. Islam had freed them from the prison of Islamism.

I have no disagreement with Husain. My argument is with liberals who assume reactionaries can be indulged as long as they stop short of planting bombs on the London Underground. Garton Ash says we should listen to Tariq Ramadan, grandson of the founder of the Muslim Brotherhood, who does not want to ban the stoning of women, merely to impose 'a moratorium' on murder.

He is not alone in advocating appeasement. Jack Straw has sent civil servants to seek Ramadan's advice on how to combat extremism. The law officers charged Derek Pasquill, one of Straw's former civil servants, under the Official Secrets Act for the alleged crime of embarrassing the FCO by leaking details of how Labour planned to send public money to Islamist groups in the Middle East. While he waited for his day in court, Liberal Democrat politicians and Sir Ian Blair, Commissioner of the Metropolitan Police, joined a Muslim Brotherhood rally whose star speaker was a Saudi cleric who until recently had called for jihad against coalition forces in Iraq.

They would do better to profit from the experience of a woman who is more principled than the lot of them. Ayaan Hirsi listened to Garton Ash and came back with two devastating questions neither he nor our political class can answer. If liberal secularists, like my heckler, did not have pride and confidence in their principles, why should they expect anyone else to take them seriously? And if, like Garton Ash, they turned away from democrats and insisted on treating European Muslims as children who can only be spoken to in the baby language of gobbledegook, what right did they have to be surprised if European Muslims reacted with childish petulance rather than the maturity of full citizens?

Observer, November 2007

Social Democrats and Theocrats

AT THE END OF 2007, Westminster magistrates remanded into custody a bookish civil servant called Derek Pasquill on six charges of breaking the Official Secrets Act. Anyone old enough to remember Soviet moles of the Cold War must have thought they could predict the rest.

The state would accuse the spy of betraying his country to an enemy that loathes liberal democracy and human rights. The prosecution would reveal how he converted to totalitarianism as a student and worked to get himself into a powerful position where he could best serve his new masters. Shocked by the duplicity of an outwardly respectable man, the judge would send him down.

But the Cold War is long gone and nothing about the Pasquill case was predictable. Far from betraying his country, the prosecution accused him of defending Britain from those who mean it nothing but harm. Far from betraying liberal principles, the prosecution alleged that he exposed appeasers in the Foreign and Commonwealth Office who sponsored Islamists working to create a theocratic empire. His crime was to leak documents to the *Observer* and *New Statesman* that revealed how New Labour brought Islamists to the heart of policy-making.

In domestic policy, the tilt towards fanaticism was evidenced by Labour's decision to treat supporters of the

Muslim Brotherhood and its sister organisation Jamaat-i-Islami on the Muslim Council of Britain as the authentic voice of British Islam. If they had been white, they would have been condemned as far rightists. The Brotherhood was founded by Hassan al-Banna, an admirer of European fascism. In the sixties, its chief ideologist, Sayyid Qutb, began the wave of murder that is sweeping the globe when he decided all existing Muslim and non-Muslim governments were pagan states that must be attacked with extreme violence. In what was then British India, Jamaat's founder, Maulana Maududi, complemented Qutb's thought by becoming the first to propose that an Islamic totalitarian empire should rule the world.

Supporters of both parties say they now want to take power by peaceful means, but remain the sworn enemies of Muslim leftists. Few knew until the press published the leaked documents that a leftist Labour government was going along with them. The dominant figure in a group the FCO established – 'Engaging with the Islamic World' – was Mockbul Ali, its twenty-six-year-old 'Islamic issues adviser'.

As a student at the School of Oriental and African Studies, he promoted the Muslim Brotherhood's spiritual leader, the Qatari preacher Yusuf al-Qaradawi – and continued to support the cleric when he joined the civil service. Although Qaradawi justified suicide bombing in Iraq and Israel, and propagated the standard medieval superstitions about women, gays and Jews, Ali lobbied to have him admitted to Britain. His view was that, apart from suicide bombings in Israel, Qaradawi had consistently condemned terrorism. He assured his superiors that, although Qaradawi's ideology was not that of the British government, it was 'shared by a majority of Muslims in the Middle East and the UK'.

As informed advice to ministers, this was nonsense. The majority of British Muslims are no different from their apolitical fellow citizens. At the time he was writing, a Populus poll found that 16 per cent justified suicide bombings.*

Qaradawi was duly admitted to Britain, to the dismay of Arab liberals who had the right to expect a Labour government to be on their side.

Mockbul Ali then moved on to Delwar Hossain Sayeedi, a Jamaat MP in Bangladesh. Eric Taylor, a senior Home Office official, worried that the Bangladeshi human rights organisation Drishtipat had alleged that Sayeedi had claimed that the UK and the US 'deserve all that is coming to them' for overthrowing the Taliban, compared Hindus to excrement and appeared to defend attacks on Bangladesh's Ahmadiyya Muslim minority. Given that Sayeedi's previous speaking tours in Britain had been accompanied by reports of violence against Bangladeshi elders who disagreed with his version of Islam, Taylor wondered whether he should be readmitted to the country. Mockbul Ali asserted that there was little reason to worry because Sayeedi was a 'mainstream' figure.

Ali was not a lone loose cannon. All around him, the urge to appease seized diplomats. In one leaked document, Angus McKee, of the Middle East and North Africa Department, said Britain should cultivate the Muslim Brotherhood in Egypt and its Palestinian subsidiary Hamas and consider passing them taxpayers' money. 'Given that Islamist groups are often less corrupt than the generality of the societies in which they operate, consideration might be given to channelling aid resources through them, so long as sufficient transparency is achievable,' he wrote.

The FCO's naivety was its most striking feature. It is not only that Saudi Arabia and Iran prove that the more religious a regime the more corrupt its officials, but that McKee and his

---

* Still a large number, I grant you.

colleagues talked as if the twentieth century had not happened. The FCO seemed to think that if it offered totalitarians tea and sympathy they would convert to democracy and recognise the rights of women.

As the case came before the magistrates, the Royal Court theatre in London revived *The Arsonists*, Max Frisch's absurdist classic on the rise of Nazism and communism, to satirise today's liberal delusion that Islamists do not mean what they say. A middle-class couple bend over backwards to be kind to arsonists who make it perfectly clear they hate them and want to set fire to their house. Gottlieb and Babette Biedermann shower them with hospitality, spurred on by the pathetic hope that they can avoid a conflagration by engaging with arsonists.

BIEDERMANN: If I report them to the police, I know I'll be making enemies of them. What good's that going to do us? One match is enough to set the whole house ablaze. What good's that going to do us? Whereas, if I go up and invite them to supper – assuming they accept my invitation ...

BABETTE: Then?

BIEDERMANN: Then they'll be our friends.

In the true modern style, Biedermann worries about being 'judgemental' and holding hidden prejudices against 'the Other'.

'All right,' he declares to his worried wife, 'I'll come straight to the point. I've had enough. You and your arsonists. I don't even want to meet my friends any more, it's all they ever talk about. In the end, you only live once. If we assume that everyone is an arsonist, how are things ever going to get better? We need to have a little bit of trust, a little bit of goodwill. That's what I think. Not always seeing evil round the corner. Not everyone's an arsonist, for God's sake! That's what I think. A little bit of trust. I can't live in fear all the time.'

As the arsonists carry barrels filled with petrol into his attic, the nervous bourgeois turns to the audience and agonises about his inability to confront his avowed enemies. 'It's not like you think, you know. It doesn't dawn on you just like that. It starts slowly and then suddenly: suspicion. Well, I had my suspicions right from the start, you always have your suspicions, don't you? But be honest, in my place, what would you have done? And when?'

He never acts on his suspicions, even though the arsonists never pretend to be anything other than arsonists. In the scenes before his house explodes, the best he can manage are nervous questions.

BIEDERMANN: Mr Eisenring, to be absolutely honest, I didn't sleep all night. Is it really petrol in those drums?

EISENRING: Don't you trust us?

BIEDERMANN: I'm only asking.

EISENRING : What kind of people do you think we are? To be absolutely honest?

BIEDERMANN: I don't want you to think I've got no sense of humour, but I must say, your jokes can be, well, a bit ... unusual.

EISENRING : It's something we're working on.

BIEDERMANN: What is?

EISENRING : Our jokes. You see, comedy is the third best tactic. The second best is sentimentality. You know, the stuff that Joe comes out with: miner's family, childhood poverty, orphanage, all that bollocks. But in my experience, the best and the most reliable tactic is still the naked truth. Because, funnily enough, nobody believes it.

The ghost of Herr Biedermann stalks the Foreign Office. You don't have to take my word for it. One of our leading authorities on the Middle East, Sir Derek Plumbly, the ambassador to Egypt, watched the contortions of his colleagues with amazement.

'I detect a tendency to confuse "engaging with the Islamic world" with "engaging with Islamism" and to play down the very real downsides for us in terms of the Islamists' likely foreign and social policies, should they actually achieve power,' he wrote in a 2005 memo to his superiors, which was leaked to the *Statesman*. 'I suspect that there will be relatively few contexts in which we are able significantly to influence the Islamists' agenda.'

So it was to prove. Morally and practically, appeasement was a failure.

Pasquill's official secrets case was a case like no other because while he was wondering whether he would end up in jail, New Labour changed its mind. The leaks and protests from liberal-minded British Muslims persuaded Ruth Kelly, David Miliband and Jacqui Smith to stop engaging with Islamists.

Pasquill stood accused of leaking against a policy the government itself admitted was wrong. Ministers told my colleague Martin Bright, who broke the story, that reading the documents made them rethink. The documents also revealed that the FCO did not know – and did not want to know – whether the Americans were using British airspace for the 'extraordinary rendition' of suspects. Ministers have again admitted that their deliberate ignorance was a mistake.

Official secrets cases are political because the attorney-general must approve them. Before Tony Blair resigned, Lord Goldsmith, the then attorney-general, ordered the police to stop their enquiries into the corruption surrounding arms deals to spare the blushes of the Saudi regime. That same regime pours anti-democratic and anti-liberal propaganda into British mosques. It would not only be hypocritical but revolting for law officers to spare Saudis who want to fuel fanaticism while imprisoning a public servant for the alleged crime of trying to fight it.

After weeks of disastrous news, New Labour has very few

friends left. It will have fewer still if it does not drop the case against Pasquill.*

Observer, December 2007

---

* I can't claim that this barely concealed threat that the *Observer* would turn on Labour if it didn't drop the case was the most subtle sentence I've written. Nor can I prove that the *Observer* forced the government to drop the case. All I can tell you is that the government *did* drop the case after a confidential document came to the attention of the lawyers, which showed the Foreign Office thought that Pasquill had done no damage to his country. Labour did not invite him to return to work, however, even though ministers could have done with his advice.

PART 4

Tyranny and the Intellectuals

'You have disgraced yourselves – *again!*'

W. B. YEATS
to the Dublin intelligentsia, 1926

Martin Amis Meets Liberal London

WHEN LIBERAL INTELLECTUALS go on one of their periodic berserkers, the targets of their rage experience three emotions. The first is astonishment as men and women who boast of their independence of mind turn into a gang of screeching children. Outrage follows as they hear supposedly respectable academics and journalists propagate demonstrable lies. Finally, they settle into a steady contempt, as they realise that many liberal intellectuals are neither liberal nor noticeably intelligent.

Neutral observers watching Martin Amis at the Institute of Contemporary Arts realised that he had reached the serene terminus of the emotional journey. He sat toying with a transgressive cigarette while all around him a herd of otherwise thoughtful people went wild.

As anyone who reads the liberal press knows, the cause of their fury was Amis's insistence that there are worse ideas in the world than America, and radical Islam is among them. That liberals cannot make a stand against a global wave of religious mayhem that is 'inquisitional and genocidal' is a moral failure as great as their predecessors' inability to see Josef Stalin for what he was and offer support to the victims of communism.

The meeting grew angrier as he and his fellow liberal renegade Andrew Anthony elaborated on the self-evident. Chris Morris, a comedian who thinks it is daring to attack rather than defend conservative positions on British television, cross-questioned Amis on the Muslim Brotherhood, whose members have become the legitimate voice of Islam for the Labour Party, the liberal press and academia.

'Are you're saying they're all murderers?' Morris demanded.

'I think Islamists subscribe to a murderous ideology,' replied Amis.

'So you mean they're all murderers?'

'No, but I believe the ideology they subscribe to is murderous.'

This continued for some time, but Amis strove to find a common ground.

During his talk he had tried to get through to his audience of anti-sexists and anti-racists by warning them that the West had 'become nervous about making a judgement about anything at all, and unable to identify anything that is clearly bad in itself.

'I want to put this question to you: Do you feel morally superior to the Taliban? Hands up who does.'

Only one third raised their arms.

A little taken aback, Amis tried to explain. 'Do you not feel morally superior to people who at a stroke at the fall of Kabul in 1996 dismantled the health and the education system of their country by banning women from work?' he asked. 'That's a pretty good beginning to a regime. No more health. No more education. Not satisfied with getting women off the street, they consigned them to houses where they blacked up the windows so that no sunlight got through to them so they couldn't be seen. The Taliban have organised many a massacre of the Hazara and other sects and other ethnicities in Afghanistan. You don't feel superior to that. The trouble with us in the West is that we have succumbed to a pious paralysis.'

When I went to his house by Regent's Park – which is, by the way, the first genteel home I have visited in years where you can smoke indoors – he thought about the two-thirds who sat on their hands. 'The only people they allow themselves to feel morally superior to are the Americans and the Israelis,' he said. 'But maybe some of what I said about the Taliban sunk in. Perhaps more trembling hands would have gone up if I had asked for another vote.'

I didn't have the heart to tell him that it wouldn't have made a difference if Osama bin Laden himself had appeared from behind a curtain and declared that listening to Amis had prompted him to mend his ways. Certainly, the audience at the ICA gave no indication that their dogmatic uncertainty, their absolute relativism, had been shaken by his arguments. They sat sullenly through the talk, wondering how best to get even. An angry man at the back had a '*Eureka!*' moment and came up with a killer question.

'What about Israel?' he shouted.

Outsiders may need me to add here that in contemporary leftish circles Israel is the great Satan, whose sinister Jews control if not the whole world, as Adolf Hitler maintained, then at least the foreign policy of the United States of America.

Amis replied that educated people should be able to combine a desire for a just settlement for the Palestinians with an understanding that Israel is a small country surrounded by enemies who want to wipe it off the map.

He was being over-optimistic, and the meeting erupted.

'*Ohmigod* he's defending Israel now!' squealed Morris.

'You could read views like this man's in the *Daily Telegraph*!' cried an outraged pensioner.

'With this, the fight was over,' Padraig Reidy of *Index on Censorship* noted in his account of the meeting. 'For if there is one thing worse than killing Palestinians, which Amis obviously does on a daily basis, it is having a view that might, possibly, be agreed with by someone who writes for the *Telegraph*. The good people of liberal England could go home reassured that Amis was a bad, bad man with bad, bad ideas.'

* * *

ALTHOUGH MARTIN AMIS has written well about communism and nuclear weapons, he was never a politically controversial figure before today's arguments. Unlike his friend Christopher Hitchens, he is not an essayist who bounces off each morning's headlines. Unlike Salman Rushdie, another old friend, death threats from radical Islam have not forced him to make politics his priority. Literature always came first, and he is still getting used to being in the middle of a polemical war.

He quotes me Saul Bellow's line from *Herzog*, 'don't contradict your times, just don't contradict your times, if you want a peaceful life'. But he means it ironically, and the nature of our times has made his late emergence as controversialist all but inevitable. Totalitarian movements exaggerate men's worst death lusts, but none has been as unequivocally misogynist as jihadism. In the introduction to *The Second Plane* Amis explains that 'Geopolitics may not be my natural subject, but masculinity is. And have we ever seen the male idea in such outrageous garb as the robes, combat fatigues, suits and ties, jeans, tracksuits and medics' smocks of the Islamic radical?'

He emphasises the point by describing a satire he eventually abandoned on how fear of women breeds male violence. Amis's character Ayed becomes a potential terrorist when his family moves from the badlands of Pakistan:

> Back home in Waziristan, a boy of his age would be feeling a lovely warm glow of pride around now, as he realizes that his sisters, in one important respect, are just like his mother: they can't read or write either. In America, though, the girls are obliged to go to school. Before Ayed knows it, the women have shed their veils, and his sisters are being called on by gum-chewing kaffirs.

There is a second reason why Amis's current notoriety is not such a surprise. The grandees of the liberal mainstream have never taken to him. Juries for the Booker Prize honoured contemporaries from the seventies and eighties, many of whom are now unread, but passed over his novels. The usual explanation is that Amis's explorations of the male psyche are unsettling, but I wonder whether the arts administrators and the critics, the elderly politicians with a literary bent and the governors of the BBC, did not also have the uneasy feeling that he was laughing at them.

A passage from the opening of his 1995 novel *The Information* presciently captured the conformism of middle-class liberal opinion years before it turned on him. At the end of the long period of Tory rule, Richard, the wretched hero, is visiting the Holland Park mansion of Gwyn Barry, a literary rival who, unconscionably, has become an immense success. Richard's envy is heightened when he walks into the study to find a sycophantic colour-supplement journalist seeking Gwyn's opinions on the issues of the day.

'Are you a Labour supporter?' the interviewer asks Gwyn.
'Obviously.'
'Of course.'
'Of course.'

Of course, thought Richard, yeah of course. Gwyn was Labour. It was obvious. Obvious not from the ripply cornices 20 feet above their heads, not from the brass lamps or the military plumpness of the leather-topped desk. Obvious because Gwyn was what he was, a writer, in England, at the end of the 20th century. There was nothing else for such a person to be. Richard was Labour, equally obviously. It often seemed to him, moving in the circles he moved in and reading what he read, that everyone in the land was Labour, except the Government. All writers, all book people were Labour, which was one of the reasons why they got on so well.

Today's Gwyn Barrys aren't Labour now – Tony Blair and the second Iraq War saw to that – but their herd instinct is as persistent as ever. In Amis's case, the herd chewed the cud and with a triumphant moo concluded that he was 'a racist'. Like Sir Kingsley, his father, he is meant to have gone from left to right and ended up a bigot of the most brutish sort.

Here's how they stitched him up.

In the summer of 2006, the Metropolitan Police announced that their officers had arrested twenty-five people in connection with a plot to use liquid explosives to murder about three thousand people and destroy ten aircraft. Flying became more of a pain than ever as airports banned passengers from taking all but tiny amounts of liquid on to planes. The British government finally cut its ties with the unelected leaders of the Muslim Council of Britain after they failed to condemn mass murder unequivocally and chose instead to say British foreign policy was the root cause of terrorism. John Reid, the then Home Secretary, described their statement as 'a dreadful misjudgement'. The former Conservative leader Michael Howard described it as 'a form of blackmail' – change your foreign policy or your aircraft get it.

In an interview a few days later, Amis joined the politicians in arguing that the unelected leaders of British Islam needed to change.

> There's a definite urge – don't you have it? – to say, 'The Muslim community will have to suffer until it gets its house in order.' What sort of suffering? Not letting them travel. Deportation – further down the road. Curtailing of freedoms. Strip-searching people who look like they're from the Middle East or from Pakistan. Discriminatory stuff, until it hurts the whole community and they start getting tough with their children. They hate us for letting our children have sex and take drugs – well, they've got to stop their children killing people. It's a huge dereliction

on their part. I suppose they justify it on the grounds that they have suffered from state terrorism in the past, but I don't think that's wholly rational. It's their own past they're pissed off about; their great decline. It's also masculinity, isn't it?

If I were a British Muslim, I would not like this on first reading – or on second reading either. It's not only that Amis's urge was discriminatory, but that it was also pointless given that a sizeable proportion of the latest batch of terrorists are converts to radical Islam whose parents had other religions or none. I hope, however, I'd retain enough composure to notice that Amis was talking about an urge felt after the revelation that a crime against humanity had just been foiled; that the urge passed and that Amis had not, in fact, gone on to demand discriminatory measures against anyone. Maybe I would also notice something else: *The Times* published the interview in September 2006. There was no fuss, no controversy and no outraged denunciations in the liberal press, nothing until October 2007, when Terry Eagleton, a quasi-Marxist professor, announced that 'In an essay entitled "The Age of Horrorism" published last month, the novelist Martin Amis advocated a deliberate programme of harassing the Muslim community in Britain.'

'That was three mistakes in the first sentence,' Amis drawled. 'It wasn't an essay, it didn't appear the month before and I didn't advocate the deliberate harassing of Muslims.'

Schoolboy errors from a professor of literature no less were, of course, not inadvertent mistakes, but the point of the exercise. Amis was out of step and had to be turned from an interesting thinker who should be treated with a minimum of good manners into the advocate of a racist, police state who could expect nothing but howling abuse. It does him no good that he tells me and every other interviewer that 'despite all its faults, despite a million ills Britain is an extraordinarily successful multi-racial society, and I love it because all novelists love variety'. He has been damned and will have to live with his damnation for the rest of his days.

He is not angry about it. He is not bellowing out great rants, or not in the presence of journalists anyway. Writers can turn their enemies into material, and Eagleton and all those ideologues who have bayed along with him in the pages of the *Guardian* and the *Independent* now fascinate Amis. Friendly journalists have made knowing remarks about how the professor had a book out, and a controversy would do its sales no harm. Amis finds their explanation of Eagleton's behaviour too shallow.

> That's just ordinary, the cynical calculation. It's a drag being a cynic, it's like being a snob or a racist, you're always on duty finding reasons for being cynical, but I can understand how that type of cynicism works. These kind of attacks are something more than 'I've got a book coming out and I want a bit of attention'. It's a super-cynicism, the cynicism that says, 'Sling the charges out there. It doesn't matter if he didn't really say it. It will stick them to him, and I will get the approval of my ideological peer group.' If you're ideological you've got two people living with you, the cheer-leader and the commissar, the frowning commissar. The cheerleader kisses you and the commissar pats you on the back for doing what's necessary to uphold the party line. To be ideological means to fear individuality. You must see safety in numbers, in the herd, so your vanity is always protected. The ideologue can't live by himself; he needs the validation of the like-minded.

If you know Amis's world, and mine, you will have experienced its desire for conformity. Comedians who shriek '*ohmigod* he's supporting Israel!' expect only applause for defending the faithful against the heretic. Their condemnations are social, not intellectual. They mark the borders the tribe cannot cross. 'Anyone who has violated a taboo becomes taboo himself because he possesses the dangerous quality of tempting others to follow his example,' said Freud. Considerable ideological effort goes into making an example of those who might tempt the tribe to abandon its old ways

I once asked Christopher Hitchens about the conformism and heresy-hunting of modern liberal life; why it was that after ten seconds' conversation with standard exponents of the ideology you would not just be able to guess their opinion on one issue but on all issues. Hitchens thought the politically committed feared that if they stepped out of line on one issue, stopped believing that, say, the comprehensive school system was a good idea, they would indeed change their minds on every issue; that their leftish political personality was like a badly made rug which would unravel if one thread came loose.

HE MAY HAVE been speaking truer than he realised about Amis. *Money*, the portrait of John Self, a porn-obsessed, junk-food-guzzling monster, turned him from being a successful eighties writer into a star. As he and everyone else said, *Money* was inspired by the greed of the Thatcher years. Looking back, he now wonders whether he and many other artists of the period got Thatcher wrong.

'I've a lot of faith in the British people,' he told me.

I think we're a good lot on the whole. The only time I hated England was in the class war of the seventies when there was a real sense of bloody mindedness, a deep disobligingness, an almost a Soviet view of 'what's in it for me'. That stopped with Thatcher, bloodily, but it did stop. She's amazing for ending the class system and the union system. She disidentified the Conservative Party from the old aristocracy with her Keiths and her Normans and her Cecils and at the same time neutralised unions. So she worked both ends of the spectrum in what seems to have been a sanitary way. Britain is no longer a class society.

At this point the PR man in me wanted to cry 'steady on, Martin'. It is one thing taking on the left for kowtowing to fascistic movements and regimes, quite another to say that Thatcher was not so bad after all. He was inviting everyone who has never read him to say he was metamorphosing into Sir Kingsley.

Then it struck me he didn't care what was said. Two young daughters from his second marriage dominate his home. The only time his mind wanders is when he thinks it is time to get their tea. They repay his affection by bossing him about whenever he tries to light up – 'They can get away with being little authoritarians about it because they know they're right,' he says, sighing. His sons from his first marriage are men now, and he enjoys their company too. When they were young, he worried about global nuclear war. Now he thinks about the small, half-forgotten conflict between Israel and Hezbollah, and what it may foretell for his daughters' future.

'Part of the crisis in the world is a crisis of weaponry and that strange neurotic war showed it,' he says. 'The Israelis are very impressed by the rockets that are coming in from Lebanon because they know that in ten or twelve years' time there will be much better rockets and some of them will have dirty warheads supplied by Iran. Israel for that reason is going to cease to be habitable.'

Not only Israelis, I mutter to myself, and was as sure as I could be that at some level Amis's many critics have been struck by the same thought. The hubbub he and writers like him are provoking is a symptom of a buried fear. 'If only we don't incite them,' the cowardly voice at the back of the head whispers. 'If only liberals don't raise their hands and say we are morally superior to men who would subjugate the women, kill the homosexuals, kill the unbelievers, kill the Jews, kill the apostates … kill everyone who doesn't agree with them. Then the psychopaths will leave us alone.'

On my way out I wondered whether Amis was learning to be careful about what he said now that he is a political figure, and was cheered by his reply.

'I hope not. I hope I will still be able to talk as someone who is basically a novelist. I don't want to have to court opinion. I don't want to have to watch my words like a politician. Hitchens loves it when he finds opposition in an audience. I thought I had absolutely no appetite for that. Now I find I do have a slight appetite for that. I'm prepared to be unpopular.'

Arena, January 2008

Neoconitis Sweeps Broadcast News

ROGER COHEN OF the *New York Times* can claim the credit for diagnosing a new disease 'neoconitis' which has raged through liberal Manhattan. Its sufferers no longer saw neoconservatism as a specific doctrine that developed in the seventies among American liberals who still supported the New Deal but had no time for the left's excuses for the Soviet Union. Neocon 'has morphed into an all-purpose insult for anyone who still believes that American power is inextricable from global stability and still thinks the muscular anti-totalitarian US interventionism that brought down Slobodan Milosevic has a place'.

Other writers extended the diagnosis by showing that it was also a codeword for 'Jew'. Alan Johnson, the editor of *Democratiya*, took from the thousands of available examples this effort by John le Carré in *Absolute Friends*. A character says, 'what would happen if we allow present trends to continue to the point where corporate media are absolutely at the beck and call in the US of a neo-conservative group which is commanding the political high ground, calling the shots and appointing the state of Israel as the purpose of all Middle Eastern and practically all global policy'.

Resist the temptation to ponder what George Smiley would have made of this Bill Hayden-style rant, said Johnson. 'Note instead that a side-effect of neo-conitis is often an openness to some motifs – in this case the idea that a small cabal controls

"all global policy" in the interests of the Jews, er, sorry, Israel –
that would have barred one from polite society until recently.'

Johnson captured the lure of conspiracy theory to minds too
inflamed to cope with the international crisis, but missed the
scope of the neoconitis epidemic. The accusation of neocon-
nery is now a showstopper and a debate-closer. You do not have
to be a conservative to be called a neocon, or a believer in the
occasional justness of American intervention or even a Jew.
When the British Muslim Ed Husain wrote an account of his
disillusionment with radical Islam, the *Guardian* accused him
of being 'a poster boy for neo-cons'. In the blogosphere a belief
in universal human rights is neoconservative, as is opposition
to tyranny. To name an opponent a neocon is to assert your
virtue and his wickedness. In the words of the old Catholic rite
of exorcism the speaker declares, 'Depart, then, transgressor.
Depart, seducer, full of lies and cunning, foe of virtue, persecu-
tor of the innocent. Give place, abominable creature, give way,
you monster.'

The New York intellectual Paul Berman advised readers that
they would not feel the force of the 'neocon' insult if they
repeated it as they would any other political label. 'You should
say it out loud in falsetto, as if a mouse had just run across your
foot,' he explained. 'Otherwise you will not have captured the
right tone.'

By law, British broadcasters should be impartial men and
women, able by temperament and training to dissect the hysterias of our time. In practice, they are no strangers to the
hitched-up skirt and high-pitched scream. It echoes through
Jon Snow's autobiography, *Shooting History*. In the imagination
of *Channel 4 News*'s anchorman, neocons have surpassed their
enemies' worst fears and attained supernatural powers.

They are time travellers responsible for 'overthrowing
Mossadegh in 1953 and Arbenz in 1954', he asserts, apparently
unaware that the neoconservative movement wasn't born until

the seventies, two decades after the liberal Republican administration of General Eisenhower organised coups in Iran and
Guatemala.

They are shape-shifters who authorised the 'carpet bombing
of Cambodia' in 1970 and the coup against Salvador Allende on
11 September 1973, he continues, apparently unaware that this
would be news to the historians who say that the man responsible for both crimes was Henry Kissinger, a 'realist' who no more
believed in the neocon dream of using force to spread democracy than he believed in fairies at the bottom of the garden.

Worst of all, they are body-snatchers who prey on gullible
members of the aristocracy. Allow me to explain. Snow tells us
that he is the son of a high-Tory bishop, and in my view, he
retains a part of a traditional conservative's resentment of the
Americans, who usurped Britain's status as a world power and
shrunk the horizons of his father's class. When he left university
in the early seventies, he applied for a job at Lord Longford's
drop-in centre for homeless teenagers at King's Cross. His Lordship assured him there was no need to worry about the competition. He had already determined to hire the young Snow
because 'I think your father must have taught me at Eton'. Longford argued for prison reform as well as the homeless, and Snow
praises him for that. But he also became a figure of fun when his
quixotic campaign against pornography led to him making in-
depth studies of the strip joints of Copenhagen.

Snow defends his benefactor in the only way he knows how.
'Frank Longford was really pretty broad-minded, despite his
reputation,' he writes, 'and seemed to me to have been hijacked
by some early neo-conservatives.'

A man so ignorant of recent history he believes that one of the
first tasks of the nascent American neoconservative movement
was to target a slightly potty Anglo-Irish peer is hosting Britain's
premier current affairs show. Surely, the charge from British and
American conservatives that a thoughtless and narrow-minded

group of upper-middle-class liberals has smarmed its way through broadcasting is proven beyond reasonable doubt.

It is easy to feel that way, particularly when you watch *Channel 4 News*. Snow provoked protests from soldiers after the Drudge Report broke the media silence on Prince Harry's service in the Afghan war. 'I never thought I'd find myself saying, "thank God for Drudge"', Snow declared in his daily bulletin for viewers. 'Editors have been sworn to secrecy over Prince Harry being sent to fight in Afghanistan. Drudge has blown their cover. One wonders whether viewers, readers and listeners will ever want to trust media bosses again.'

Never mind that reporting troop movements in wartime stands alongside shouting 'fire!' in a crowded theatre as a restriction on freedom of speech that all but the most anarchic journalists accept, and consider the double standard. If the *Sun* were to reveal the secret location of Maxine Carr, Snow would be incandescent with rage and say that a populist tabloid was endangering her life. Yet when editors decide not to endanger British soldiers in battle, they are guilty of a breach of trust.

While I was writing this article, the Ministry of Defence announced the 100th death in Afghanistan. *Channel 4 News* said that it was 'duty-bound' to examine Gordon Brown's claim that our soldiers had died in a noble cause. 'Reliable measures' were hard to find, it concluded with a shake of the head. The conservative *Spectator* magazine pointed out that the army had pushed the Taliban back to the Pakistani border, allowed the preparations for the upcoming elections and stopped al-Qaeda re-establishing an Afghan base. The failure of Channel 4 to grasp that the struggle against a movement that executes teachers for the crime of teaching girls to read and write was a liberal struggle struck me more forcibly. Its report could not allow the notion that radical Islam was against every good liberal principle to take root in the minds of its liberal audience. Doubts and awkward moral questions might follow.

The bias feels all the more insidious because of the huge advantage politically committed broadcasters enjoy. Politicians realised long ago that taking them on is like swearing at the referee or throwing your racket at the umpire – a mug's game they can never win. As soon as interviewees challenge them, broadcasters retreat behind the mask of impartiality and present themselves as mere adjudicators. It is no good using the normal tactics of argument against them by highlighting the previous failures of their ideology or their hypocrisies and blind spots. Take them on, and they will insist they have no ideology, and make you look like a spoilsport who won't play by the rules of the broadcasting game.

Yet because they need to duck for cover, their influence is limited. Conservatives generally make too much of bias in broadcasting. It is not simply that Radio 4's *PM* and *The World at One* are models of public-service journalism, but that the more dubious programmes cannot always be dubious. *Channel 4 News* is straight most of the time and often provides the evening's best coverage. Even when Snow let rip about the decision of editors not to turn Prince Harry into a Taliban target, he had to watch his back and add the nervous caveat: 'But perhaps this was a courageous editorial decision to protect this fine young man.'

Reviewing Snow's autobiography, the Labour MP Denis MacShane paraphrased Karl Marx and wrote, 'Television reporters offer an interpretation of the world. Snow, one suspects, would prefer to have changed it.' MacShane's use of the past tense was instructive. If you want to report the world, go into television, but if you want to change the world, go into politics, or argue your case as a polemicist or join a protest group. You suffer the disappointments of political campaigning but also feel the satisfaction that comes from making a commitment and fighting for it. Broadcasting brings the politically engaged celebrity and money, but extracts a dreadful price. It allows them only to push the impartiality rules so far by, typically, asking tough questions of a political foe while giving powder-puff interviews to a friend. When challenged in debate, their employers will not allow them to stand and fight their ground. They must scuttle away and pretend to be nothing more than civil servants of the airwaves.

Lord Longford may have made an ass of himself on many occasions but there was nothing surreptitious or snide about his public career. For better and for worse, he stated what he believed in and fought in the open. Partisan broadcasters can never fight neoconservatives, real or imagined, openly. They can get away with the sneak attack and the deniable smear, but not with honest engagement. To use a word they would never use, their chosen careers are 'unmanly'.

Conservatives should pity rather than condemn liberals locked in the gilded cage of broadcast news. For theirs are lives half lived.

Standpoint, June 2008

It's the Jews, Once Again

I HAVE HAD PROFESSOR Ted Honderich's books on my shelves all my adult life. I won't pretend I reach for them often, but the argument of his 1976 essays on violence has stayed with me. Inequality kills, it runs. The poor have shorter lives than the rich, not only in famine-ridden Saharan hellholes but in Europe and North America, too. We should, therefore, overcome squeamish liberal objections to the violence of the left and consider the possibility that it might end the greater violence of poverty. Honderich did not dwell on the record of revolutionary violence in Stalin's Soviet Union and Mao's China in promoting the equality of the mass grave. Nevertheless, it struck me that his initial claim – that our failure to alleviate poverty was a kind of complicity with murder – stood up.

Thirty years on, and the world has been transformed. In the seventies, there were revolutionaries from Peru to Cambodia. Today, with the exception of the Maoists of Nepal, no radical movements of the far left are close to seizing power. Everything has changed except Ted Honderich, who is churning out books on how 9/11 and all that has happened since are a payback for our sins of commission and omission. I cannot say they convince me. I am suspicious of the belief that irrational movements have rational causes, but maybe I'm wrong. Everyone, from the *Independent* to the *Daily Mail*, is asserting with varying degrees of vehemence that we are the 'root cause' of Islamist violence. Who better to dissect my faulty thinking than University College London's Grote Professor Emeritus of the Philosophy of Mind and Logic?

Our meeting began badly and got worse. I had arranged to talk to him at a conference at the Royal College of Art in London's museum district: a bland, modernist building overshadowed by the exuberantly Gothic Natural History and Victoria and Albert museums. The college is an anonymous place where it is easy to miss people, but there was no missing Professor Honderich. Six foot five inches tall and seventy-three years old, he was all flowing grey hair and dramatic poses as he marched up to me and began to denounce a Channel 5 documentary by the *Times* columnist David Aaronovitch. I missed it and had not the faintest idea what he was going on about, but so vigorous were his condemnations that I assumed Aaronovitch must have pilloried him.

Only later did I learn that Honderich himself had made a documentary for the channel (which the *Guardian*'s critic described as a 'fatheaded' attempt to blame Islamist terrorism on 'almost everyone but Islamist terrorists'). The station's controllers then commissioned Aaronovitch to argue that Islamist terrorists did indeed carry a portion of the blame for Islamist terrorism. At no point did he mention Honderich. Nevertheless, the professor was furious that Channel 5 had aired a contrary point of view.

It took me a while to work that out, and I responded with polite bafflement when he pressed a closely typed, sixteen-page attack on Aaronovitch into my hands. I glanced at it and saw the professor was suggesting that Aaronovitch was a part of 'Israel's fifth column'. I should have realised then that I was in front of an academic who was more used to giving lectures than listening to them.

What interested me, I said, as I tried to calm him down, was that in the seventies, when he had originally argued that revolutionary violence might be justified, there actually were movements of the revolutionary left. Now, nearly all the violent threats to the status quo come from radical reactionaries. Did it make a difference to him that the proponents of violence were the Iranian ayatollahs, al-Qaeda and the Muslim Brotherhood, organisations which had incorporated parts of classical fascist tradition?

At the mention of fascism, the professor's head shot back. 'Fascist tradition? I think that's an amazing utterance, as a matter of fact. It's an utterance, by the way, which is gone for by the makers of that Aaronovitch programme.'

Dear God, I thought, the man's obsessed. I stemmed the flow by doing what I suspect few of his students had ever done.

'Er, yes, fascist,' I interrupted. 'Surely you will admit this is the radical right dressed up in religious robes?'

He would not, of course, and could not. I had asked him earlier whether he still called himself a socialist, and there had been a long pause – a very long pause – before he replied that he remained a member of the Labour Party 'in the hope of one day getting rid of Blair'. As our meeting progressed, I began to understand the reasons for his hesitation. A positive commitment to left-wing politics might have trapped him; might have compelled him to stand with his comrades in, say, Iran or Iraq against their persecutors. As it was, Honderich was free to explain away their oppression with root-causery, and deny its true nature.

'First, fascism is a nationalist movement,' Honderich said as he got into his stride. 'Second, it has a leader principle, and there's nothing like a leader principle in Islam. Fascism lacks, above all, the overwhelming element of humanity; there is a humane element, a humanity element, in Islam. The idea that al-Qaeda or Islam is properly called fascist is really an extraordinary idea and is, if you will allow me to say so, an attempt to cook the books against al-Qaeda and Islam.'

His voice was as monotonous as a metronome, and it was only after a minute that I shook myself and noticed that he was conflating Islamism and Islam. I have my problems with the accusations of Islamophobia that pseudo-leftists throw around so freely. I can develop reasonable phobias about any religion which places the supposed dictates of its god, or gods, above the laws of free parliaments. But I fully accept that to say all the world's billion or so Muslims support al-Qaeda is false and prejudiced. Yet here was an emeritus professor of logic, a philosopher who drops the names of his friends 'Freddie' Ayer and Stuart Hampshire, doing just that.

I pointed out his error.

He boomed back: 'I'm happy to take the correction. Rewrite the thing in terms of al-Qaeda.'

No chance, I thought, and moved on to his philosophy. Honderich is a consequentialist. He believes that the consequences of a decision, or failure, to make a decision, are more important than motives. For Honderich, if you do not give money to Oxfam or the Red Cross, you are killing Africans as surely as if you had deliberately stopped a food convoy reaching a refugee camp. That you may never have given Africa a second's thought is unimportant.

After the Terror, his response to 9/11, begins with heart-rending descriptions of world poverty. The insinuation is that he believes that the attacks on New York and Washington were a consequence of the failure of the rich world to tackle malnutrition and disease.

'Surely, you don't believe that,' I say. 'Al-Qaeda has no connection to famine in Chad or Aids in Malawi.'

Surprisingly, given the space he devoted to the state of sub-Saharan Africa, he accepts my argument without reservation. 'I think that's the kind of utterance we've really got to fight against. To say that radical Islamist movements are the result of poverty is the last thing I would say.'*

Al-Qaeda isn't the fault of poverty, it turns out.

It's the fault of the Jews.

'With respect to 9/11, its prime necessary connection is neo-Zionism. Not the establishment of Israel but the expansion of Israel into the last fifth of historic Palestine and I stick to that absolutely.'

I put the usual objections, that we have had Baathism, the Iranian revolution and al-Qaeda campaigns from the Philippines to his native Canada. Wasn't he worried that he was sounding a little anti-Semitic when he blamed all this violence on a filthy little war over a patch of land on the eastern Mediterranean? Wasn't he once again turning the Jew into a paranormal figure responsible for half the violence on the planet? He would not accept that. Nor would he accept that he had switched from defending the far left to defending the far right. 'There is a great deal of continuity in my work,' he said with orotund satisfaction. 'There is, and I'm perfectly happy about that.' He was 'delighted' not to be like 'a lot of people, of whom perhaps you are one, who have managed, as you would say, to educate yourself and change your views under various pressures. One of them, by the way, is the pressure of being Jewish.'

This was getting ridiculous. You don't have to be Jewish to oppose psychopathic movements. You just need to have had an education in the anti-totalitarian tradition.

But there was no stopping him. Jews in general and me in particular were responsible for mass murder.

---

* All the more surprising because in his book he asks, 'Is it possible to suppose that the September 11 attacks had nothing at all to do with … Malawi, Mozambique, Zambia and Sierra Leone? … In thinking about it, remember that the attacks on the towers were indeed attacks on the principal symbols of world capitalism.'

'Everything is very dark at the moment and you are making a contribution to it. The world is ever darker. It's a shitty place now and you are also responsible, [you] bear a part of the responsibility for 9/11 and 7/7.' Without pausing for breath, he added, 'I liked your book, by the way, on New Labour.'

Old hands at interviewing never walk out. But I was overcome by the urge to escape. More than anything else, his ability to denounce me one minute and flatter me the next unnerved me. 'Well, I've got another one on the way,' I said. 'And, trust me, you won't like it.'

With that, I headed off, past the posturing mannequins of the Victoria and Albert Museum, past the fossilised dinosaurs of the Natural History Museum and into the welcome embrace of the dangerous city. It was only when I was making my way home through Tavistock Square that I realised the 'root cause' of the errors of Honderich and the thousands of intellectuals like him. In a review of *After the Terror* for the online journal *Democratiya*, Jon Pike, a philosopher with the Open University, told me something I hadn't appreciated about the 7/7 attacks. The bus bomb in the square exploded round the corner from Honderich's University College. Pike described how mails flew across the net, as academics checked that the bomber had not killed their colleagues, and we must be grateful they found that all the philosophers could carry on theorising. University College's sole fatality was Gladys Wundowa, a Ghanaian cleaner and charity worker.

If Honderich could have brought the bus bomber Hasib Hussain back to life and asked him what kind of society he had murdered her to create, what would he have said? If that sounds too speculative, look at the societies being created by the movements Honderich explains away as the fault of others. Would feminists, socialists, liberals, religious minorities and atheists be happy living in a Palestine ruled by Hamas rather than Fatah, or modern Iran, or Afghanistan, if al-Qaeda and the Taliban come back, or Iraq if the 'insurgents' win? Would emeritus professors?

It is a poor consequentialist who cannot think about consequences. Honderich cannot because, I think, the emotional consequences of admitting that not all the darkness of the world rises in the West would be too great for him to endure.

New Statesman, November 2006

Vänster om, Höger om!*

FROM THE 1880S TO the 1980s, socialism defined the left. European leftists argued with each other about what socialism meant, while Russian, Chinese and other poor-world socialists murdered each other. Some were democrats and others were totalitarians, but on the basic point they agreed: being left-wing meant believing that the common ownership of the means of production offered the best way forward for humanity.

They arranged human societies in a hierarchy or pyramid. Socialism in one of its many forms was at the top. The next most desirable social order was what left-wingers foolishly called capitalist democracy: countries like yours and mine with mixed economies, universal suffrage, bills of rights and welfare states. At the bottom of the heap were the most detestable regimes imaginable: fascist, communalist or confessional states, which used insane conspiracy theories and pseudo-science to divide people by ethnicity or creed.

Move forward into the twenty-first century and the left is unrecognisable. Socialism is dead, destroyed by the terrible crimes of the communists and the success of market economies, most notably in Asia. There are still people who call themselves socialists but no serious political movement anywhere in the

* Left turn, right turn.

world believes in the total transformation of society. You grasp the scale of the defeat by remembering that the case for socialism was practical as well as moral. Socialism was not only meant to bring an ethically superior order but a more productive one as well. It was the economic logic of communal ownership, which, according to Marx, made its triumph inevitable. Today its failure seems preordained.

People who say they are on the left now favour higher rates of taxation and the provision of public services by state monopolies, and are justifiably wary of private corporations and financial markets. Yet when their politicians take power they often turn to the market for solutions to the practical problems of running modern societies. They bring in private businesses to run public services or allow a market in education by giving school vouchers to parents.

They are not selling out, merely reflecting the true state of parties of the left in the democratic world, which are everywhere cautious and flexible. They can no longer inspire enthusiasm for vast schemes of state control because they no longer believe in them themselves – and nor do most of their supporters when they speak honestly.

Political writers have discussed the death of socialism at length, but few have noticed how the leftism that has emerged from the wreckage finds it easy to go along with right wing and extreme reactionary ideas that the twentieth-century left at its best opposed.

I will explain what I mean with the help of a few plausible scenarios.

- You study the history of radical Islam and realise that from the Iranian revolution onwards, whenever radical Islamists have seized power they have murdered liberals and leftists. You then survey newspapers from a random sample of European countries, and find that without exception liberal and leftist rather than conservative journals excuse radical Islam.

- A bomb explodes in Stockholm killing 100 people. Within minutes, the radio broadcasts the voices of leftists who blame the Americans, the Israelis and the Swedish government for mass murder. Not one criticises the terrorists or the ideology that motivated them.
- The Sudanese regime revives its genocidal campaign against the peoples of Darfur. You want to protest, but notice there are no large demonstrations to join in Sweden or any other European country. You realise that people who call themselves left-wing rarely protest about crimes against humanity they cannot blame on the West. Such atrocities no longer stir their hearts.
- You pick up a copy of *Ordfront* and read that 'The Israeli Government Runs the Swedish Media'. You are not as surprised as you once would have been when you hear that *Ordfront* is a left-wing newspaper. In the twentieth century, those who said that a conspiracy of Jews controlled the media and governments were Nazis. Now they are leftists. You point out the shift to a friend who works on Swedish television's media monitoring programme. She can't see the story.
- At a meeting in Stockholm, you hear a Dutch Muslim feminist, who has escaped from forced marriage and sexual abuse, call on Swedish liberals to fight against the oppression of women. A distinguished social democratic thinker stands up and accuses her of being 'provocative'. When the leader of a small revolutionary party screams from the back of the hall that she is 'a tool of the neocons, racists and Zionists', the audience smiles indulgently.
- You enrol in a cultural studies course at the nearest university and notice a strange phenomenon. In the past, conservatives defended reactionary religions in the poor world, while leftists believed in progress and enlightenment. In the lecture hall, you hear radical academics condemn challenges to tradition as 'cultural imperialism' and denigrate progress as an 'oppressive' vice of the Enlightenment.

I may have exaggerated these scenarios, but not by much. The hierarchy of the twentieth century vanished with the collapse of socialism. Now the worst form of society is Western democracy, particularly American democracy. In the past conservatives made excuses for fascism because they mistakenly saw it as a continuation of democratic right-wing ideas, while left-wingers condemned it without equivocation. Now in Europe and North America leftists excuse fascistic and reactionary movements and ignore their victims, even when the victims share left-wing ideals.

Their native far-right parties are an exception. As long as racists are white, they have no difficulty in opposing them in a manner that would have been recognisable to the traditional left. But give them a foreign far-right movement that is anti-Western and they treat it as at best a distraction and at worst an ally.

If the worst side of the old left was its failure to confront communism, the best was its camaraderie. European socialists supported strangers who shared their values. Today an Iranian feminist, an Iraqi democrat or a Kurdish socialist is highly unlikely to receive a show of solidarity from Europeans who call themselves left-wing, particularly if the supposed leftists are middle-class intellectuals. At best, they will ignore their comrades. At worst, they will denigrate them.

If you think the phenomena I am describing are simply the result of the disastrous Bush administration, I would agree with you up to a point. But they were developing long before Bush came to power and show every sign of continuing after he has gone.

In any case, a left that still had life in it and a European liberal tradition that meant what it said would have had no difficulty in dealing with Bush in an honourable manner. It would have opposed the second Iraq War, deplored the errors and brutalities of the occupation while supporting those Iraqis who fought al-Qaeda and insisted that they wanted something better after thirty-five years of the genocidal Baathist regime. Support was forthcoming from parts of the old and declining labour movements, but the dominant voices on the liberal left in the media, universities and political parties stayed silent as al-Qaeda slaughtered Iraqis without compunction. 'Internationalism', 'solidarity' and 'fraternity' now feel like dead words from a lost age.

Even the one foreign cause that does inspire the European left, the Israeli confrontation with the Palestinians, is far less altruistic than it seems. Very few on the left are prepared to support Fatah, which for all its faults is a recognisable national liberation movement that may build a Palestine worth living in, while deploring Hamas, which wants to impose intolerable burdens on Palestinian women, gays, trade unionists, secularists and Christians.

The inability to discriminate between democrat and theocrat is a sign of vacuity. Today's left cannot tell its friends from its enemies because it has no programme for a better world. Blaming its decadence on Bush is as foolish as holding America responsible for every conflict. Deeper historical trends explain the crisis of our times.

1. The rise of consumer politics

In the sixties, those who longed for a radical transformation of the status quo, as many people do at sometime in their lives, could draw comfort from revolutionary leftist movements that were sweeping the poor world, as well as the support for student radicals in their own countries. History was on their side. Millions were moved by their slogans.

Since the fall of socialism, revolutionary leftism has died everywhere except in Latin America, and even there it is sickly and shallow.

The main threat to the status quo comes from radical Islam and the corrupt nationalisms of China and Russia. Far leftists are open in their support for jihadis. The apologias from some liberals are so comprehensive that they must also support radical Islam in their hearts. A love of violence and hatred of their own societies – well merited or otherwise – leads them to conclude that any killer of Americans is better than none.

Noam Chomsky in his political writings, and Michel Foucault and the postmodernists in their cultural theorising, anticipated the twenty-first-century left ideology. Read them and you find that a leftism without a practical political programme has taken the place of socialism. All they have is a criticism of the existing order. In this mental universe, no movement that challenges the existing order can be unambiguously condemned.

Say what you like about them, but a communist or social democrat in the forties had clear ideas about how to transform society. Today, there is no radical alternative that serious people believe they can use, just practical ways of adapting to changes in the economy and environment.

A paradoxical consequence of the death of the socialist idea is that leftism now suits the consumer society. Because there is no coherent left-wing political programme, anyone can affect a leftish posture, just as anyone can walk into a shop. For example, if I were a socialist addressing a meeting decades ago, the audience might have agreed with a specific point I was making. If I said that we should do more to improve the treatment of prisoners or provide free health services, it might have nodded vigorously. But because I believed in socialism I would not be able to stick to a single issue. I would be compelled to add that I also wanted the nationalisation of the commanding heights of the economy, penal taxation and workers' control. Members of the audience might then have backed away, saying that they thought these policies were disastrous and so they could not possibly define themselves as left-wing.

Modern leftists do not have to risk alienating potential sympathisers by putting forward a general programme that might make their listeners uncomfortable. Indeed, they rarely have a programme for a new ordering of society. They are merely against the West in general or America in particular, both of which, God knows, provide reasons aplenty for opposition. If someone points out that as leftists they have a duty to fight crimes committed by ultra-reactionary movements, the new left ideology instructs them to say that it is 'hypocritical' for Westerners to criticise when they carry so much guilt. The correct course is to do and say nothing.

The collapse of socialism also explains the general inability of leftists in Europe and North America to work on behalf of feminists, democrats and leftists in the poor world. If you do not have a positive programme yourself, how can you see strangers as comrades who have the right to your support?

These perfidies may be scandalous but they chime with the psychology of modern consumerism. Shoppers do not like altruistic commitments. They have no appetite for boring meetings to raise public consciousness and the lobbying of politicians to change policy.

When I go into the homes of the richest people I know, I see Naomi Klein and Michael Moore on their shelves and think, 'Why am I surprised? The left is no threat to the wealthy any longer. Being a leftist is a lifestyle choice. It carries no costs and no obligations.'

2. Liberal disillusion

So far, I have been dealing with the consequences of defeat. But the second half of the twentieth century also saw enormous liberal triumphs. European left-wing movements gave the masses better housing, full-time education, employment rights and comprehensive health cover. If you could travel back in time, and tell the reformers of 100 years ago what Sweden and the rest of Europe would look like today, they would be astonished and delighted.

You would then have to explain to them that the triumph of leftish ideals had the unexpected consequence of turning the liberal intelligentsia against the white working class. The workers let down the intellectuals. They did not lead the charge towards a socialist society as the intelligentsia told them to. They did not always use the relative affluence the welfare state gave them to acquire a taste for avant-garde art and atonal music. Worse still, they voted in large numbers for politicians the middle-class left despised – Reagan, Thatcher, Bush and Sarkozy. And all too clearly in the cities of Europe and North America, the utopian plans of the twentieth-century social reformers did not always create a better society but welfare dependency, family breakdown and crime.

You can see the disappointment of the leftish middle class in their attempts to prevent democratic votes and deny freedoms. The centralisation of decision-making in the undemocratic bodies of the European Union, the fondness for asking unelected judges to take political decisions and politically correct speech codes all flow from a belief that the working class cannot be trusted to think as the middle classes would like it to think.

Beyond a fear that they cannot win majorities in open elections, the liberal middle class across the developed world feels a deeper unease. History no longer seems to be going its way. Market economies undermine the status and comparative wealth of the public sector managers who dominated modern states at the high tide of social democracy in the mid-twentieth century. Financiers and industrialists have acquired fantastic wealth and political status, while the liberal middle classes lingered in jobs their rulers despised for their failure to be market oriented.

Modern democracy is a system that no longer pleases them. They are less likely than they once would have been to stand up for the best values of their societies.

3. Multiculturalism and its discontents

Our progressive intellectual of 100 years ago would be as astonished by the triumph of human rights as by the growth of the welfare state. Women, homosexuals and blacks – groups which had been discriminated against for centuries – have won full legal equality. A measure of the transformation is that it is now impossible for a conservative politician who is against equal rights for homosexuals to become the leader of a mainstream European centre-right party, let alone go on to win a national election.

Again, there is an ambiguity, however. Although the extraordinary success of campaigns against sexism, racism and homophobia improved the lives of millions of individuals, postmodern liberals did not see them as individuals but as categories. They developed an identity politics based on group definitions that was anti-individualist in its assumptions. They treated women, members of ethnic minorities, gays and others as blocs with communal interests. Multiculturalists took the liberal idea of tolerance and pushed it into an extreme relativism which held that it was wrong for liberals to attack previously disadvantaged groups – 'the other' – even when 'the other' espoused ideas which were anti-liberal.

In short, it has become racist to oppose sexists, homophobes and fascists from other cultures.

Such attitudes are a disaster for progressive forces in the poor world, most notably in the Arab countries, and in Europe's immigrant communities. We are now in the extraordinary position where liberals consider it 'left-wing' to argue that the emancipation of women is good for white-skinned women in Stockholm but not for brown-skinned women in Tehran. Postmodernists have picked up the reactionary, anti-universalist philosophies of the counter-Enlightenment and dressed them in modern clothes.

4. Fear

From the 9/11 atrocities on, the stupidest citizens of Western democracies could be in no doubt that forces were swirling around the globe that would murder them on a vast scale. This is a short and simple point to make, but we are frightened and think it is better to say nothing about the treatment of women, the attacks on freedom of speech, the psychopathic ideologies, medieval hatreds and raging conspiracy theories in case we provoke our potential killers.

FEAR IS THE most powerful of human motives. Add in the despairing and reactionary turn modern leftish thinking took after the collapse of socialism, the tolerance of the intolerable inculcated by postmodernism and the doubts about democracy in the liberal mainstream, and I hope you can see why so many can't oppose totalitarian movements of the far right or even call them by their real names.

However understandable the denial, it remains as pitiful a response to Islamism as climate change denial is to global warming. Both sets of deniers believe that we can carry on as before living our safe, consumerist lives as if nothing has changed.

We cannot in either case, and must face the threats of our time. Reasonable men and women can disagree about how we face them, but we will not be able to see them plainly until we have cleared away the mountains of rubbish that block our view. The twenty-first century will not have a left that is worth having until we do.

Axess, Stockholm, Summer 2008

Nicolas Sarkozy Woos
Bernard-Henri Lévy

Review of *Left in Dark Times:*
A Stand against the New Barbarism

IN 2007, a few months before the French presidential election, a gleeful Nicolas Sarkozy phoned Bernard-Henri Lévy. André Glucksmann, who had been Lévy's comrade in the struggles against totalitarianism since the seventies, had announced in *Le Monde* that he had had it with the left. He was crossing the line and backing Sarkozy, the candidate of the right he had once opposed.

Sarkozy quickly exhausted his limited supply of small talk and got down to business. 'What about you?' he asked Lévy. 'When are you going to write your little article for me? Huh, when? Because Glucksmann is fine. But you ... you, after all, are my friend.'

Lévy was embarrassed. He had indeed known Sarkozy for years, and had briefed him before a famous television debate with Tariq Ramadan, the leading Muslim Brotherhood apologist in Europe. Sarkozy confronted Ramadan over his support for a 'moratorium' – instead of an outright ban – on the stoning of Muslim women found 'guilty' of adultery.

Sarkozy: A moratorium ... Mr Ramadan, are you serious? Muslims are human beings who live in 2003 in France, since we are speaking about the French community, and you have just said something particularly incredible, which is that the stoning of women, yes, the stoning is a bit shocking, but we should simply declare a moratorium, and then we are going to think about it in order to decide if it is good. But that's monstrous – to stone a woman because she is an adulterer! It's necessary to condemn it!

Ramadan: Mr Sarkozy, listen well to what I am saying. What I say, my own position, is that the law is not applicable – that's clear. But today, I speak to Muslims around the world and I take part, even in the United States, in the Muslim world ... You should have a pedagogical posture that makes people discuss things. You can't decide all by yourself to be a progressive in the communities. That's too easy.

Sarkozy: Mr Ramadan, if it is regressive not to want to stone women, I avow that I am a regressive.

Soon after that put-down, Ramadan decided to leave France. He couldn't move to America, the Homeland Security Agency had barred him from entering, so he came to Britain. As if to prove Glucksmann's point, British progressives did not treat him as an ideologue for a reactionary movement. The nominally liberal academics of Oxford University feted him, and ministers in the nominally left-of-centre Labour government sought his advice. Was this the left Lévy was meant to support?

Meanwhile Lévy didn't need Sarkozy to tell him (although that didn't stop Sarkozy *from* telling him) that Ségolène Royal, the socialist candidate and his leading opponent, had already met the leaders of Hezbollah, who in 2002 had welcomed the gathering of Jewry in Israel because it 'saves us the trouble of going after them worldwide'. Royale had also murmured kind words about the efficiency of the Chinese justice system, which condemns about ten thousand prisoners a year to death.

'It's over, Bernard,' Sarkozy told him in effect. 'You know it better than I do. The nobility has gone. The altruism fled. All that's left of the left is malice and cowardice. Join your friends. Join me.'

But Lévy couldn't. 'Personal relations are one thing,' he replied. 'Ideas are another. And no matter how much I like and respect you, the left is my family.' It wasn't much of an answer – and Levy knew it. *Left in Dark Times* is his more considered attempt to explain why he still saw himself as a man of the left, even though the left liberalism he had dedicated his life to had gone wrong in Europe – and could easily be perverted in America too.

The French leftist culture in which he has flourished will strike most as strange beyond measure. America has no Marxist tradition worth mentioning and no experience of Nazi occupation. The totalitarian temptation of communism that enchanted so many French men and women in the twentieth century never enchanted many Americans. Lévy's assault on the ideology of their successors in twenty-first-century France may seem to have little to do with anyone outside Europe.

Lévy adds to the impression of otherness by cutting an exotic figure. I met him when we argued against a motion that 'democracy isn't for everyone' at a debate in London. He appeared in the green room in an immaculate white suit, looking every inch the dandy, as beautiful in his way as his wife, the actress Arielle Dombasle, who dazzled by his side. Bob Geldof walked across to talk to him, and as my eyes flitted from Geldof to Lévy and back again, I was hard pressed to tell which was the rock star and which the philosopher. The audience, exhausted by Iraq, was dead against us when we went on stage, but we swung the meeting around and routed our conservative opponents. I like to think that it was the force of our arguments which won the night, but the spectators may just have been bowled over by Lévy's glamour.

The celebrity thinker is not a feature of American politics – do John McCain and Barack Obama crave the support of the equivalents of Glucksmann and Lévy? Do they know who they are? Do you?

But Americans would be wrong to dismiss Lévy as a fascinating foreigner for a reason I don't think many liberals have grasped. Americans on the left may not thank me for saying so, but they have been lucky in one respect to have had George W. Bush as their enemy. He has united the opposition; he has been the glue which has held men and women with madly contradictory ideas and aspirations together. Hatred of Bush has given the American left a new salience and a new power, something it hasn't had since the early days of the Clinton era, but it has not given it a unified vision.

Bush has gone, but little else has changed. President Obama still faces a psychopathic variant of Islam prepared to murder without limit, an Iran pushing for the bomb and the newly confident autocracies of China and Russia. If he has the nerve to take them on, Obama will find that the American leftists or progressives or whatever we are meant to call them these days are nowhere near as united as they now seem. Former allies will soon start raging against him, as they raged against Bush; in some corners of the movement, the clenching of fists and the pursing of lips have already begun. The arguments we are having in Europe are about to hit the States. Lévy is worth taking seriously because he forewarns in the hope that Americans will be forearmed.

THE FIRST PART of *Left in Dark Times* explains what Lévy meant when he told Sarkozy that he was still a member of the family of the left. He sees the best of leftish conscience as a series of responses: the Dreyfusard reflex, which encourages us to defend the individual against Church and state; the anti-Vichy reflex, which rejects any version of racism or anti-Semitism; the reflexes of the 1968 protest movement, which opposed author-itarianism and censorship; and finally, an anti-colonial reflex, which revolts against the oppression of one people in the name of another. Lévy knows that from the Dreyfus Affair through the Nazi occupation to 1968, there were many on the French left who sided with the enemy. Overall, however, the causes that inspire him were fought by the left against the right.

Not now. As the wily Sarkozy realised, in Europe men and women who believe in universal human rights, the emancipa-tion of women and freedom from tyranny spend more time fighting leftists than rightists.

What was truly exotic about our debate in London was not Lévy's tailoring but the fact that our opponents were traditional conservatives. Nine times out of ten, the motion that democ-racy isn't for everyone isn't sponsored by right-wing, establish-ment believers in privilege and cultural determinism, but by apparent leftists who regard it an extension of 'imperialism' to argue that it is always wrong to stone women to death.

Anti-Americanism is everywhere – and this is a second reason why stateside readers should pay attention. Today anti-Americanism is the main, often the sole, defining feature of European leftist opinion. Lévy produces the best analysis I have seen since Richard Wolin's *The Seduction of Unreason* of the manner in which European liberals are taking over a reac-tionary idea. In the early twentieth century, fascist and proto-fascist writers were appalled by America's 'unnaturalness', he writes: its rejection of tradition, hierarchy and organic bonds between people and place; and its celebration of consumerism, standardisation, racial mingling and mass culture. For good reason, they feared America's appeal to the European masses. Liberals, by contrast, respected the emancipatory potential of a society built on a social contract rather than racial ideas of blood and soil. Today it is the leftists of *Le Monde Diplomatique* who pick up the tropes of the old far right and echo the

Islamists when they warn that American culture is colonising our brains, insidiously corrupting innocent Europeans by turning them into the dupes of the supposedly all-powerful US corporations. As Lévy says, the only America that most of his comrades want is the isolationist America of Michael Moore and Pat Buchanan, a faraway America, an America which is happy for the rest of the world to go to hell.

Anti-Americanism didn't start with Iraq, and it is not limited to the European left. In the days after the Islamo-fascist attacks on New York and Washington, the apologia did not come only from right-wingers, as it would have in the thirties, but from the likes of Noam Chomsky and Susan Sontag. Nor was it only Bush's foreign-policy activism which provoked their opposition, but any American activism, including the sort of activism they once supported. Lévy captures the left's shift from universal values with a vignette of a confrontation with a former friend, Rony Brauman. He once travelled the world helping the victims of crimes against humanity, regardless of whether their suffering could be blamed on America or not. Over the years, Brauman's indignant voice grew quieter, until he stopped condemning atrocity and began picking fights with the liberal interventionists whose cause he had once supported. In 2007, during a radio debate about the genocide in Darfur, Lévy tried to find out why. When Lévy brought up the killing of Jews by Vichy France as an analogy, Brauman cried that the two were not comparable. 'The war in Sudan is more complicated, and the Sudanese should sort it out themselves.'

At that moment, Lévy thought he understood the new mindset. Behind his former ally's casuistry lay the recognition that there was a powerful movement in American public opinion to stop the crimes in the Sudan. But like other wised-up intellectuals, Brauman had read his Chomsky and his Baudrillard. He knew that America was not a democracy, but 'the command post' of an empire which brainwashed the masses by manufacturing consent. Support America on one thing and you would have to support her on everything – and you were not going to catch a guy as wise as Rony Brauman falling for that. 'I was looking at a champion of human rights,' Lévy writes, 'who was telling me, without the slightest hint of embarrassment, that he'd decided to sit out Darfur, to write it off as just another piece of our era's collateral damage.'

As I was writing this article, I guessed that I could find Braumans of my own in the American liberal press. I clicked on the *Nation*'s website, and was not disappointed. 'It remains to be seen whether an Obama administration can articulate a coherent progressive purpose for American foreign policy in the post-Bush era,' announced the first article I read. 'So far, at least, his team appears to be falling back on the liberal interventionist notions of the Nineties.' Thus a random dip into America's leading leftist journal instantly gave me the argument that it would have been 'progressive' to leave Bosnia's Muslims to be murdered and driven into exile in the nineties and – by extension – that it is equally 'progressive' to allow Robert Mugabe to condemn Zimbabwe to a man-made famine today.

The American left is not as different from the European left as readers may imagine, not least because several of the ugliest features of European leftism are American imports. Lévy finds it significant that when the American academics Stephen Walt and John Mearsheimer disinterred conspiracy theories about powerful Jews to explain away the Iraq War, they were not embraced by right-wing European journals, as anti-Semitism was in the early twentieth century, but by their left-wing rivals. I speak from experience when I say that among English academics, the duo's notion that a Jewish cabal organised the second Iraq War is ubiquitous, and those who hold it think that their regurgitation of the oldest fantasy of the far right is proof positive of their liberalism. Denunciations of 'Jewish warmongering' came from Charles Lindbergh and 'America Firsters' in the thirties and forties, Lévy says. Now we have 'a left that makes your head spin – a left that, if words have any meaning at all, is sometimes more right-wing than the right wing itself.'

The inevitable consequence is the abandonment of solidarity with those victims of oppression whose suffering does not fit into the 'anti-imperialist' world view. If crimes cannot be blamed on America, the West, Israel or the Empire, they vanish from the leftish consciousness. In a magnificent passage, Levy asks

> What happens to you if you think, like the Burundian Tutsi, that the fantasy of Hutu Power, and not a scheme carried out by Texas oilmen, is the source of your problems? Or like a survivor of the extermination of the Nuba, in the most distant corner of the Sudan, that it's your uniqueness that singled you out for misfortune and explains the determination of the Islamist regime in Khartoum to get rid of you? What happens if you're Burmese, Tibetan, a Syrian Kurd, a Liberian? What is to become of you if the disaster you're dealing with has nothing to do with the evil of the Empire, its conspiracies, its plots – but everything to do with the corruption, for example, of a state apparatus, or of unscrupulous national elites?
>
> Well, nothing. You're out of luck. You're a thousand times less important, a thousand times less interesting to 'progressive' consciences, who have much less reason to fret about your particular case than about, for example, a humiliated Muslim who has resorted to terrorism in response to that humiliation.

LEVY DELIVERS INTELLECTUAL argument at its most urgent and engaging. But because he is an intellectual historian and a *soixante-huitard* to boot, he can't always understand the social forces propelling the ideas he so effectively demolishes. He does not notice, for example, that a side effect of his generation's admirable campaigns for the emancipation of women, an end to racism and equal rights for homosexuals is that modern liberals are reluctant to criticise oppression in once-subordinate cultures, nations or communities. In Western minds, much of the planet has been effectively depoliticised – become a no-go zone for argument. Instead of seeing a conflict in Iran between liberals and reactionaries and taking the side of the liberals, a large swathe of Western opinion feels that it is illiberal to fight the theocratic enemies of every good liberal principle. The struggles within cultures no longer stir their souls or move their hearts.

Europe's Muslim minorities are suffering the consequences. When the liberal-minded among them turn for support to those who call themselves liberals, they find that their supposed allies are in bed with the enemy and pretending that the most reactionary variants of Islam are the voice of the oppressed. The English progressives who supported Tariq Ramadan or marched on demonstrations against the Iraq War organised by the friends of Saddam Hussein are all too common.

Lévy dissects their ideological contortions with brio, but his second failing is that he doesn't grasp how comfortable with the consumer society many European leftists have become. Their unwillingness to intervene and their fervent condemnations of the 'hypocrisy' of those who would uphold universal human rights have a radical ring. But in truth they aren't so different from the corporate leader who doesn't want ethical foreign policies to restrict his profitable investments in despotic countries, or the bore at the bar whose says the African savages should be left to murder each other.

Lévy is an exhilarating writer because he has a Protestant contempt for orthodoxy. If he were a minority of one, he would still see himself as the true voice of the left. Yet there is an equally convincing Catholic view of intellectual life which holds that you cannot be right against the world. If the Pope and all his cardinals agree on doctrine, then that is doctrine. Even if they are wrong, even if they are standing previous doctrine on its head, you cannot break with them and still call yourself a Catholic.

Likewise, if the majority of people on the European left continue to have no project beyond anti-Americanism, display no willingness to confront misogyny, homophobia and anti-Semitism when they appear in other cultures and have no interest in the oppressed if they are oppressed by the wrong type of oppressor, can Lévy carry on calling himself left-wing? Should he want to?

When Lévy told Sarkozy that he could not vote for him because the left was his family, Sarkozy cried, 'What? Those people who have spent thirty years telling you to go fuck yourself? Do you really think I'm an idiot, or do you really believe what you are saying?'

The language of the leader of the French right was rough, but he asked a good question, which I am not sure Lévy answers. True American liberals should set out now to win the ideological battles that will come, so that no gleeful conservative can ever ask it of them.

Democracy, Autumn 2008

PART 5

The Silence of the Hams

'Mr President, are we no longer to be permitted to condemn misogyny, homophobia, or calls to kill – if they are made in the name of religion? Are we obliged to respect religious practices that we find offensive? Is lack of respect for such practices to be considered a crime? Are ideas, are religions now to be accorded human rights? Surely, when religion invades the public domain it becomes an ideology like any other, and must be open to criticism.'

The International Humanist and Ethical Union
pleads with the dictatorships on the UN Human
Rights Council, July 2008

The Rout of the Avant-Garde

IN THE SMARTEST corner of the East End of London, I paid my respects at the funeral of the avant-garde. At first glance, Gilbert and George's 'Sonofagod Pictures: Was Jesus Heterosexual?' exhibition at the White Cube did not look like a wake. The bright and glistening gallery is in Hoxton, a corner of town that has been full of bohemian vitality since it was colonised by the 'Young British Artists' in the early nineties. As fashionable visitors move between its loft conversions and cafés, 'edgy' is the highest compliment they can bestow and 'taboo' the gravest insult. Taboos are taboo in Hoxton.

Even on a wet Thursday lunchtime, there were plenty of sightseers from the metropolitan intelligentsia enjoying the show rather than mourning the passing of their world. In puffery that might embarrass an estate agent, the novelist Michael Bracewell told them in the catalogue that Gilbert and George were engaged 'in rebellion, an assault on the laws and institutions of superstition and religious belief'.

Burbling critics agreed. Gilbert and George still get a 'frisson of excitement' by including 'f-words, turds, semen, their own pallid bodies and other affronts to bourgeois sensibilities' in their work, wrote a journalist with the impeccably bourgeois name of Cassandra Jardine in the *Daily Telegraph*. 'Is it the perfect Christmas card to send George Bush at Easter? Yeah, yeah,' added groovy Waldemar Januszczak of the *Sunday Times*.

Their justifications for edgy art won't work any longer, and not only because the average member of the educated bourgeoisie likes nothing better than f-words and pallid bodies on a visit to the theatre or gallery. After the refusal of the entire British press to print innocuous Danish cartoons, the stench of death is in the air. It is now impossible for the arts to boast about their fearless disregard for easily offended sensibilities when artists lack the courage to offend those who might fight back.

Sonofagod was trading under a false prospectus. The exhibition was not a brave assault on all religions, just Christianity and in particular Catholicism. Gilbert and George narcissistically presented themselves as icons towering over a shrivelled Christ. 'God loves Fucking! Enjoy!' read one inscription. The gallery owners knew that although Catholics would be offended, they were very unlikely to harm them. That knowledge invalidated their claims to be transgressive smashers of taboos. An uprising that does not provoke a response is not a 'rebellion', but a smug affirmation of the cultural status quo.

If they were to do the same to Islam, all hell would break loose. In interviews publicising the show, Gilbert and George showed that they at least understood the double standard. They are gay men who live in the East End where the legal groups of the Islamic far right – Hizb ut-Tahrir and the Muslim Association of Britain – have been superseded by semi-clandestine organisations which push leaflets through their letterbox saying: 'Verily, it is time to rejoice in the coming state of Islam. There will be no negotiation with Islam. It is only a short time before the flag of Islam flies over Downing Street.' Even if the artists found the audacity to take on the Islamists around them, they know no gallery would dare show the results.

The fear of being murdered is a perfectly rational one, but it is eating away at art's myths about itself. In the name of breaking taboos, the Britart movement has tittered at paedophilia

(Jake and Dinos Chapman) and rubbed salt in the wounds of the parents of the Moors murderers' victims (Marcus Harvey). The avant-garde cannot go on playing at rebellion because the contradictions between breaking some taboos but not others are becoming too glaring and the postures of its pseudo-radical members too preposterous.

Their absurdity was on display when the Almeida Theatre, the White Cube of theatreland, showed David Mamet's *Romance*. His characters hurled anti-Semitic and anti-Christian abuse at each other and very edgy they sounded. Mamet's justification for the venom was that he had set the play against the backdrop of Palestinian–Israeli peace talks. He meant the hatreds on stage to reflect the hatreds of the Middle East. Readers with an interest in foreign affairs will already know that the Palestinian–Israeli conflict is between Muslims and Jews, not Christians and Jews. Islamophobic abuse ought to have followed the anti-Semitic abuse if the play was to make sense. Neither Mamet nor the Almeida had the nerve to do that. Their edginess was no match for the desire of the prudent bourgeois to save his skin.

The insincerity extends way beyond the arts. Rory Bremner will tear into Tony Blair, but not Mohammed Khatami. Editors will print pictures of servicemen beating up demonstrators in Basra, which may place the lives of British troops in danger, but not Danish cartoons, which may place their own lives in danger.

You cannot be a little bit free. If you are not willing to offend Islamists who may kill you, what excuse do you have for offending Catholics, the families of murdered children and British soldiers, who won't?

Observer, February 2006

Now It's the Art Galleries

THE SATANIC VERSES, *Behzti*, Theo van Gogh's *Submission*, *Jerry Springer: The Opera*, the Danish cartoons of Muhammad ... now we must add the London exhibition of the work of Maqbool Fida Husain to the rapidly expanding list of works of art and satire targeted by militant religion.

The show at the Asia House gallery in the West End's fine-art district should have been essential viewing for admirers of Indian culture. Husain is the grand old man of Indian art. He began as a boy painting cinema hoardings for 6 annas per square foot before getting his first break at the Bombay Art Society in 1947. His international appeal lies in his mixing of classical traditions with modern styles. Art from all over the world inspires him – Emil Nolde and Oskar Kokoschka were early influences – but you only have to glance at his pictures to know an Indian must have painted them.

The Indian high commissioner, Kamalesh Sharma, said at the opening that Husain was India's greatest modern artist. The exhibition was to run for four months, to allow visitors to decide for themselves whether he was right.

No longer. Asia House closed the show after threats of violence from anonymous Hindu fundamentalists. Arjun Malik of the Hindu Human Rights campaign assured me his supporters had nothing to do with it, but said his group had been willing to do everything short of violence to stop the public seeing two of Husain's works.

Fundamentalists had already deluged the gallery with letters, phone calls and emails complaining that Husain's 'so-called art' offended the 'sentiments of the Hindu community of the UK'. (A ludicrous claim, as the Indian government would never have endorsed an attack on Hinduism, and no one has elected the Hindu Human Rights campaign to represent the Hindu or any other community.) The protesters also went for Hitachi, which had given Asia House plasma TV screens, and demanded public apologies from everyone involved, including the high commissioner.

They called off a planned demonstration in London yesterday because, like the managers of the Birmingham Repertory Theatre who closed *Behzti* after the demonstrations by conservative Sikhs* and the national newspaper editors who refused to publish the Danish cartoons, Asia House buckled under the pressure to censor.

The apparently separate protests from different faiths are connected. We are seeing rival fundamentalists egging each other on in a politics of competitive grievance. Every time one secures a victory, the others realise they cannot be left behind. If satirists are frightened of mocking Islam because they believe they may be killed – and they are – why shouldn't Christian fundamentalists decide to become more menacing?

A comedian who takes a pop at the Pope sends the subliminal message: 'We can deride your religion as despicable because

---

* Gurpreet Kaur Bhatti's play about the abuse of Sikh women by Sikh men was greeted with riots outside the theatre by abusive Sikh men. Far from condemning them, the Home Office minister, Fiona Mactaggart, whose constituency includes many Sikhs, cooed, 'I think that when people are moved by theatre to protest, in a way that is a sign of the free speech which is so much part of the British tradition. I think that it is a great thing that people care enough about a performance to protest.' According to her logic, the suppression of Bhatti's freedom of speech was a triumph for freedom of speech.

we know you are not so despicable you will resort to violence.'
There is a limit to how long the ultras for any religion will put
up with that before they change the ground rules.

After abusive Sikh men closed *Behzti*, Christian Voice upped
the ante against *Jerry Springer: The Opera*. The show had previously run at the National Theatre for months without attracting
protest. But when BBC2 came to broadcast it, London Christians imitated Birmingham Sikhs, and BBC executives needed
the protection of private security guards.

You can see the same pattern in the hounding of Husain. The
paintings the demonstrators targeted were nudes of the Hindu
goddesses Draupadi and Durga. Arjun Malik went into all kinds
of verbal convolutions when I asked what he had against them,
before coming out with the explanation that 'according to tradition, they should not be disrobed'. The reason for his tongue-
twisting is that nude gods and goddesses have been a part of the
Indian tradition for 5000 years. As Husain said in India, 'nudity
is not nakedness; it is a form of innocence and maturity'.

It is no longer innocent because, after the state-sponsored
violence of the Danish cartoon protests, Hindus from the religious Indian right looked around for a grievance of their own.
They picked on Husain because he was born into a Muslim
family, and joined a confessional arms race. Earlier in the year, a
Muslim politician in the Indian state of Uttar Pradesh offered a
large reward to anyone who beheaded a Danish cartoonist. A
Hindu politician responded by saying he would pay the same to
anyone who would kill Husain.

Depressingly but predictably, given the cowardice that
suffuses the arts, the closure of a major exhibition by fanatics
has passed without comment or protest from the cultural elite.
No press coverage, no denunciations from ministers. Violent
men can censor in Britain without anyone standing up to them.

British troops are fighting in Afghanistan and Iraq against
forces motivated by the religious fervour of radical reaction.

British police officers arrest suspects inspired to kill because they, too, have a psychotic religious mission. Yet, comedians, art gallery owners, TV producers, newspaper editors and Home Office ministers give in to religious extremists. This is no way to win a war.

Observer, May 2006

The Broadcasters Bite Their Tongues

FAR IN THE DISTANCE, a protracted scream comes out of a dark tunnel. As it rises, the ground begins to shake. A dot of light speeds towards the viewer. In seconds, it fills the screen and a rattling blur of cold steel shrieks past the camera.

The director cuts to the forecourt of King's Cross station. Hasib Hussain, a gawky eighteen-year-old with soft eyes, looks imploringly at the authoritative figure of Sidique Khan.

'Sidique … wait …' he says, with a voice full of fear and uncertainty. The older man calms the boy with a bear hug.

'There is nothing to fear in death, Hasib,' he says. 'When the time comes, we'll face towards Makkah together, as one.' He looks Hussain in the eyes. 'Our lives begin today.'

Hussain nods. Khan ruffles his hair, and disappears to slaughter commuters on the London Underground. Hussain screws up his courage and prepares to murder an equally random collection of passengers on a bus heading out from King's Cross.

So begins *The London Bombers*, one of the most thoroughly researched and politically important drama-documentaries commissioned by British television. A team of journalists, one of whom was a British Muslim, reported to Terry Cafolla, a writer who won many awards for his dramatisation of the religious hatred which engulfed the Holy Cross school in Belfast.

The reporters spent months in Beeston, the Leeds slum where three of the four 7/7 bombers – Sidique Khan, Hasib Hussain and Shehzad Tanweer – grew up. They didn't find that the 'root cause' of murderous rage was justifiable anger at the 'humiliation' America, Israel, Britain and Denmark and her tactless cartoonists had inflicted on Muslims.

Instead, they inadvertently confirmed the ideas of Ernest Gellner, the late professor of anthropology at Cambridge. In *Postmodernism, Reason and Religion* (1992), Gellner asked why a puritanical version of Islam was in the ascendant when godless-ness was flourishing everywhere else. His answer was that Wahhabism and its ever more zealous theocratic variants could appear as modern as secular humanism. They represented the pure religion of scholars of the city, which could free Muslims from their peasant parents' embarrassingly superstitious faith. Accepting fanaticism was a mark of superiority: a visible sign of upward mobility from rural idiocy to urban sophistication.

And so it proved in Leeds. The picture of Beeston the BBC presents is a disorientating mixture of the provincial and the cosmopolitan. On one hand, Beeston is almost as much of a village as the ancestral homes of its Pakistani inhabitants. It is an isolated suburb, cut off from the centre of town by an urban motorway. On the other, its parochialism is an illusion. Cheap flights make the madrasas and terrorist training camps of Pakistan easily accessible. The Internet connects them to the global jihadi network.

In one scene, Hasib Hussain hears a message ping on his mobile. He flips it open and finds a beheading video. He watches the snuff movie impassively, showing no emotion when the killer cuts a hostage's throat. Later Khan and Hussain learn how to make a bomb, not by infiltrating an army regi-ment, but by the simple expedient of going to an Internet café and logging on to an Arab jihadi site. 'What did people do before Google?' the admiring Hussain asks.

Sidique Khan is the dominant figure. He turns against the traditional Sufism of his father, who remains stuck in the tribal and religious loyalties of the subcontinent. By breaking with both, Khan escapes an arranged marriage designed to keep wealth within the extended family, and enters into a love match with a fellow student at Leeds Metropolitan University. His father's pir, or Sufi priest, demands a hearing. While Khan waits to talk to him, he sees the elder hang a miracle cure – a miniature Koran – round a child's neck. Khan looks on in disgust. 'What you do here is not harmless, it's dangerous,' he thunders. 'How dare you contaminate Islam? There is only one Allah and he does not share his power, not with anyone … Your tradition of Islam, your parlour tricks, they belong in the hills of Pakistan.'

The London Bombers works so well because it is a family drama about inter-generational conflict as well as an account of the largest massacre in Britain since Lockerbie. The BBC captures the claustrophobic milieu of bodybuilding and vigilantism into which the men retreat. The bomb-making in a tiny terraced house becomes a male bonding ritual in which the members of a cult of death quash each other's doubts. 'How can we keep Muslims off the Tube that day?' asks Abdullah Jamal, the fourth bomber. 'They'll go straight to paradise,' answers Sidique. 'It is *quadaa* [fate] that they're there. And if it is Allah's wish …'

(Pause)

'We need more acetone.'

So psychologically convincing is the portrayal of macho loyalty and the lure of barbarism that viewers can understand how these men turn into mass murderers. Except that they can't and won't understand, because the BBC will not give them the opportunity. This is a review of a drama that was never made.

The reporters convinced the families of three of the four bombers to cooperate. By the end, they agreed that the BBC's account of their sons' and brothers' lives and deaths was accurate. Cafolla submitted five versions of the script. He was working up to a final draft when the BBC abandoned the project. The official reason is that the drama did not make the grade. The script is circulating in samizdat form, which is how it reached *Standpoint*, and every writer and director who has read it disagrees. As do the journalists. They say that BBC managers did not tell them they were stopping production because their work was substandard but because it was 'Islamophobic'.

Eh? The defining characteristic of Islamophobic prejudice is the belief that all Muslims are potential terrorists, and yet here, apparently, is the BBC seconding that motion by arguing that a dramatic examination of terrorism would be offensive to all Muslims.

It makes no sense until you understand the moral contortions of the postmodern liberal establishment. This may not be a complete list, but my best reckoning is that to date the Foreign Office, the Home Office, the West Midlands Police, the liberal press, the Liberal Democrats, the Metropolitan Police, the Crown Prosecution Service, the Lord Chief Justice and His Grace the Archbishop of Canterbury have either supported ultra-reactionary doctrines or made libellous accusations against the critics of radical Islam. All have sought to prove their liberal tolerance by supporting the most illiberal and intolerant wing of British Islam, and by blocking out the voices of its Muslim and non-Muslim critics as they do it.

As the sorry history of *The London Bombers* shows, they have left us a country that cannot tell its own stories; a land so debilitated by anxiety and stupefied by relativism that it dare not meet the eyes of the face that stares back at it from the mirror.

Standpoint, August 2008

A Cartoon Crisis

FOR THREE WEEKS, there were demonstrations across the planet about a great injustice done to Muslims. After baton-wielding cops inflicted dozens of injuries, the fear of death is in the air. George W. Bush's State Department warned of 'systematic oppression', while secularists and fundamentalists revealed their mutually incompatible values. I am not talking about the global menace of Scandinavian cartoonists that terrified our fearless free press into silence, but the mass arrests in Iran.

The media barely mentioned the story, even though it cuts through the garbage about a clash of civilisations between 'the West' and 'the Muslims'.

The Muslims of Tehran are proving themselves to be anything but a monolithic bloc happy to follow the orders of the ayatollahs and their demagogic president, Mahmoud Ahmadinejad. There are huge class divisions to begin with. Close to the bottom of the social hierarchy lie the city's bus drivers. The authorities refused to allow them an independent trade union and ruled that members of an 'Islamic council' in the offices of the Tehran and Suburbs Bus Company should represent their interests instead. Perhaps unsurprisingly, Islamists have not proved the doughtiest fighters for better pay and conditions, and did nothing about the bus drivers' claims that managers were stealing from their pay packets. The workers abandoned the clerics, formed their own union and threatened to strike.

Ahmadinejad won the rigged Iranian elections last year with a promise to stand up for the little man against the Islamic Republic's corrupt elite. Faced with a choice between sticking to his word or supporting religious despotism, he showed his true colours by allowing the most ferocious crackdown Tehran has seen since the religious authorities crushed dissident journalists and students in 1999.

The company's managers called in the paramilitary police, who arrested the union's six officers and beat workers until they agreed to renounce the strike. Bravely, the majority refused. So the state's thugs targeted their wives and children.

Mahdiye Salimi, the twelve-year-old daughter of one of the strike leaders, told a reporter that they had poured into her home in the early hours of the morning trying to find her father. When his wife said she did not know where he was, the assault began. 'They kicked my mum's heart with their boots and my mum had an enormous ache in her heart. They even wanted to spray something in my [two-year-old] sister's mouth.'

No one knows how many people the authorities arrested. The highest figure the British TUC has heard is 1300. International trade union federations and the British embassy in Tehran estimate that somewhere between four hundred and six hundred people are still in prison.

Owen Tudor, the TUC's international officer, went to the Iranian embassy to protest and was overwhelmed by the hatred of unions he met. Unconsciously, Iranian officials parroted the language of Margaret Thatcher and told him unions were 'the enemy within'. From their perspective, you can see why they would think so. Unions instil democratic habits and encourage solidarity with others regardless of colour and – more importantly in this case – creed. Neither of these admirable traits is likely to appeal to your average theocrat who believes he is following God's orders.

Human Rights Watch, Amnesty International, the US State Department and the British Foreign Office have all protested. Trade unions, Iranian exiles and gay groups have demonstrated. Yet the media ignores them. The failure is due to journalists' perennial inability to walk and chew gum at the same time. We consider stories one by one and the story of the moment was 'Muslim' anger with cartoonists.

I am not saying it was not newsworthy, but too many forgot that it was conjured out of nothing by hard-line Danish imams who hawked the cartoons round the Muslim world for four months (and, somewhat blasphemously, added drawings of their own which were far more sacrilegious than anything the cartoonists produced). The religious right and Syrian Baathists took up their cause and proved, yet again, that secular and theocratic dictators need to incite frenzies to legitimise their arbitrary power.

Iran has seen all the stunts before because it has endured Islamism longer than any other country. Cheeringly, the old tricks are no longer working. The Associated Press's reporter said that about four hundred people demonstrated outside the Danish embassy in Tehran, most of them state employees obeying orders from their masters.

Even if you take the lowest estimate, there are as many striking bus drivers in prison in Tehran as rioters prepared to play the worn-out game of throwing Molotov cocktails at Western embassies. No one ever made money by being optimistic about the Middle East, but after nearly thirty years of Islamist rule, Iranians seem sick of it.

It cannot be said often enough that this is not a clash of civilisations but a civil war within the Islamic world between theocratic reaction and the beleaguered forces of liberty and modernity. As I believe I have tried to emphasise before, the best service the rich world's liberal left can render is to get on the right side for once.

Observer, February 2006

State Britain

BRIAN HAW'S 'ANTI-WAR' protest in Parliament Square is still going, years after he first planted his ragged banners on the grass in the traffic island. Politicians have tried to censor him, the police have forced him to shorten his once straggling display, but he survives and looks as if he will stay there until he drops.

I found his banners a bleak sight when I trudged by. Like so many others, Haw cannot ask who is killing whom in Iraq. There are no slogans expressing his disgust at the death squads of the Baathists and Iranian-backed Shia militias. No condemnation of Abu Musab al-Zarqawi, the late leader of al-Qaeda in Iraq, who explained that he would murder Iraq's Shias indiscriminately so that they would retaliate and 'show the Sunnis their rabies and bare the teeth ... and drag them into the arena of sectarian war'. Haw's placards about Afghanistan are as worthless, and do not manage a word of criticism of the Taliban's crimes and ideology. Western governments are responsible for the suffering of humanity; no one else is worth mentioning.

The best justification for Haw's morality is that if British and American troops in Iraq and Afghanistan cannot guarantee order, they are indirectly responsible for atrocities committed by their opponents. As the inevitable conclusion is that they should try harder to defeat their enemies, it is not a point that I expect Haw wants to acknowledge.

For all his double standards, I was not as shocked by his protest as I expected to be. Familiarity breeds indifference as well as contempt, and in any case, the arguments around Haw were never about whether he was right or wrong, but whether the government had the right to silence him. As freedom includes the freedom to be silly, it did not. The efforts of New Labour to close down his demonstration, like its laws against the incitement of religious hatred, showed it did not understand the need of a free society for vigorous debate.

Haw has ceased, however, to be an embattled protester you must defend regardless of his views. His ideology has gone mainstream, and he has become the darling of the art establishment.

The Turner judges gave Mark Wallinger the 2007 prize for his recreation of Haw's original line of banners denouncing 'baby killers' and 'B-liar', at Tate Britain. The judges praised Wallinger directly and Haw by implication for 'the immediacy, visceral intensity and historic importance' of a work that 'combines a bold political statement with art's ability to articulate fundamental human truths'.

Hyperbole of this intensity usually masks insecurity, and I wonder whether the Turner judges blustered because they knew in their hearts that in the current climate in liberal England Wallinger would have made a bolder political statement if he had put a piece defending the government in the Tate.

As it was, he produced lifeless propaganda that even the converted found preachy. His *State Britain* is merely a copy of Haw's protest – the Tate's equivalent of an Airfix model – and an aesthetically and politically inferior one at that. Even after the police have cut back their number, Haw's tattered banners stained with mud and rain are more powerful, not least because of their location opposite the parliament whose politicians he despises. Wallinger's clean-cut copy, by contrast, sits in a gallery where it runs no risks: a sanitised protest that will never worry the authorities.

Just to make sure gallery visitors get the message, a history of the demonstration accompanies the exhibit. No one, not Wallinger, not the staff of the Tate, not the Turner judges, found it odd that Haw the 'peace campaigner' began his protest in the summer of 2001 months before 9/11 and almost two years before the start of the second Iraq War.

The chronology should have alerted them that they were celebrating a man happy to duck into the darkest corners of the left. Haw says he was moved to demonstrate by George Galloway's Mariam Appeal, a charity which was meant to help Iraqis who were the victims of both United Nations sanctions and Saddam Hussein's genocidal regime. If Haw knew in 2001 that Galloway was an admirer of Saddam, it did not bother him. He probably could not have known at the time that Saddam had turned the UN's oil-for-food programme from a relief operation to help starving Iraqis escape the worst effects of sanctions and his rule into a scam to enrich him, his sons and his supporters overseas. Among the beneficiaries was the Mariam Appeal, which received hundreds of thousands of dollars from a Jordanian businessman who was selling Iraqi oil.

Haw has no excuse for not knowing about the Mariam Appeal now. The Commons Standards and Privileges Committee reported that 'there was strong circumstantial evidence that the oil-for-food programme was used by the Iraqi government, with Mr Galloway's connivance, to fund the campaigning activities of the Mariam Appeal'. Similarly, he also ought to know that al-Qaeda was responsible for the slaughter on 9/11 – it is hardly a secret. But in a video for an 'alternative' news site, Haw announces that '9/11 was an inside job, yes it was', organised by the American government and Hollywood, apparently.

Like Holocaust denial, 9/11 conspiracy theories are too fascistic for the type of person who sits on the Turner Prize jury, but anything else goes. Call me a cockeyed optimist, but I don't think the moral blindness of the intelligentsia can last much longer. Obviously, some who have lost their bearings after Iraq will be stuck that way for the rest of their days, but the hysterical mood is lifting from others. When they regain their wits, I hope they will see the decision of art grandees to celebrate Haw and his hagiographer as the low point from which the only way was up.*

Observer, February 2008

* At the time this book went to press, there was no sign that the intelligentsia was regaining its wits. So by all means do call me a cockeyed optimist.

Labour's Contemptible Election Trade-off

IN HIS YEARS in the Commons, Evan Harris, a Liberal Democrat MP, has earned a reputation as a diligent defender of civil liberties. Lord Lester, the distinguished Liberal Democrat lawyer, is equally committed to human rights and anti-racism. Both men assumed that their reputations would win the delegation from the self-appointed Muslim Council of Britain round to the liberal cause. Like the Tories and many writers and actors, the Liberals were appalled by the government's plans to introduce a new offence of incitement to religious hatred: revolted as much by Labour's cynicism as its authoritarianism.

Ever since the Iraq War, Muslim voters have been turning from Labour to the Liberals. Harris and Lester tried to explain to the delegations why New Labour's plans to woo them back by suppressing free speech would be disastrous.

Devout believers in each religion inspire hatred of other religions because they suppose that theirs is the one true way. This hatred shows itself when they seek to save the souls of others by converting them. Is proselytising to be a criminal offence?

Meanwhile, even in these PC times, it is not a crime to hate others, any more than it is a crime to envy them – if it was then Gordon Brown and Tony Blair would be in prison for hating each other. In any case, what the Saudi religious police do to women, and what the Catholic Church's rules on contraception do to men, women and children in Aids-ridden Africa, are hateful. Surely, it is morally wrong *not* to seek to inspire hatred of the hateful, rather than to stay silent and let the hateful triumph.

If Labour has its way, the law officers may prosecute the next Salman Rushdie for his blasphemies. If they do not, there could be riots against the state's failure to call upon a statute that seems to guarantee action against those who offend the faithful. Either there would be censorship or dashed hopes would fuel superstitious passions. Whatever course the government took, it would be giving reactionary clerics the power to damn dissident voices in minority communities as un-Islamic, or un-Hindu or un-Sikh or un-Jewish.

It cannot be said often enough that a religion is not an ethnicity or a gender but a system of ideas, no different in principle to socialism, Thatcherism or liberalism. As with all ideas, religion must be open to fair, unfair and even hateful criticism. Abandon this principle, and we might as well have had a law against inciting hatred of Blairism. (I know, I know: I shouldn't put ideas in their heads.)

Lord Lester understood the theoretical arguments as well as anyone, but he was as interested in the practicalities. The government said that all it wanted to do was frustrate neo-Nazi groups, which cannot attack Pakistanis directly because of the law against racial hatred and therefore put out propaganda against 'the Muslims'. Lester pointed out that the existing law against inciting racial hatred already covered 'racism by proxy', and every prosecutor knew it. He told the Muslim Council that he and his Liberal Democrat colleagues had proposed that the statute should be rewritten to make it clear that racial hatred disguised as religious hatred was still racial hatred.

Labour risked turning white supremacists into free-speech martyrs, he continued. Liberal middle-class opinion would turn against minority religions and the white working class would feel that they could not speak their minds in their own country. Far better to concentrate on what hurts people in real life. Lord Lester said the Lib Dems had proposed a bill to punish daily acts of prejudice – taxi drivers who refuse to pick up women wearing veils, shopkeepers who refuse to serve customers fondling a string of beads. He said they wanted to promote the principle of equality, and the government had agreed to do it, although when it would bring legislation to Parliament was anyone's guess.

Oh, quite soon, the men from the Muslim Council of Britain told him. They sent us a copy of the draft bill for our comments.

Lester and Harris went very quiet, for no one in the Lords or Commons had seen this bill. No one knew what it was likely to contain, or when, if ever, the government would release it. No one apart from the Muslim Council of Britain, which was already studying the draft and proposing amendments, and evangelical Christian groups, which had had the same courtesy extended to them.

The Liberal Democrats learned at that moment what many of us had suspected for months: a deal was going down. Her Britannic Majesty's government was prepared to sacrifice Britain's liberties and run the risk of religious riots for the sake of grabbing back the votes of fundamentalists alienated by Iraq. Labour was prepared to write off freedom of speech as collateral damage in the war against Saddam Hussein.

A Labour minister, Mike O'Brien, spelled out the terms of the surrender in an article in *Muslim Weekly*. All right, he said to the readers, you are furious about Iraq and ready to storm away from Labour in a righteous rage. But where will your rage take you? *To the Tories?* 'Ask yourself what will Michael Howard do for British Muslims? Will his foreign policy aim to help Palestine? Will he promote legislation to protect you from religious hatred and discrimination? Will he give you the choice of sending your children to a faith school? Will he stand up for the right of Muslim women to wear the hijab?'

Stick with New Labour, ran his unsubtle message. If you tell us to, we will allow you to force your children to be indoctrinated in sectarian schools and your women to hide behind veils. You can count on us to deliver, O'Brien continued. 'Recently Iqbal Sacranie, the general secretary of the Council, asked Tony Blair to declare that the government would introduce a new law banning religious discrimination. Two weeks later, in the middle of his speech to the Labour party conference, Tony Blair promised that the next Labour government would ban religious discrimination.'

As for the Liberal Democrats, O'Brien continued, they were no better than the Tories. 'A new crime bill, announced in the Queen's Speech, is coming before parliament to toughen the laws on incitement to religious hatred. This has upset some MPs such as Evan Harris MP, the Liberal Democrat spokesman, who has said he will oppose it because it is unnecessary!'

Harris was an odd choice of target for Labour to present to *Muslim Weekly*. The Oxford MP is not even on the Lib Dem front bench. Why not pick on the leaders of the Liberal Democrats? But then, they're not Jewish and Harris is – as is Michael Howard. 'I am appalled by the way the Labour minister went out of his way to name me specifically,' Harris remarked. 'Is it because I am the only Jewish Lib Dem MP?'

It is hard to tell, but for what it is worth, I doubt whether Labour is playing with anti-Semitism. Ministers are not trying to win over one group of fundamentalists by alienating another but to maximise votes by making an ecumenical appeal to fundamentalists of all religions.

At a time of low turnouts, the party knows that motivated minorities can turn elections. Hence the ecumenicism. What Rushdie calls 'the currently fashionable Blairite politics of religious appeasement at all cost' is based on the calculation that, in the lazy, postmodern world, those who used to stand up for free speech won't become as angry as religious fundamentalists. The faithful will refuse to vote Labour if it does not meet their demands for censorship, but liberals will stay with the party even if it caves in on freedom of speech. The next few months will show whether this contemptible calculation is correct.*

New Statesman, January 2005

* In the end, the House of Lords neutered the bill, not public opinion. It says much about the dismal condition of liberty in Britain that its least bad defenders are quangocrats and aristocrats.

Inequality before the Law

ANTI-DISCRIMINATION LEGISLATION once aimed to ensure that society treated citizens equally. By removing irrelevant criteria, the law allowed the victims of prejudice to receive the same rights as everyone else.

When the Commission for Racial Equality investigated racism in the building industry, it said that a man's skin colour was irrelevant to whether he would make a good worker. A black bricklayer should have the same opportunities as a white bricklayer. Today's supporters of homosexual adoption say that the sexuality of a couple is irrelevant. If they can show they would make good parents, they should have the same rights to adopt as everyone else. The argument among economists about the gender pay gap is, at root, an argument about relevance as well. Are women paid less because they take time off to have children or because of misogynist employers' irrelevant prejudices?

Now politicians, judges and the godly are trying to turn religion into an equal opportunities cause. The language sounds the same as in the twentieth century, but the consequences could not be more different. Instead of fighting for equality, they are demanding special treatment and the social fragmentation that goes with it.

Mr Justice Silber has ruled that Aberdare Girls' School in South Wales had been guilty of racial discrimination when it excluded Sarika Watkins-Singh for insisting on wearing a religious bracelet which broke its uniform code. It was a trivial case, which made you wonder about the dogmatism of both sides and the quality of their lawyers. The school might have given way – the bracelet was little more than a slim band. Watkins-Singh's parents might have accepted that they had a duty to uphold the authority of the teachers even if they did not agree with every one of the school's decisions. Still, for all the pettiness, Mr Justice Silber's judgement was remarkable for his inability to recognise that a just society should treat people equally. He did not rule that all the girls at Aberdare had the right to wear bracelets, just Watkins-Singh, because she was its only Sikh pupil. In his willingness to use the law to discriminate, he was typical of contemporary politicians and judges. So imbued with biased thinking have they become that they think that it is liberal to grant privileges to the few and are shocked when citizens ask for the true liberalism of equality before the law.

When Ed Balls was at the Treasury, the Plymouth Brethren told him that they and their more fundamentalist offshoot – the Exclusive Brethren – were the victims of religious prejudice at the hands of that unlikely source of bigotry, the tax authorities. Both sects believe that God decides when you die. To their members, compliance with the state's requirement to take out an annuity at seventy-five forced them to second-guess the Almighty by blasphemously betting on the date of their deaths.

The obliging Balls created an alternative pension scheme and then spluttered when pensioners of all faiths and none saw his generous loophole and shifted large sums of money through it. He seemed to think he could legislate for one group without the law applying equally to everyone.

If he did not have the strength of principle to stand up for equality, he ought to have had the wit to realise that the

Plymouth Brethren may not have been as devout as they appeared. If you sincerely believe that an omnipotent god controls every aspect of your life, you place your fate in His hands. You do not ask accountants to lobby ministers for tax-efficient changes to pension law.

The same lack of seriousness applies to others who shout that they are the victims of religious discrimination. Watkins-Singh was not a perfect example because the law treats Sikhs and Jews as racial as well as religious groups. But before her, Lillian Ladele persuaded an employment tribunal that it was discriminatory for Islington Council to require her to perform her duties in a register office. She objected to organising gay civil partnerships on the religious grounds that she was an evangelical Christian who regarded homosexuality as a sin. When the tribunal found for her, it not only endorsed homo-phobia and ruled that religion took priority in a register office – where gay and straight couples go to *escape* religion – but failed to see a glaring inconsistency.

If Ms Ladele thought homosexuality sinful, she should not have wanted to work for an institution that organised 'gay weddings'. The same objection applied to the Muslim checkout staff at Sainsbury's who refused to scan alcohol. If alcohol was as offensive to their religious principles as they claimed, they would no more want to work for a company that sold it than a pacifist would want to join the SAS.

The old questions about equality and relevance surge back in these cases. The courts offer no protection to workers who have no religious justification for their homophobia but merely a visceral loathing of gays. Employers are still free to fire them just as teachers in South Wales are still free to send home girls who want to wear bracelets because they think they look pretty. The law is, however, intervening to stop employers taking the same action against religious workers, even though they are unwilling to do their jobs properly.

I wonder how far the judiciary and the government are prepared to go before they realise that they are reducing their principles to absurdity. The Exclusive Brethren tells its members not to watch television. If the BBC refused to hire one of their number on the relevant grounds that he or she was not allowed to watch television, would it be guilty of religious discrimination? Believers in some versions of Orthodox Judaism hold that women can't be witnesses in religious cases. Muslim believers in sharia say that the testimony of a Muslim woman or non-Muslim man is worth only half as much as evidence from a Muslim man. If an ultra-orthodox Jewish or misogynist Muslim barrister stands by these principles in an interview, would the law officers be guilty of religious discrimination if they said he was unfit to be judges in an English court because they did not accept the equality of the sexes?

The way out of the mess is for the state to commit itself to secularism, and offer full religious freedom in the private sphere, while striving to keep religion out of public life. Leaving all considerations of principle aside, secularism is the only ideology that can make a multi-faith society work. The alternative is a future of competitive religious grievance and incessant vexatious litigation.

Observer, August 2008

PART 6

Bread without Freedom

'Take up the White Man's burden –
Send forth the best ye breed –
Go send your sons to exile
To serve your captives' need
To wait in heavy harness
On fluttered folk and wild –
Your new-caught, sullen peoples,
Half devil and half child.'

RUDYARD KIPLING,
1899

Lesser Breeds without the Law

'SIR,' WROTE MR H. W. SCOTT of Hemel Hempstead to the editor of the *Daily Telegraph*, 'Bob Geldof hopes to raise an army of a million protesters against world poverty. Instead of sending them to Scotland to lobby the G8, he would do better if he divided his troops into groups of, say, 50,000, and sent them to protest repeatedly in front of the London embassies of the countries everyone knows to be the worst offenders in failing to reduce poverty in their own countries.'

An argument can be true even if it is made in the *Telegraph*, and no one can deny that the regimes that preside over the African disaster will get off lightly in the protests against the G8 summit. If the Make Poverty History manifesto were implemented, the Common Agricultural Policy would be scrapped; the World Bank and the International Monetary Fund would no longer be able to force weak countries to open their markets before they were ready for free trade; debt which can never be repaid would be cancelled; and the rich world would provide more aid for hospitals and schools.

It is an admirable programme, but the reader can be forgiven for believing that Africa has no dictators and rich, white men direct its affairs. Corruption doesn't feature in Geldof's manifesto and human rights are mentioned in passing just once, and then only in a sideswipe at world trade rules rather than a direct assault on tyrants and torturers.

Workers for Make Poverty History became exasperated when I raised the point, and with good reason. The political parties barely mentioned Africa in the 2005 election campaign. The outside world surfaced in Michael Howard's sly attacks on Tony Blair's alleged leniency towards asylum seekers, and that was it.

The electorate returned New Labour exactly one month before the protest, but the election felt like half a lifetime away. Make Poverty History made Africa news, and I would not be writing this piece if it were not for its efforts. It has won the support of the Prime Minister and the Chancellor. It will persuade hundreds of thousands of people to march on the streets of Edinburgh, many of whom had never given the wretched of the earth a second's thought until Geldof reached for his megaphone. After all these achievements, the charities then have to deal with niggardly critics who insist that they tackle oppression and corruption as well as trade, aid and debt.

No, they told me, we do not. The concerts, the marches and the television dramas are being organised to lobby the G8 summit. By definition, they are about what the rich can do for the poor. Contrary to what you read, we do not believe in helping countries that can't show that resources freed by debt relief will be well used. Steve Tibbett of Action Aid, a member of Geldof's coalition of charities, explained that the very act of targeting aid at the poorest strengthens the hands of those who are most likely to fight for basic political freedoms: teachers, doctors and the citizens' groups which monitor how the money is spent.

I could understand the frustrated note in his voice. Here are development charities trying to confront apocalyptic outbreaks of hunger and disease. Isn't that enough? Why should whining berks who have never lifted a finger for anyone but themselves demand they take on every other crime and injustice when there are plenty of articulate campaigners banging the drum for human rights? The argument makes sense until you turn round and listen out for the campaigners for human rights, and realise that the drumbeat of those who once swore that they would support and defend them has become muffled of late.

WHO IS THIS talking?

> If you look globally today and want to talk about human rights, for the vast majority of the world's population they don't mean very much. To talk about freedom of expression to a man who can't read the newspaper, to talk about the right to work to someone who has no job; human rights means nothing to them unless it brings some change on these particular issues.

These clunking and sinister sentences did not come from a colonial administrator explaining that freedom of speech and conscience were all well and good for freeborn white men but not for lesser breeds without the law. Nor was it a communist apparatchik saying that there was no need for bourgeois freedoms in the proletarian paradise of the Soviet Union. Nor was it Edward Heath or Henry Kissinger announcing that the Chinese liked autocracy or Abu Musab Zarqawi and Osama bin Laden denouncing democracy as a Greek heresy. Rather, the assertion that human rights don't 'mean very much' to the poor, the black and the brown who make up the majority of the world's population, fell from the lips of Irene Khan, the new secretary-general of Amnesty International, an organisation that once believed that human rights meant everything.

Her shift in policy provoked no stern questions because Amnesty has an almost canonical status. I cannot name another institution whose word is accepted without challenge. When anyone else with power from the prime minister downwards utters an opinion, journalists scrutinise and round up opponents to put the contrary view. They accept Amnesty as a purveyor of incontestable truth because it has built up its reputation over the decades with tens of thousands of scrupulous investigations into the treatment of prisoners of conscience.

Since it was founded in 1961 after an article in the *Observer* about the arrest of two students by the old fascist dictatorship in Portugal, Amnesty has campaigned relentlessly and patiently for the rights of political prisoners for fair trials and freedom of speech. Opposition to the death penalty was added to the list in the 1970s, despite the protests from traditionalists that the organisation was in danger of distracting itself from its original goal. The small dilution in the purity of its cause had little effect and it remained an unfaltering opponent of political persecution.

No longer. To Khan, the human-rights agenda is passé. Demands for freedom of speech and the rights to vote and protest were not the concern of the majority of the human race. 'Amnesty has a middle-class, Western, complacent, white image in many parts of the world,' she told the *Financial Times*.

Her nervousness is a part of the wider crisis of liberalism. Liberals prefer abandoning liberal principles to running the risk of seeming a white imperialist democrat, maybe even a neocon. Khan would avoid the nasty name-calling by expanding Amnesty's remit to include campaigns against poverty because, as one of her sympathisers put it to me, 'more children die of lack of food or water than [are] killed by torture and the death penalty'.

This is true, but beside the point. Amnesty is crowding into a crowded field. All the charities in the Make Poverty History alliance campaign for access to clean water and decent food; what they are not doing is standing up for human rights. Amnesty says it will continue to do so and I hope it will; it still has many good people working and its story isn't over yet. But ever since Khan took over, I've had an uneasy feeling that it is losing universal principles and treating the abuse of rights by the United States as worse than similar or more grotesque abuses by dictators who aren't white, middle-class or Western. That feeling was transformed into a certainty when Amnesty described Guantanamo Bay as the 'gulag of our times'.

By all means, Amnesty and everyone else should loudly deplore America's failure to treat prisoners of war in accordance with the Geneva Conventions. But when they've finished, they should check the figures. If they exclude the millions who died of starvation, disease and exhaustion, they will find that the communists murdered 776,098 gulag prisoners by summary executions between 1930 and 1953. At Guantanamo Bay, no one has died of starvation, disease or exhaustion and no prisoners have been executed. Not one. If Amnesty's American obsession prevents it from seeing the worst crimes of the twentieth century for what they are, how will it sound the alarm about the worst of the twenty-first?

A barely reported exchange showed why the arguments against Khan matter. Journalists in Johannesburg tackled James Morris, head of the United Nations World Food Programme, who had promised hundreds of thousands of tonnes of emergency supplies to Zimbabwe. Try as they might, they could not get him to condemn Mugabe. According to Morris, Zimbabwe was on the edge of famine because of drought and Aids, not because of the dictatorship's destruction of agriculture and suppression of dissent. The mistake the UN made with Saddam's Iraq was to be repeated. Food would go to the regime rather than the needy and the regime would be able to use it to reward friends and punish enemies.

In April, Zimbabwe was re-elected to the UN Human Rights Commission for the third year running by satirically minded African states, so Morris may have to play the diplomat. To anyone who does not, it is obvious that he and Khan are letting dictators off the hook. Zimbabwe is on the edge of starvation because it does not have freedom of expression, among other human rights. The great lesson of the twentieth century was that tyrannical regimes – the British Empire, Mao's China, Stalin's Russia, Mengistu's Ethiopia – presided over enormous famines. Democracies did not. Amnesty does not know it, but the choice between human rights and social justice is not either/or but both/neither.*

Observer, June 2005

---

* Although Amnesty staffers and volunteers continued to do brave and necessary work, the organisation's managers abandoned themselves to relativism and its attendant double standards. The *Observer*'s Andrew Anthony noted of the 2008 Secret Policeman's Ball, Amnesty's annual fund-raising comedy show, 'The real comic turn of the evening was Professor Germaine Greer. Introducing a film that showed only examples of American ill-treatment of detainees, she announced: "Torture is barbaric and stupid." She called upon the watching public to oppose the practice. Amen to that, yet her words would have carried more authority if she didn't believe that outlawing female genital mutilation was "an attack on cultural identity".

The White Woman's Burden

OXFAM WAS FOUNDED IN 1942 to bring aid to the oppressed of Nazi Europe, a cause that did not make it popular with the Churchill government. After the Germans occupied Greece, the Royal Navy blocked the shipping lanes. Famine spread across the mainland and the islands. Lifting the blockade might have helped the starving, but Whitehall wondered whether food meant for the hungry would end up in the bellies of German troops instead, and gazed with some disdain on the new lobbyists.

They were easy to mock. The Oxford Committee for Famine Relief was composed of stereotypical members of the great and the good: the bishops, academics, retired teachers and Quaker philanthropists, who had been at the forefront of liberal causes for generations and the butt of satirists' jibes for just as long. In *Bleak House*, Dickens gave us Mrs Jellyby, who had 'very good hair but was too much occupied with her African duties to brush it'. She was so infatuated with her plan to bring education and coffee cultivation to 'the natives of Borrioboola-Gha, on the left bank of the Niger', that her neglected daughter declared: 'I wish Africa was dead! I do! Don't talk to me, Miss Summerson. I hate it and detest it. It's a beast!'

Yet Churchill's coalition government found it no easier than its successors to dismiss the new charity. Mock if you like, implied Gilbert Murray, Regius Professor of Greek at Oxford, founder of Oxfam and friend of half the worthy causes of the mid-twentieth century, but 'be careful in dealing with a man who cares nothing for comfort or promotion, but is simply determined to do what he believes to be right'. Murray was better at predicting the power of organised conscience than Dickens. The ad hoc response to the Greek famine turned into the most visible charity on the high street. It was infused with the amateur air English liberals adopt when they go out into the world to do good. The first head office was in a cramped room above the original Oxfam shop in Broad Street in the city centre; the second in a dingy parade of shops in Victorian north Oxford.

The tweeds and piles of dusty pamphlets are gone now. Under the leadership of Barbara Stocking, Oxfam has moved to a huge HQ at a new business park on the edge of town. Old hands find the identikit postmodern box with its dispiriting views of the cars jammed on the ring road soulless, and I saw why when I got there. This might be the head office of any corporation in any ribbon development anywhere in the world. Once inside, however, there was no denying the efficiency of the place. Charity workers sit in an open-plan office the size of a football pitch. Neat shelving units hold research papers, while a GM-free, organic canteen offers succour and fair-trade coffee, possibly from the left bank of the Niger, to those who need a break from rescuing Africa.

The businesslike atmosphere reflects the personality of the director. Stocking is a former regional director of the NHS who, according to rumour, was in the running for the top job. Corporate cant litters her talk – 'making a difference', 'meeting the challenge' and all the rest of it – but it would be a mistake to see her as another empty suit. The charitable world is notoriously uncharitable, but I could not find a director of a rival charity with a bad word to say about her. Meanwhile her own staff describe an honest and popular manager who is, above all else, a success.

Under her leadership, turnover has hit £300 million. Oxfam now has more than 750 shops in the UK, 6000 staff all over the world and sister organisations in thirteen countries. Oxfam officials have gone from the charity into government and helped make New Labour the most charitable administration ever. Tony Blair and Gordon Brown were the 'Lennon and McCartney' of poverty reduction, cried an approving Bono, and if you can forgive the cheesy comparison, you can see his point. I would be exaggerating if I said that aid was a major political issue in Britain, but it matters more to voters here than in any other European country.

The *annus mirabilis* for Oxfam was 2005, when Blair and Brown pushed for the G8 nations to agree to an extraordinary programme of debt relief and subsidies for Africa, Live 8 played Hyde Park and the Asian tsunami provoked an outburst of altruism. 'It was a time when people recognised that we are part of the global world,' Stocking remembers with a warm smile. 'For the first time, the new horizons of travel and the Net came together and made people realise that if we're going to live happily in the global world we're going to have to make it better.'

I was not convinced then and am less so now. Even at the peak of Make Poverty History's campaign, you did not have to be a *Telegraph*-reading Tory to think the aid movement was taking a wrong turn. It presented a picture of a world as much the white man's to direct as it was at the zenith of empire. No one told the audience at Live 8 that Africa had blood-drenched dictators in power or kleptomaniac families in office. The pop stars stayed silent about genocidal movements and spy-ridden regimes. All that was needed to rescue Africa from poverty was for the developed world to agree more aid, fairer trade and debt relief and – poof! – the suffering would end.

This almost colonialist world view remains in place. An Oxfam study of global warming says, truthfully, that pollution from the rich world will hurt the poor world, but fails to ask how Africa can develop without increasing its output of greenhouse gases. A report on foreign policy says, again rightly, that the Iraq War has made humanitarian intervention harder to justify, but it contains no condemnation of Baathist and Islamist 'insurgents' or one gesture of solidarity with their victims. A report in advance of this summer's G8 summit condemns rich governments for failing to honour promises made in 2005, but assumes the problems of the world are the fault of the West and, therefore, that the remedies lie in Western hands.

The usual justification for lopsided vision is that pressure groups can best influence their own governments. A demonstration in London against the massacres in Darfur will have no influence on the regime in Khartoum, but a march to demand that the British government commit more money to, say, education in Africa might. If double standards and myopia follow, then so be it. What matters is what works. But the easy ride given to Oxfam, Christian Aid and the other charities overlooks a structural problem. The aid charities are hybrids with incompatible aims. On the one hand, they provide relief regardless of the political consequences – like the Red Cross – and, on the other, they lobby for political change – like Human Rights Watch. As Amartya Sen showed, democracies don't have famines. The great hungers of the past hundred years were presided over by colonial administrators, communist tyrants and African nationalists and gangsters. Dictatorships do not tolerate censure from anyone inside their borders. If Oxfam were to speak out against the obscenity of Robert Mugabe's Zimbabwe being elected to head the UN Commission on Sustainable Development, there is a fair chance Mugabe would stop Oxfam workers from relieving the suffering inflicted by his economically unsustainable regime.

Its hybrid status means Oxfam has to direct disapproval at governments that will not respond to criticism by deporting aid workers, but, rather, will invite Stocking in for a chat and a cup of tea. The aid charities are therefore treacherous guides to global politics. They are dependent on dictators and must overlook their crimes. They are respected by democrats and can therefore safely blame the democracies for the crimes of others.

Stocking has the strength of character to face hard questions candidly. In Darfur, I said, Oxfam is feeding 600,000 refugees on the Chadian border. Is that why it refuses to call the Darfuri genocide 'genocide'?

'It is a dilemma for us,' she said. 'We think we've got to save lives today while trying to get the international community to sort out the bigger problem. Now we will do our absolute utmost to go to the edge of that. We will try to give as much information out, but not in ways that are challenging to the Khartoum government.'

I asked whether she could imagine circumstances in which Oxfam would choose to speak plainly, even if telling the truth endangered famine relief. There were two, she replied. First, if charitable aid was a 'sticking plaster' that allowed the international community to feel that conditions in, say, Darfur were not so bad. Second, if aid was keeping an oppressive government in power, as may soon be the case in Zimbabwe.

I suggested that a better policy would be to help African progressives set their countries free by championing their causes and highlighting the massacres of their oppressors. If I had confessed to stealing second-hand books from my local Oxfam shop, she could not have been more shocked. 'No, no, that's not our mandate,' she cried. 'We want to offer a way out of poverty that makes them feel they have economic opportunity and provides them with a right to be heard. It's not our job to help groupings that want to overthrow their governments.'

She sounded reasonable as she marked out her limits, but I left wondering how long the aid charities could stay in British politics while staying out of African politics. The strongest criticism she would make of governments in the poor world was that some of them were corrupt. But the trouble with Africa is less that its post-colonial elites are corrupt – there are corrupt governments all over the world – but that they are unpatriotic. From Côte d'Ivoire to Zimbabwe, post-colonial rulers have shown that they would rather bring the roof down on their wretched peoples than let potential forces of opposition grow in business, agriculture and trade unions.

A thought experiment shows future dangers for Oxfam. Suppose the G8 meets all its 2005 promises. Suppose the World Trade Organisation stops the rich world subsidising its farmers. Then suppose that nothing changes or, as Sen would predict, that change for the better comes only in those countries already on the path to constitutional politics. Would Oxfam be able to rouse governments and publics for another Live 8? Or would governments and publics echo young Miss Jellyby and say that Africa was a beast?

At its birth, Oxfam had to decide whether destroying tyranny was more important than relieving immediate suffering, and sixty-five years on it seems no closer to an answer.

I asked Stocking whether she expected to see Africa break away from the demeaning need for other people's charity by the time we retired. Yes, she replied. Absolutely. Look at the strides made in combating poverty in India. The naysayers said change was impossible, but it happened, for all their sneers. I forgot about the question and moved on, but it evidently niggled away. As I was preparing to leave, she went back to it and corrected herself: 'Perhaps not by the time we retire, but maybe before we die.'

New Statesman, May 2007

Let Them Eat Organic

THE MILLENNIUM WAS meant to bring with it a wave of violence from maniacal cultists. Just before Christmas 1999, the Italian intelligence services warned the Pope that Satanists, who had grouped together under the banner of the Followers of Beelzebub, were preparing to attack St Peter's Basilica. The secret policemen also fretted about trouble for the Vatican from New Acropolis, a mysterious and mystifying sect dedicated to avenging the death of Giordano Bruno, an obscure philosopher burned at the stake by the Inquisition in 1600.

The Israeli police, meanwhile, were looking out for one Monte Kim Miller, a self-proclaimed messenger of God, who told his followers he would die in Jerusalem and be resurrected three days later, as is traditional. Previously, the marketing manager with Procter & Gamble had predicted that an earthquake would destroy his home town of Denver, Colorado, on 10 October 1997. His followers sold their homes and furniture. They were too hasty. Denver was still standing on 11 October 1997. Eighty-five members of Miller's Concerned Christian cult vanished. The FBI feared they would regroup in Jerusalem and attack holy sites on 31 December 1999.

As it was, not much happened in Rome or Jerusalem. The religious maniacs who were to do real damage waited until 11

September 2001, and they were not interested in anniversaries of Christ's birth.

In 2000, the ravings of Satanists and New Acropolites were less hysterical than the sober predictions of respectable men and women, who thought themselves to be incubated from frenzy and delusion. Investors, who believed that markets were rational, poured money into dotcom and telecom shares. They inflated the bubble to a point where a crash was inevitable.

Meanwhile, managers and governments, who believed that computer programmers were objective assessors of technological risk, spent somewhere between £150 billion and £500 billion warding off the millennium bug. Full-throated doomsters predicted that the bug would lead to planes falling out of the sky, the infrastructure collapsing, nuclear missiles launching of their own accord and riots spreading as looters snatched what few cans of food were left on the shelves. Less excitable Mystic Megs confined themselves to warning that a global recession would follow the huge disruption to business the bug would bring, but stopped short of predicting an outright apocalypse.

As it was, nothing worth mentioning happened to the computers. Either the global effort to exterminate the bug was more successful than anyone dared hope, or empire-building computer technicians created a pandemic of panic about a phantom menace. The latter option seems more likely to me, and historians will look back in wonder at the many maniacal beliefs reasonable people held to be sensible at the turn of the century. After gazing at the stock market and millennium-bug fantasies, will they then turn to the repulsion millennial Europeans felt for genetically modified food?

It is too early to be certain, but GM food has been around for over a decade in America and there is an embarrassing shortage of diners dropping dead and genetically modified super-weeds rampaging across the prairies. The Royal Society, Britain's national academy of science, told the government's 2003 review of GM crops that there was no evidence that they created allergic reactions, damaged health or reduced the nutritional quality of food.

They sounded confident, but I doubt that the scientists managed to convince a single discerning eater. Just as the wised-up were certain that computers were going to crash at one minute past midnight on New Year's Day, so they are now certain that GM food is unsafe and inferior; a threat to the health of humans and the genetic diversity of the environment.

The conditions that created the bug panic perfectly match the causes of the GM phobia. Anthony Finkelstein, professor of software systems engineering at University College London, warned that government and business were wasting billions in the fight against the bug in the late nineties. In January 2000, vindicated by the non-arrival of the catastrophe, he identified three reasons why policy-makers refused to listen and allowed themselves to be swept up by a millennial mania.

The first was the developed world's state of ignorant dependence. People could not manage without computers but few knew much about them. They were ready to be scared. Similarly, with genetic modification, everyone depends on food, but most of us are ignorant of biology and cannot understand how scientists can transplant bacterial DNA into a plant. All we know is that it sounds spookily unnatural.

Second, said Finkelstein, someone must have an interest in promoting fear. The millennium bug made technicians rich. With GM food, the commercial interest appears to be all on one side. Monsanto, the biggest supplier of GM crops, began lobbying to get GM food accepted in Europe in 1998. Its timing was terrible. Capitalist triumphalism was at its height and European publics did not trust US corporations that seemed able to persuade weak governments to let them make as much money as they could. But GM foods also upset the cultural and financial interests of the setters of style and taste, who were busy promoting a cult of the authentic. Just as Marie Antoinette and her courtiers dressed up as peasants and shepherds, and pretended to live the simple life while the real French peasantry was close to starvation, so their heirs play at being natural, when an overpopulated world needs an agricultural revolution. They propagandise for 'natural' childbirth, even though genuinely 'natural' childbirth for most women in the Third World is about the most dangerous experience of their lives. They dine on the 'natural' ingredients the peasantry allegedly used to produce, even though natural farming for real peasant farmers is as unpleasant as natural childbirth for the majority of mothers: backbreaking drudgery, predominantly undertaken by the women who survived the pains of natural childbirth. Opposition to GM food swept Europe because it affronted the lifestyle of the middle classes, and all those who made money from catering to it.

Last, but by no means least, is the media. The millennium bug was a fantastic story. The clock was ticking. Robots were about to run amok. There was a race against time to save the planet. After that, the hacks needed a follow-up, and mad scientists playing God and not thinking about Mother Nature's terrible retribution suited their requirements nicely.

Which is not to say that the environmentalists have been proved wrong. Whatever the Royal Society says, absence of evidence is not evidence of absence. Just because no one has proved that GM food can damage your health does not mean that it cannot. Friends of the Earth and Greenpeace have a checklist of dozens of tests they want carried out. They say it is hard to find out whether GM food has poisoned Americans because there has been no proper monitoring of who eats what.

The power of the biotech business to push regulators about is as feared now as it was in the 1990s, and with justice. I suspect, however, that for all the apparent fastidiousness on the part of the Greens, scientific propriety is not their chief concern. Even if every test were passed and another ten years go by without so much as one case of GM-induced diarrhoea, Greens would still be against genetic modification, as would millions of European consumers. Their reaction against it is visceral, not rational, and no amount of contrary evidence will change their prejudices.

What fussy Europeans choose to eat does not matter greatly. The government is angry that the Greens are driving biotech industries offshore, but the customer is king and customers in Britain and the rest of the EU have made up their minds that they don't want GM. They may be being fools, but parliaments cannot legislate against folly. When it comes to the poor world, however, resistance to GM turns vicious. The opponents of biotech emphasise that the industry is not interested in feeding the hungry any more than the pharmaceutical companies are interested in treating malaria. The developed world is where the profits are. But their arguments are contradicted by inventions such as 'golden rice', created by Dr Ingo Potrykus of the Swiss Federal Institute in Zurich, which clearly is designed to relieve suffering. Dr Potrykus modified rice to help the 200 million or so children who risk death or blindness from vitamin A deficiency. If it works, and if it is taken up in Asia – two big 'ifs' – children will live who would otherwise die.

Dr Potrykus is an independent thinker, yet the Green movement accuses him of being a tool of the biotech companies. When he learned that Greenpeace had reserved the right to take direct action against golden rice tests plots, he said it would be guilty of a 'crime against humanity' if it did.

Historians are likely to write more in anger than amusement

if European opposition turns out to have been a millennial mania with fatal consequences for the rest of the world.*

Observer, May 2003

---

* In 2008, the Royal Society announced yet another inquiry. In the intervening five years, no one had fallen sick from eating GM food, and supporters and opponents continued to argue about the technology's environmental impact. It was time for a real expert to settle the controversy, and a man claiming to be the 'next King of England' stepped forward. In an interview with the *Telegraph*, Prince Charles declared, 'Millions of small farmers all over the world are being driven off their land into unsustainable, unmanageable, degraded and dysfunctional conurbations of unmentionable awfulness!' he cried. Soon we will face 'the absolute destruction of everything'!

Of everything, your highness?

Yes, and if agribusinesses thought they were going to prevent the absolute destruction of everything by using 'one form of clever genetic engineering after another', they would cause 'the biggest disaster environmentally of all time'.

The Menace of the Quaint

AT THEIR LAST annual meeting, faith healers gathered at Roots & Shoots in south London to discuss how to treat Aids with magic pills. They did not say they were faith healers, of course, or shamans or juju men. They presented themselves to the world as 'homeopaths': serious men and women whose remedies are at least as good as conventional medicine.

According to the advance publicity, Hilary Fairclough, a homeopath endorsed by no less a medical authority than Jeanette Winterson, intended to describe the 'impressive' results from her clinic in Botswana. Harry van der Zee, co-founder of the Amma Resonance Healing Foundation, would say how 'in just a few days or weeks' the African Aids patients he treated became 'symptom-free and able to return to their jobs and schools or to look after their children again'. The Society of Homeopaths promised that they and other speakers would provide 'fascinating insights' for World Aids Day.

It will be a true miracle if they had managed to do that. Of all the pseudo-sciences, homeopathy is the most evidently spurious. Devised by Samuel Hahnemann in the late eighteenth century, it holds that the smaller the dose of a mineral or herb the more potent it is. In a homeopathic sulphur remedy marked 30C, the proportion of sulphur to inert packaging in a pill is 1 to   100,000,000,000,000,000,000,000,000,000,000,000,000,000,

253

000,000,000,000,000,000,000. A glass of water is more likely to cure you.

Yet dismissing homeopathy as quackery given by and for the feeble-minded is surprisingly hard. Anti-elitism dominates our society and many feel uncomfortable saying that the 6 million people who take alternative medicines are idiots. They sincerely believe in phoney remedies and sincerity trumps sense in modern culture.

In rich and privileged societies where the 'worried well' take their good health for granted, homeopathy feels somehow natural when set against cold, conventional medicine. Today's audiences for fiction certainly have no difficulty believing that conventional doctors and drugs companies are more villainous than their natural and holistic rivals. Scrabbling around for a new plot after the end of the Cold War, John le Carré came up with *The Constant Gardener*, a story about drug manufacturers murdering Africans. 'Big pharmaceuticals are right up there with the arms dealers,' declares one character, who could not tell the difference between an antibiotic and a cluster bomb. Far from ignoring or deriding him, the public cheered le Carré on. *The Constant Gardener* was a commercial and critical hit as both a novel and a film.

You might have thought that the medical establishment would fight back and make a stand for science. The reputations of the Chief Medical Officer and the Department of Health and the doctors they regulate depend on their ability to say that the remedies they approve have been tested in double-blind trials, but they go along with fake treatments that can't stand up to passing scrutiny.

GPs use homeopaths as a dumping ground for hypochondri-acs – or 'heart-sinks', as they're known in the doctoring busi-ness, for the reaction they provoke on entering a surgery – and the state pays for five homeopathic 'hospitals'. With the Trea-sury about to stem the flood of money to the NHS, Whitehall ought to close them and concentrate scarce resources on medicine that works. A minister bold enough to argue for the effective use of public funds would, however, face strong opposition.

About one hundred MPs signed a Commons motion asserting that homeopathic hospitals were 'valuable national assets'. They have 'the potential', as the MPs carefully phrased it, 'to offer clinically effective and cost-effective solutions to common health problems faced by NHS patients, including chronic difficult-to-treat conditions such as musculoskeletal and other chronic pain, eczema, depression, anxiety and insomnia, allergy, chronic fatigue and irritable bowel syndrome'. Well-known loons were joined by otherwise intelligent politicians, who were nevertheless content to have their constituents cozened.

Maybe they believed the standard justification for homeopathy that the 'placebo effect' is a real psychological phenomenon. Patients suffering from minor ailments can feel better after taking a sugared pill. I have never liked the argument because there would be no placebo effect if doctors told patients the truth. To endorse homeopathy on the NHS is to endorse state deception.* In his book *Counterknowledge*, Damian Thompson of the *Daily Telegraph* goes farther and makes a persuasive case that what we tend to dismiss as harmless fads for Cherie Blair and her kind cause immense suffering in the wider world. In Britain, the NHS's backing for public homeopathic hospitals

---

* The argument for treating homeopathy as a placebo echoes the classical argument in favour of hypocritical religious belief. Educated men did not believe in the gods, of course. But they put on a show of piety because they thought religion was a useful means of keeping the lower orders and slaves docile. 'Religion is regarded by the common people as true, by the wise as false, and by rulers as useful' – Seneca. Ophelia Benson of the *Philosophers' Magazine* describes supporters of useful lies as exponents of the 'Tinkerbell Mechanism': the notion that unsupportable ideas will stay in the air as long as the childlike believe in them.

legitimises the private homeopaths who work in their shadows. An investigation by *Newsnight* showed ten private operators putting patients' lives in danger by rejecting anti-malarial drugs for pills containing infinitesimal quantities of garlic and citronella oil.

Beyond Britain, in the Africa John le Carré couldn't see, the obsessions of people we think of as eccentrics have had lethal consequences. For years, South African president Thabo Mbeki has done his best to hinder the distribution of anti-retroviral drugs. He stood by while a foundation run by the German vitamin entrepreneur Matthias Rath launched propaganda campaigns in the townships against conventional Aids treatments. He listened to Peter Duesberg, a biologist who argued that to prevent Aids, all you need to do is eat well and avoid recreational drugs. After hearing Duesberg speak at a conference, Anthony Fauci, the usually mild-mannered Aids adviser to the American administration, said: 'This is murder. It's really that simple.'*

Unregulated 'nutritionists' in Britain and Germany also claim vitamin C is as effective a treatment for Aids as anti-retrovirals and, as we have seen, homeopaths shout 'hallelujah' and tell the congregation they have seen Africans walk out of their clinics 'symptom-free'. Don't think that just because they seem obscure cranks that their ideas can't have influence, when the Net makes them available to anyone anxious to deny the established facts about Aids. The notion that governments do not need to spend money on Aids has found a grateful audience

---

* In September 2008, Rath pulled out of a libel action against the British science writer Ben Goldacre and the *Guardian* newspaper. Goldacre had excoriated Rath for buying 'full page adverts denouncing Aids drugs while promoting his vitamin pills in South Africa, a country where hundreds of thousands die every year from Aids under an HIV denialist president and the population is ripe for miracle cures'. The ANC belatedly reclaimed a little of its lost honour by removing Mbeki from office at around the same time.

among kleptomaniac elites anxious to find reasons to keep public money in their Swiss bank accounts. African nationalists want to believe that white pharmaceutical companies are conning them, and are grateful for alternative healers who say the same. In Zimbabwe, Robert Mugabe has announced that Aids is the result of poverty, not HIV. Muslim Africa dismisses Aids as God's punishment of homosexuals. In India, China and Vietnam doctors accuse their governments of failing to acknowledge the scale of the public health crisis. The most shameful case for those of us who once supported the ANC, however, remains South Africa, where doctors had to lobby until 2006 to persuade Mbeki to support the distribution of anti-Aids drugs. Many of his comrades still propagate the conspiracy theory that white drugs firms are sucking the wealth out of black Africa.

Suppose apartheid had not fallen and a white minority government was indulging Aids denialists. I think it is fair to imagine the streets of the world's capitals filling with demonstrators accusing a white regime of being complicit in the mass killing of blacks. Geldof and Bono would organise concerts. Fiery orators would make accusations of 'genocide' and 'ethnic cleansing', and denounce those who provided spurious arguments to justify the neglect of South African Aids victims as the accomplices of a criminal policy.

As it was, there were no mass demonstrations because a black rather than a white government presided over the disaster, and its accomplices were not in big pharmaceutical companies but eccentric little alternative institutes we too casually dismiss as quaint.

Observer, October 2007

PART 7

Cuckoo Land

'Right! Officer Krupke
You're really a square
This boy don't need a judge
He needs an analyst's care
It's just his neurosis
That oughta be curbed
He's psychologically disturbed.'

WEST SIDE STORY,
1957

Pathologising Everyday Life

BRIAN BLACKWELL GOT a disorder and got away with it, so why shouldn't you? He battered his parents to death with a claw hammer and then went on holiday with his girlfriend. But, instead of imprisoning him for life, Mr Justice Royce allowed him to plead manslaughter on the grounds of diminished responsibility. He will be eligible for parole in five years and seven months, which, for a defendant who might have spent the rest of his days in prison, was a notable victory. Five psychologists agreed that he was suffering from Acute Narcissistic Personality Disorder. When they said he was a narcissist, they did not simply mean he was selfish – most killers are selfish – but that he had a verifiable mental illness which meant he was no more fully responsible for his crimes than a blind man would be fully responsible for bumping into you in the street.

According to the textbooks, acute narcissists have five or more of the following traits: an extravagant sense of self-importance; fantasies of unlimited success; the belief that they are special and can be understood only by their equals; an unreasonable sense of entitlement; a yearning for admiration; a willingness to exploit others; a lack of empathy; a tendency to fly into a rage when thwarted; a visible arrogance or hauteur; and an envy of others and a belief that others envy them.

It sounds frightfully specific, but look again at that list. How many people do you know with five or more of its grandiose vices? My diffident self aside, I would say it encompasses most managers of my acquaintance, all actors, many politicians and every editor of a national newspaper.

After the Blackwell case, Oliver James, the most garrulous of the Fleet Street shrinks, declared that 80 per cent of convicted prisoners had a personality disorder, and 74 per cent had more than one. James did not follow his argument through and say that 80 per cent of convicts should ask the Court of Appeal to cut their sentences on grounds of diminished responsibility. But then his trade is rarely logical.

It is not only criminals who can plead mental disorder in mitigation. The late twentieth century brought an explosion of psychiatric diagnoses, as the history of the bible of therapy, the American Psychiatric Association's *Diagnostic and Statistical Manual of Mental Disorders*, shows. The first edition (*DSM-I*) was published in 1952. It was little more than a pamphlet, and listed a mere sixty disorders. At 134 pages, the second edition of 1968 might have been mistaken for a novella. The third, in its revised version of 1987, had 567 pages and was longer than many Victorian novels. *DSM-IV*, the current dictionary of delusion, was published in 1994 and would be easier to handle if it had appeared in two volumes. It has 886 pages and even in paperback weighs 3lb 4oz. *DSM-V* will be out in 2011. No one is expecting a haiku.

Herb Kutchins and Stuart A. Kirk, two sceptical American academics, argue that psychiatry has expanded by pathologising everyday life. To give a sense of how its empire has inflated, they took ordinary human troubles and showed how they could be, and indeed were being, reclassified as disorders.

- An ambitious friend is striving for promotion and says he's not sleeping well. (Not sleeping equals Major Depressive Disorder.)

- A former classmate says she has never forgotten how you humiliated her in the playground. (Bearing grudges equals Paranoid Personality Disorder.)
- A colleague won't go for a drink after work and spends his weekends at home by himself. (A desire for solitude equals Schizoid Personality Disorder.)
- A wife says that after ten years of marriage she is no longer aroused into a state of passionate anticipation by the sight of her naked husband. (Absence of sexual interest equals Hypoactive Sexual Desire Disorder.)
- Your sister cannot stop thinking about a boyfriend who left her. (Infatuation equals Obsessive-Compulsive Personality Disorder.)
- Your child won't listen to his teacher. (Lack of respect for authority equals Oppositional Defiance Disorder.)
- A husband says his wife worries all the time. (Nervousness about the future equals Generalised Anxiety Disorder.)

The list could go on, and indeed does go on in *DSM-IV* for 886 pages. Whether you are happy or sad, neat or messy, chaste or promiscuous, bumptious or withdrawn, fat or thin, drunk or sober, you have the symptoms of at least one mental disorder – probably more.

The cynical thing is to say that the spread of psychiatry is very profitable for therapists – there are 200,000 in Britain indulging in 300 varieties of therapy – and equally profitable for the makers of Prozac, Xanax and beta-blockers, who were heartened by the announcement in *DSM-IV* that there were 12 million sufferers from generalised anxiety disorder in the United States, all of them potential customers.

As important as following the money is questioning the medical status of the definitions of disorder. You do not have to trail behind Foucault into the postmodern wilderness and pretend that all mental illnesses are social constructs to wonder what a therapist means by 'disorder'. There are chronic illnesses such as schizophrenia and severe depression, which are no more of a social construct than cancer, but what about the ocean of ordinary human unhappiness, in which most shrinks swim and nearly all disorders lie?

If a psychiatrist says you have Narcissistic Personality Disorder, would every competent psychiatrist who examined you say the same? You can prove that you do not have a tumour by having a scan, but how can you prove that you are not a narcissist? If you cannot, wouldn't psychiatry fail Popper's falsification test and be a pseudo-science? Above all, what does a psychiatrist's diagnosis of narcissism predict about behaviour? A doctor can warn a heavy smoker that he has a one-in-three chance of contracting lung cancer. Could a psychiatrist say to a sufferer with a narcissistic personality disorder that the chances of him taking a claw hammer to his parents are one in three, 300, 3000?

There is a long history of empirical scepticism about psychiatry, which goes back to Freud's original critics. A proud place in it belongs to Thomas Szasz, a Hungarian refugee from Nazism who found sanctuary in America. In 1980, he testified for the prosecution in the case of Darlin Cromer, which was not so different from the Blackwell trial. As with Blackwell, no one disputed that Cromer had kidnapped and murdered her victim, a five-year-old black boy. Witnesses described how she had talked of 'killing niggers' and of it being 'the duty of every white woman to kill a nigger child'. None the less, the defence argued that she was a victim of 'schizophrenic paranoia', and should receive a reduced punishment.

Szasz would have none of it. He asked the jury to think about how psychiatrists who had interviewed Cromer weeks after the crime could know what had been in Cromer's mind at the time of the killing. When the defence lawyers asked him to explain why she had killed, Szasz refused to use medical language.

Cromer 'was a bad student', he said. 'She was a bad wife. She was a bad mother. She was a bad employee, in so far as she was employable. Then she started to engage in illegal drugs, then she escalated to illegal assault, and finally she committed this murder … Life is a task. Either you cope with or it gets you. If you don't know how to build, you can always destroy.'

The jury preferred his explanation, and convicted Cromer. Szasz's words sound harsh. It feels better to the liberal mind to explain away crime by invoking biology or psychiatry, and find comfort in rational explanations for irrational behaviour. Those who think it a kindness to treat a criminal as a patient should remember Hannah Arendt's warning that 'if everyone can be innocent, than everyone can be guilty'. Or to put it another way, if criminals can be patients, then patients can be criminals, and the burden of proof and presumption of innocence can go to hell.

In the end, it is not an apposite question to ask whether the effect of psychiatry is liberal or conservative as medicine cannot be judged by political standards. We need to know instead whether the hundreds of disorders it claims to have discovered are proper objects for scientific study or vague generalisations.

Reviewing a recent collection of essays on Szasz in the American journal *Reason*, Jacob Sullum said that the most heretical point he made about his colleagues was that they were in a losing fight against advances in neurology, which had the potential to explain real and terrible mental diseases by examining biological causes.

We are a way from there yet, but the genetic revolution is moving on. My guess is that, when our understanding of the brain improves, disorders will return to where they were before Sigmund Freud: sufferers will talk to friends or relatives or look within themselves. They may pay money for a psychiatrist's time, but they will have ever fewer reasons for believing they are talking to a scientist. Today's psychiatric mania will one day be seen as an example of imperial overreach: the last spectacular expansion of a doomed intellectual system.

'Just think,' people will say, 'before the genetic revolution you could get away with murder.'

New Statesman, July 2005

The Genetic Revolution (Postponed)

WHETHER WE LIVE in a golden age of science is disputed, not least by Professor Steve Jones, but we certainly have lived through a golden age of science writing. Richard Dawkins, Stephen Jay Gould, E. O. Wilson, Steven Pinker and Steve Jones himself have taken evolution out of academia and engaged the educated public. For all their skill, watching them has been like watching a concert party for troops in a war zone: an interesting diversion from the main event. They have been arguing about selfish genes, punctuated equilibrium, sociobiology and atheism, while barely noticing the biological catastrophe around them. The 'Holocene extinction event', a destruction of flora and fauna by the human race so extensive that it is comparable with the five other mass extinctions in the 550-million-year history of complex life on earth, is ravishing the planet, but great writers on evolution have stayed silent as man destroys their raw material.

Jones makes ample amends in his new study of the poisoning of the coral reefs, but I put it to him that, for most of their careers, he and his contemporaries have missed the dying elephant in the room.

His answer shows Jones's many virtues. First, he corrects my sloppy generalisation; Jared Diamond and E. O. Wilson have written well about man's catastrophic effect on other species, he points out. Then he's off with the incisive fluency that makes editors hire him and readers buy him.

'What's interesting is that biologists are as distanced from the world of natural history as any member of the public. Most of us just study humans, fruit flies, bacteria or snails.' He points across the senior common room of University College London. 'Look, there are two extremely eminent mathematical biologists. They probably couldn't recognise the difference between a sparrow and a starling. Biologists' minds are focused on a very narrow range of things. I would say 90 per cent of students in the faculty aren't particularly concerned about what is going on in the natural world. They want to cure brain cancer.

'I'm unhappy about it, but I'm unhappy about it more as a concerned human being than as a professional biologist. I'm not minimising the horrors of what's going on, but I don't think biology is going to solve the horrors. Even the work that tells you about the size of reserves you need to protect endangered species brings generally bad news – you need huge reserves.'

Listening to him, I think that if ever I have to be trapped in a lift with anyone, it might as well be Jones. In talking as in writing, he combines wit and pace with a backlist of references he began accumulating when he was a bookish boy in Nonconformist Wales who buried himself in his grandfather's Bible. *Almost Like a Whale*, his rewriting of *The Origin of Species*, offers a small example of his range. It begins by laying out the dogma Charles Darwin had to combat: that God fitted every creature for its place in creation. An ordinary writer would have simply presented the argument against natural theology and left it there. Jones digs out a poem by one John Hookham Frere, a justifiably forgotten Georgian, and quotes with relish his anti-Enlightenment verse of 1798 that explains the argument for design with two of the worst lines in English poetry:

> The feather'd race with pinions skim the air –
> Not so the mackerel, and still less the bear!

He pays readers the compliment of assuming they are as knowl-edgeable as he is – the classic strategy of a natural teacher who knows how to flatter his pupils into keeping up. When I meet him to share the atrocious sandwiches UCL forces on its academics, he is angry that 'supposedly liberal' rules will make him retire from teaching in two years, when he reaches sixty-five. Many academics would welcome the chance to write books and address appreciative audiences around the world. Not so Jones. Teaching comes first.

All of which makes his success appear an easy matter to explain. We would have to give up on intellectual life if a writer who loves learning and knows how to communicate it couldn't find an audience.

Jones's appeal has a mysterious element, however. He is a wary, even gloomy thinker, out of step with the current culture of exhortation and moral uplift. Prince Charles, virtually every celebrity who opines on the environment, the serious media, the British government and all the other signatories to the Kyoto treaty, insist that changes in lifestyle and energy produc-tion can limit the effects of climate change. The underlying assumption of the homilies on recycling and cutting back on air miles is that relatively painless adaptations can 'make a differ-ence' and limit the degradation. True, serious Greens aren't so cocksure, but even they believe that dramatic change can have dramatic effects. Jones has no time for optimism of any variety. *Coral* is subtitled *A Pessimist in Paradise*, and he sees the destruction of the coral polyps as foretelling the destruction of humanity. The reefs themselves make some firm, and sombre, predictions about our own apocalypse. We shouldn't be surprised – extinction is the fate of all species – though Jones cheerily says his best guess is that disease will get us before the heat.

Pessimism is a persistent feature. For all his suavity and atheism, I wonder if it is cheap psychology to speculate whether his grandfather's Bible gave him a touch of the Old Testament prophet. He delights in taking apart the confident pretence of sociobiologists that their study of evolution has given them the key to human nature. 'An awful lot of stuff about human behaviour and society one reads would not get into a scientific journal if it were about fruit flies,' he says, sighing. 'It's not good enough. Science is about facts.'

When I give him a sociobiological account from Pinker's *The Blank Slate* of how humanity's sense of justice developed from an evolutionary need of early human beings to punish those who threatened to take their mates, he all but bursts out laughing. 'Now design the experiment. Give me the data to suggest that's true. This is arts-faculty science. People sitting down and inventing stories without the smallest fact to support them. It's dangerous because evolution has been used as an alibi by everyone. Marx sent Darwin a copy of *Das Kapital*. Hitler used it to justify his crimes. You have to be careful about the naive application of these ideas. In the States, defence lawyers are trying to use genetics to spare defendants from death row. In Georgia, lawyers for Stephen Mobley [who murdered the manager of a pizza parlour in 1991] tried to save him from lethal injection by arguing he had a gene that predisposed him to violence. The state of Texas, home to our friend George W. Bush, responded by changing its rules in a very subtle way to say that anyone deemed to be a continuing threat to society would be liable for execution. In effect, if the defence uses a genetic argument that a prisoner is genetically predisposed to violence, the state will use the genetic argument to kill him because it can't cure him. Although I despise that view, it has the same logic as the alternative that genes deny criminal responsibility. You have to be very careful to disentangle biology from its use in society and it's not clear to me that sociobiology has tried to do it.'

Nor does Jones hold back from saying that his fellow geneticists are as guilty as sociobiologists of 'grossly overselling' what they can do. He does not doubt that genetic discoveries will improve many lives. They may influence whom we decide to marry and which pregnancies we decide to abort. Insurance companies may be able to demand higher premiums or even refuse cover to customers with suspect genes. But Jones wonders why the quid pro quo for the afflicted in the form of new cures from gene therapy is so late in arriving.

Medicine assured us it was on its way. The mapping of the human genome led to euphoric predictions of sensational cures. The mania caught managers at UCL, who proposed renaming one of their hospital buildings the UCL Institute of Gene Therapy.

'Thank God they didn't,' says Jones, eyes wide with disbelief at the folly of it all. 'The amount of egg we would have on our face for doing that! Until very recently, gene therapy hasn't worked. It has now worked in some cases – inborn immune deficiencies for babies in the womb – and that's wonderful, and it's been remarkably promising for some varieties of inherited blindness, but it's only worked in dogs so far. That's it. That's all we've done. But I've had the horrible experience of giving lectures to sixth-formers and twice girls have come up to me at the end and said, "You're talking about cystic fibrosis and I've got it, but I'm not worried because I'm going to be cured by gene therapy." And I've thought, "Oh my God. Where did you get that from?"' Well, the answer is scientists and science teachers – that's where they've got it from.

'Where did that come from?' is a question Jones is asking ever more regularly. Creationism, once an unthinkable mental deformation for educated men and women, is flourishing among his Muslim students. When the publishers of the Turkish edition of *Almost Like a Whale* flew him out, he was astonished when they introduced him to his bodyguards. I ask how he copes with students who come to university with closed minds.

'At the end of the course I ask, "Was I lying to you about chromosome structure?" and they say no. Then I say, "Was I lying to you about cell structure?" and they say no. So I ask why on earth they think I'm lying to them about evolution, and of course they can't answer, because they're not allowed to.'

Cautious in the face of intellectual manias, caustic about superstition and pessimistic about the future … his students may not always appreciate it, but the great virtue of Professor Jones is that he doesn't lie.

New Statesman, June 2007

The Clairvoyants

STEVEN SPIELBERG'S *Minority Report* starred Tom Cruise as a detective in the Washington, DC of 2054. He is a 'pre-crime' solver who acts on tip-offs from 'precognitive' humans who drift in a flotation tank, their brainwaves tapped by computers. The 'precogs' are telepathic. They pick up the thoughts of potential criminals as they think about committing crimes. Forewarned, Cruise and his team catch the perpetrators before they can perpetrate.

'Mr Marks,' he declares as he arrests a husband who is about to kill his cheating wife and her lover, 'by mandate of the District of Columbia Precrime Division, I'm placing you under arrest for the future murder of Sarah Marks and Donald Dubin that was to take place today, April 22 at 0800 hours and four minutes.'

Billboards in Washington announce, 'Pre-crime: it works!' A grateful populace agrees because there hasn't been one murder in six years. Cruise is a hero until, inevitably, the precogs accuse him of plotting to kill.

Science fiction at its best is a comment on the present, not a prediction about the future. Although we don't have clairvoyants in tanks, pre-crime policing is in vogue. Take the following assertions the authorities hold to be self-evident. Half of all crime is committed by just 10 per cent of criminals, who are well known to the police. The intelligence services are watching

Muslim fanatics who are willing to commit atrocities. Instead of being held in asylums for the public's protection, known madmen have been freed from mental hospitals to rape and kill in the community. Computer databases can track potential paedophiles and prevent them working with children.

The more the public hears that criminals can be identified in advance, the greater the yearning for pre-emptive action grows. If the police know who the villains, terrorists, psychos and perverts are, why can't they lock them up and prevent unnecessary suffering?

These sentiments were once confined to the bar at the Police Federation annual conference. Now pre-emptive justice is government policy. It isn't a coherent policy and it isn't being applied uniformly, but in Whitehall and beyond, there is a half-articulated desire to dispense with the traditional insistence that a crime or a conspiracy to commit a crime must have taken place before a criminal is pronounced guilty as charged. Lives would be spared and scheming defence lawyers foiled if the state could pronounce suspects guilty without charge.

A faintly annoyed Tony Blair explained to the 2003 Labour Party conference that the old safeguards were all very well in their day but now did more harm than good. 'Of course the criminal justice system with its rules and procedures was a vital step of progress when poor people were without representation unjustly convicted by corners cut. But today in Britain in the twenty-first century it is not the innocent being convicted. It's too many of the guilty going free.'

Accordingly, the fourteen al-Qaeda suspects who have been scattered around England's maximum-security prisons and hospitals are not going to go free any time soon. They haven't been charged or tried. They haven't seen the evidence against them or had the opportunity to challenge it. They are being held indefinitely because the security services assert that they are involved in international terrorism.

The government rejected a recommendation by MPs from all parties to end the internment of foreign nationals. This is an emergency measure aimed at potential terrorists, replied ministers. Let them go and you risk a British 9/11.

How does the government know that, if a court has not tested the evidence from the security services? As far as journalists can work out, only one of the detainees is a serious threat to anyone. Abu Qatada is an inspiration for Islamic death cults, videos of his sermons are always being found in the flats of mass murderers. But if he is the inciter of jihadis he gives every appearance of being, why not prosecute him under Britain's sweeping anti-terrorist laws? Abu Qatada aside, the other detainees look like nobodies. One's all but dead from polio, one's gone mad and is in Broadmoor and another seven are on the way to losing their minds. No matter. They must stay in jail because of what clairvoyant spies say they may do rather than because of what they have done.

Suicide bombing is a phenomenon that makes cowards of us all. The faint risk that internment may stop a plane loaded with passengers smashing into a skyscraper has meant that scarcely anyone is prepared to take to the streets in protest.

But the government cannot be allowed to get away with the pretence that the suspension of the rule of law for terror suspects is an emergency measure for exceptional times. British government and British society are everywhere kicking against the constraint that defendants are innocent until proved guilty whether suspects are terrorists or not. Whitehall polishes crystal balls, examines the entrails of chickens and comforts the public with unredeemable promise of pre-emptive strikes against offenders.

In December 2000, the Department of Health announced reforms to the treatment of the mentally ill. They included the stipulation that people with untreatable violent personality disorders should be incarcerated in secure psychiatric hospitals.

Until then, there had been three grounds for the imprisonment of British citizens: because they had committed a crime; because they were remanded in custody while awaiting trial on the charge of committing a crime; or because they had a treatable mental illness and needed to be imprisoned while they received care.

The government has proposed a fourth. Men and women should be locked up for being bad and therefore a threat to others, rather than mad and therefore in need of medical treatment. The demand from the press and public for what was internment by any other name was enormous. From the murder of Jonathan Zito, who was stabbed in the eye at a Tube station by Christopher Clunis, a schizophrenic with a long history of violence, to the murders of Lin and Megan Russell, beaten to death on a country lane by Michael Stone, a paranoid schizophrenic who was well known to the mental health services, the nineties were peppered with stories of psychos being left at liberty to murder.

The ejection of patients from mental hospitals under the care-in-the-community policy seemed a public menace. Many people, not all of them sensation-seeking journalists, suspected that overstretched psychiatrists disowned violent men by pronouncing that they were suffering from an untreatable personality disorder no doctor could help them with.

I believed it myself, but it turns out the number of killings by people who have been in contact with the mental health services has remained constant since the sixties, even though the overall number of homicides has quintupled. They account for about forty murders each year. The closing of the asylums has not flooded the streets with dangerous lunatics. Alcoholism and the drug culture have driven up murder rates, while the proportion of killings by the mentally ill has shrunk. You are safer walking through the grounds of a psychiatric hospital than standing outside a pub at closing time. A schizophrenic on the streets is more likely to be the victim than the perpetrator of violent crime.

The government took no notice of the figures and bowed to popular pressure to incarcerate before it could incriminate. Margaret Clayton, the former chairwoman of the Mental Health Act Commission, scented a double standard. 'If you talk to any chief constable, they will tell you that they could pick out the serious criminals on their patch. But if they are not allowed to pick up known criminals without the evidence to convict, why should we allow it for the mentally disordered?' Clayton was too hasty. Pre-crime policing is spreading out across the system.

After the Soham* case, the press lambasted Humberside Police for its failure to rigorously examine the allegations of rape and underage sex against Ian Huntley and to warn the teachers at Soham Village College that he was a man of suspicious character. Every commentator took it as a given that accusations of child abuse were the same as convictions for child abuse. In future, if police forces do their jobs properly, the Criminal Records Bureau will provide employers with 'soft intelligence' on applicants seeking to work with children – rumours, accusations that never led to a conviction, and suspicions.

The use of innuendo to destroy careers does not provoke disapproval because of the disgraceful history of child victims

---

* The murder of two ten-year-old girls, Holly Wells and Jessica Chapman, by Ian Huntley, the caretaker at their school in Soham, Cambridgeshire, in 2002. As was the pattern with other recent high-profile murders, the media pushed the laws of contempt of court to the limit. I am not saying it was wrong – juries don't always need the protection they are offered and the Americans get by even though their media can report what it wants. The reporting of Soham was, however, another example of the spread of pre-judgement. Editors no longer worried about prejudicing juries by implying guilt before conviction, and the law officers no longer used the threat of contempt actions to make them worry.

having their stories ignored by the authorities that were meant to protect them. But as the pendulum swings the other way, honest people are being denied a career in teaching or social work because of unsubstantiated and malicious rumours.

A glimpse of the scale of unproven accusations was provided by the NAS/UWT teachers' union. It said that between 1991 and October 2003, there were 1378 completed investigations into accusations that its members had committed criminal abuses. Of these, 196 enquiries went to court, and a mere sixty-nine produced a conviction. The NAS/UWT is one teachers' union among several and, obviously, does not represent the hundreds of thousands working with children outside education. Its figures must be regarded as the top of the tip of the iceberg.

Those who argue that we shouldn't break old legal principles in the name of protecting the young are out of step with the spirit of our time. Of every 1000 live births in 1900, 144 children died before the age of one. Everybody, including the rich, was likely to have direct or indirect experience of the loss of a child. By 2000, the death rate had fallen to six per 1000. Now a child's death is an event that is almost unimaginable. Far from nurturing tolerance, wealthy and safe societies are ragingly intolerant of unexpected loss and suffering, and it isn't only alleged paedophiles who are having fair hearings prejudiced as a result.

As average life expectancy increases and national wealth grows, experience of untimely death diminishes. The state no longer seems authoritarian when it acts on a precautionary principle and promises to anticipate unexpected harm, and intervene before it occurs. Previous generations would never have accepted the 2003 Criminal Justice Act; they would have said it allowed the prejudicing of juries to such an extent that it risked rigging trials. Human nature being what it is, most jurors would be far more likely to convict defendants if they were told of their past crimes.

In the past, the judiciary hid previous convictions from juries except in exceptional circumstances: when the defendant falsely claimed to be of good character; or when previous convictions bore a striking similarity to the allegation before the court. After the Act, there was no more of such pettifoggery. The prosecution revealed previous convictions to the jury whether they were relevant or not. Evidence 'which shows or tends to show that [a defendant] has behaved, or is disposed to behave, in a way that, in the opinion of the court, might be viewed with disapproval by a reasonable person' became admissible. The Home Office replaced evidence that a suspect *had* committed a particular crime with evidence that he or she had a general propensity to commit crime. Thus, previous misconduct that did not lead to a conviction and even acquittals will become relevant. And in the rush to prejudgement, the innocent will surely be convicted.

Behind the faith in pre-emptive strikes is the belief that the experts can be trusted. The police know who the villains are, the spies know who the terrorists are and the psychiatrists know who the dangerous lunatics are. They are 'precogs' who can see crimes before they happen.

They aren't and they can't. The government had to postpone its mental health clampdown because the professionals admitted with uncharacteristic frankness that they did not have the faintest idea who might become a murderer. Patients could be holding themselves together until something – the ending of a relationship, the death of a parent, a seemingly trivial slight – pushed them over the edge. Risk assessment is like weather forecasting, the *Lancet* said in 2001, accurate over a few days but useless in the long term. We can tell you what has happened and what is happening, but we cannot say what will happen.

Our yearning for security takes no account of the impossibility of seeing into the future. It cannot accept that when the unhinged recover their senses and old villains go straight the past is no longer a guide. Instead, it demands with increasing rancour to find a way round the hard requirement that a case must be proved beyond reasonable doubt before a suspect can lose his or her liberty; and fails to grasp that when the innocent are convicted, the guilty go free.

'They that can give up essential liberty to obtain a little temporary safety deserve neither liberty nor safety,' wrote Benjamin Franklin in eighteenth-century Pennsylvania. In twenty-first-century Britain, it is better to say that those who trade liberty for safety will end up with neither.

New Statesman, January 2004

Criminal Crackers

IN 1876, CESARE LOMBROSO, an Italian professor of psychiatry, advanced the theory that criminals were born, not made. They were throwbacks to a primitive and barbaric stage in human evolution. Detectives should not worry about the difficult task of collecting reputable evidence. They merely had to order suspects to take off their clothes.

'Stigmata and the inversion of the sex characters in the pelvic organs' announced their guilt, Lombroso explained. 'Ears of unusual size' were always a bad sign. So, perplexingly, were ears that were 'very small or standing out from the head as do those of the chimpanzee'. Murderers had 'prominent jaws'; pickpockets 'long hands and scanty beards'.

Lombroso's anatomical obsessions were part of the explosion of pseudo-science that justified colonialism and the privileges of the wealthy. Conservative theorists argued that no reform of society could help the lower orders and lesser breeds overcome biological destiny. It was a waste of effort to try since God (or Darwin) had made them unreformable. The market for such excuses still flourishes among those rich, white Americans who are comforted by the belief that blacks are condemned by their genes to remain stuck at the poor and criminal end of the bell curve. Lombroso found many admirers. As late as the thirties, judges ordered 'Lombrosian' analyses of defendants' physiques. The courts used their ears as evidence against them.

Criminologists might still cite him if the thirties had not also been his nemesis. Like many of his contemporaries, Lombroso believed the stigmatised should be sterilised so they could not produce new inferior specimens. Hitler put eugenic theory into practice and Lombroso's name disappeared from the conversation of polite psychological circles.

Today's psychologists and psychoanalysts are far nicer. Instead of gabbling about inverted sex characters, they empathise with the sufferings of the victims of 'personality disorders' in a truly caring way. The language may have softened but the intellectual flaw is essentially the same. The ideals of justice are being undermined as effectively now as in the crackpot world of nineteenth-century academic Italy.

CRIME CORRESPONDENTS ARE a conformist bunch. They spend their days talking to detectives, and naturally grow to like their sources and share their exasperation with the many obstacles the legal system puts in their way. Friendship is the greatest corrupter in journalism and detectives are often likable and sympathetic characters. The Dando* case broke the complicity. It disturbed my colleagues on the crime beat more than any prosecution I can remember.

How, they asked, could the jury find Barry George guilty of her murder when the police had no weapon, no witness, no motive and a microscopically small piece of contested forensic evidence?

They should direct the same question elsewhere. The police,

---

* Jill Dando was shot dead outside her home in Fulham in April 1999. She was one of the stars of the BBC of the nineties, a reassuring presence on the screen, who had fronted everything from *Crimewatch* to *Songs of Praise*. Friendly without being pushy, popular without being populist, she was the habitual winner of opinion polls on the person you would most like to go on holiday, or dine, with. On the day of her murder she had been due to present the early evening news. The media is often accused of fermenting panics about crime. It had no need to in this case.

Crown Prosecution Service and trial judge have a duty to stop flimsy evidence reaching a jury. Doubtless Jill Dando's celebrity and the millions that the Met had spent on finding her murderer explain why normal scepticism disappeared. The same press that is now fretting about the integrity of the criminal justice system would have pelted any detective or prosecutor who had stopped the case.

Yet unless they are all brilliant liars, the police and prosecutors' belief that they caught the right man appears genuine. Psychology gave them their self-confidence. When detectives arrested Barry George, the Met handed him over to the shrinks. They found that he was afflicted with six mental abnormalities. He had psychopathic, paranoid, narcissistic, histrionic, somatisation and factitious personality disorders, and a version of autism – Asperger's syndrome – as well. The psychologists told the detectives that his multiple conditions meant that he was self-important, suspicious, malevolent, superficially charming and much, much else besides.

The assessment may be correct – I've no doubt they were trying to do their best – but none of the disorders they found is proof that George killed Jill Dando. The enormous category error is to think that a description of a suspect is evidence that he is a criminal. The possibility that George had a 'concurrent factitious disorder' gets you no farther towards finding out who pulled the trigger than 'ears of unusual size' or a heavy cold.

David Canter, professor of psychology at Liverpool University, wouldn't share all my worries about psychology distracting detectives – he profiles offenders himself. Nevertheless, he is alarmed about the effect on officers' judgements of medical classifications. What would be platitudinous in translation can sound convincing and conclusive to lay ears when put in psychological jargon.

'To say that George was suffering from Asperger's syndrome is very unhelpful and totally unrevealing,' he told me. 'It confuses the issue and has nothing to do with the real evidence.'

The murderer shot Jill Dando in daylight in a suburban street with horrible efficiency. The police, reasonably, believed an experienced assassin killed her. George is certainly a nasty piece of work, and no woman would want the stalker and convicted sex offender living anywhere near her. But he's also a simpleton whose life was all over the place. None of his acquaintances believed he was capable of killing Dando.

Early in the investigation, long before George was the prime suspect, Adrian West, one of Canter's old students, gave the Met a psychological profile of Jill Dando's killer. He told the police that, appearances notwithstanding, the killer might not have been a professional. The crime gave the impression that a cool, ruthless murderer had been at work, but the killer might have been an amateur who got lucky, so to speak.

West may be right, but he cannot be certain. His best guess is still a guess, but it was clutched at in the BBC's special programme on the night of George's conviction. He was a psychologist and his views were worth far more than the hunches of plodding coppers. His status was enough to confound reasonable doubt. George's conviction must be safe.

The hope that the educated outsider can solve a case that baffles the proletarian plods is buried deep in popular culture. It runs from Sherlock Holmes through to Lord Peter Wimsey and Poirot. In an oblique way, it is a yearning for justice, which is rooted in the realistic understanding that detectives are in a bureaucracy which will want to save face and cover its back as much as any other bureaucracy. Independent minds are needed to keep the cops on their toes if the innocent are to escape convenient punishment.

To the commissioning editors of TV drama departments today's brilliant outsiders are psychologists. They come from a different school than the gentlemen amateurs of the past, but they retain the ability to see what bureaucrats cannot. In

Cracker, Robbie Coltrane is a drunk and a gambler, but his vices bring insights the uptight detective can never reach. Sue Johnston in *Waking the Dead* is Coltrane's antithesis: sensible, controlled and calm. But she is also an outsider, a wise mother who can pass on her knowledge to the children working beside her in the incident room.

If drama departments wanted to break away from fantasy and show a realistic depiction of psychological profiling they should occasionally allow Coltrane to fit up an innocent man and Johnston to allow a guilty one to escape. The scandalous Rachel Nickell inquiry was led by Paul Britton, a psychologist who set an undercover policewoman, who posed as a sadistic temptress, on the suspect.* After the bombing of the Atlanta Olympics in 1996, FBI profilers decided the terrorist was a madman looking for an opportunity to pose as a hero. They

---

* Rachel Nickell was murdered on Wimbledon Common in 1992 in front of her toddler son. Britton told a policewoman who worked under the pseudonym 'Lizzie James' to pose as a seductress and extract evidence which would incriminate Colin Stagg, the local loner. 'Lizzie' won Stagg's confidence. She told him how she loved violence, and the tapes of their conversation show him desperately trying to keep up with his strange girlfriend. When 'Lizzie' claimed to enjoy hurting people, Stagg mumbled: 'Please explain, as I live a quiet life. If I have disappointed you, please don't dump me. Nothing like this has happened to me before.' When 'Lizzie' went on to say 'If only you had done the Wimbledon Common murder, if only you had killed her, it would be all right,' Stagg replied: 'I'm terribly sorry, but I haven't.' Still the police tried to prosecute him on the grounds that Stagg matched Britton's psychological profile of the killer. Mr Justice Ognall threw the case out, saying the police were guilty of trying to entrap Stagg with 'deceptive conduct of the grossest kind'. The police and their tame hacks hounded Stagg for years afterwards, nevertheless. Unsurprisingly after what her superiors asked her to do, 'Lizzie James' had a nervous breakdown and sued the Met. Finally, the police intimated in 2006 that Stagg might not have been the killer after all, and paid him £700,000 in compensation. A cold case review team cast its eyes over the DNA evidence and charged a sex offender, who was already in Broadmoor, with Ms Nickell's murder. He confessed in 2008.

told the police to direct their enquiries towards those who had rushed to help the injured. The cops marked down a brave security guard as their prime suspect. They slandered and harassed him for months, and then admitted he had nothing to do with the explosion and that the real offender had escaped. Park Dietz is one of the most quoted forensic psychiatrists in the American press. He believes that there are 3 million psychopaths at large in his country – on top of the 2 million inmates in the free world's largest prison system. Dietz earns a living advising companies how to spot psychopaths on the payroll. In an echo of social Darwinists' fears of the working class, he says that you can tell a psycho by the way he goes 'to the union with grievances'.

Not to be left out, New Labour proposed to abolish the presumption of innocence and allow psychiatrists to decide who is a dangerous antisocial. The Home Office doesn't know that almost a hundred years after Freud, there is no evidence that psychoanalysis or psychology or any of the innumerable varieties of counselling can predict behaviour. The weird must be interned.

The old lazy lie of 1876 remains with us: alleged science is still a substitute for the due process of law.*

Observer, July 2001

---

* After George had spent eight years in prison for the Jill Dando murder, the Court of Appeal agreed to a retrial. His counsel, William Clegg, QC, who had also represented Colin Stagg, told the new jury that 'the only reason that the prosecution say that this is the work of the local loner, the local nutter, the man with these serious psychological problems, is because that is the man they arrested'. The jury acquitted.

Beware of the Flowers

A YOUNG NHS psychiatrist, who blogs under the pseudonym Shiny Happy Person, described how she 'was just taking five minutes out, enjoying the sunshine in the surprisingly pleasant grounds of my new hospital, when the flowerbed spoke to me'.

She went on to reassure her readers,

> No, I'm not neuroleptic-deficient. Other people heard it too. One moment, all was quiet and the next a disembodied voice was bellowing from somewhere in the vicinity of the begonias. Strictly speaking, it wasn't actually addressing me and I know this because it said, 'This is a no-smoking area. Please put your cigarette out. A member of staff has been informed.' I gave up smoking six weeks ago. But, really, how Orwellian is that? The smokers looked understandably alarmed, glanced furtively around and then scarpered. I can't help questioning the wisdom of installing a talking flowerbed to tell people off in the grounds of a psychiatric hospital, of all places.

One of the many difficulties in reporting on the NHS is that doctors cannot speak freely about the idiocies of their managers. Threats of dismissal mean I cannot identify the junior psychiatrist or say where she works. But it is on the record that hospitals have banned smoking and some, such as the University Hospitals Coventry and Warwickshire Trust, have put smoke alarms outdoors to catch patients who nip outside for a quick fag. The makers of a new generation of alarms say their trade doesn't stop with the NHS. They are doing good business with local authorities, drug rehabilitation centres and government departments. Their Cig-Arrete (geddit?) detector provides 'a visual and audible re-enforcement of your commitment to creating a smoke-free environment'.

Sensors pick up the whiff of illicit smoke and a voice cries, 'This is a no-smoking area. Please extinguish your cigarette. A member of staff has been contacted.' Which sounds very like what Shiny Happy Person said she heard. You might think there's nothing wrong with alarms blaring out threats when smoking is the biggest cause of preventable death. But it's not illegal to smoke in hospital grounds – yet – or any other open space. NHS managers are going beyond the law and not thinking about the likely effects on the mentally ill of having flower beds shout at them while they do it.

Wagging fingers and badgering voices are everywhere. During the traditionally quiet days of August, we had example after example of British bureaucrats, grown fat on extra powers and extra funds, using an increasingly audacious authoritarianism to hide their manifold shortcomings. As psychiatric patients were fleeing from talking begonias, the Metropolitan Police threatened to use anti-terrorist legislation against climate-change protesters at Heathrow, even though the demonstrators were not, in fact, terrorists but Greens. A few days earlier, the West Midlands Police and Crown Prosecution Service referred Channel 4 to the media regulator, Ofcom, for exposing Islamists, even though what Channel 4 had said was true and the police in a free country have no business organising sanctions against journalists going about their lawful business.

Meanwhile, the Chief Constable of Cheshire, Peter Fahy, gave the clearest sign yet that boozing was replacing smoking as the vice twenty-first-century busybodies cannot tolerate. He responded to the arrest of four young men for the murder of Garry Newlove by demanding that the government lift the legal age for drinking alcohol to twenty-one. The accused were drunk at the time of the murder, but three of them were under eighteen, so were already drinking illegally. The accusation that they had broken the existing law that he and his officers had failed to enforce in no way deterred Mr Fahy from distracting attention from possible doubts about his competence by demanding a new law which would prevent eighteen- to twenty-one-year-olds having a pint and, indeed, overturning a basic tenet of English law in the process.

'At the moment, you can drink anywhere you like unless the local authority has designated that you can't drink in that area,' he continued. 'I would like to see the emphasis changed and that we say drinking in public is not permitted apart from in those areas where a local authority says, "Yes, in this particular park, this particular location, people can drink."'

It is alarming to realise that a Chief Constable charged with upholding the law has no respect for the 800-year-old Common Law principle that any act which isn't specifically illegal is legal. He and others want to stand it on its head so that all acts are illegal except those the authorities specifically say are legal.

The alternative would have been to promise to break up gangs and remove the licences of pubs and shops that sold to underage drinkers. But that would require hard police work on the part of Fahy and his officers.

The seduction of authoritarianism is that it is easier, much easier, to install screaming smoke detectors than persuade patients to stop smoking, to shoot the messengers rather than investigate totalitarian religion, to stop law-abiding people from drinking or protesting rather than take action against teenage gangs or real terrorists.

The overbearing streak in government is likely to spread. As Labour's public spending splurge ends, we will see a growth in the incentive to lash out grow among institutions, such as the NHS and the police, which need to conceal how much public money they have wasted. I imagine that in their quieter moments, our bureaucrats close their eyes and sink into a daydream. In their imaginary country, there is no need to protest about climate change because the authorities are taking the necessary measures. Sexist, racist and homophobic preachers do not really challenge the foundation of the liberal consensus but are the invention of a sensation-seeking media. People do not smoke and drink for pleasure, but out of an antisocial failure to appreciate their own and society's best interests.

Any assault on freedom becomes justifiable if it will help save their clean-living, conflict-free, multicultural England from those who would destroy it. The shrieking from the flower beds is only going to get louder.

Observer, August 2007

PART 8

Before the Banks Bust

'The 11 years of Labour have been absolutely fantastic for the super-rich. Having a friendly Labour government has almost been better than having a Tory one; it has neutered politicians on the left.'

PHILIP BERESFORD,
compiler of the *Sunday Times* Rich List

The World on Your Doorstep

AN UNDER-APPRECIATED cost of English being the world's business language is the loss of English jobs. It is difficult to imagine anyone other than Germans or Hungarians staffing a call centre for Germany and Hungary, but when half the world speaks English, half the world can handle calls from England. HSBC's announcement that 4000 jobs would go from its centres in Sheffield, Birmingham, Brentwood and Swansea to India and Malaysia made the papers only because it was one of the largest one-off transfers of British jobs overseas. Once the shock had passed, it seemed merely an extreme manifestation of a routine business practice.

BT, Goldman Sachs, Abbey National and Prudential have already sent jobs east. Business pundits predict that 200,000 more will follow soon. In Hyderabad and Bangalore, there are well-educated, English-speaking and, above all, cheap workers who can take over. As HSBC said, hiring them 'is the best – indeed the only – way of increasing productivity and allocating resources'. Optimists tell the British not to worry. In future, we will concentrate on profitable specialist services, while basic clerical and IT work will go to India, manufacturing to China and farming to Africa. The global division of labour sounds appealing until you realise that not everyone in Britain can be a merchant banker, and that in any event the gulf between the poor and the rich world doesn't run between countries but within them.

The head office of HSBC is in the Canary Wharf complex in the old London docklands. It's worth a visit, if you've never been. As you walk towards its shining towers from the slums of the East End, you don't see the old two nations but the new two worlds. For the wealthy, Canary Wharf is a gated work village. There are security guards round every corner and CCTV cameras on every wall. It is as isolated from the main centres of the capital's life – Parliament, the Old Bailey, the West End – as it is from the poverty on the other side of the security barriers. Therefore, and naturally, and of course, the owners of the *Mirror*, *Telegraph* and *Independent* groups decided that this inaccessible complex was the best place in the country to house seven national newspapers.

When I worked on the *Independent*, I hated the place. Short of putting reporters in prison, newspaper owners could not have found a more effective means of cutting them off from the public whose lives we were meant to cover. I won't pretend that all of my colleagues agreed with me, and have no doubt that most of the other 55,000 workers in Canary Wharf's banks and dealing rooms enjoyed being locked in the development. It was at once daring and safe: diverse and uniform. Bankers from every developed country took the lift from their offices to patronise expensive boutiques; restaurants advertised cuisines from all over the world; and wine bars and gyms provided rest and recreation after work. No one could fault the cultural variety on offer, but although I heard many languages, I could pass all of my day and much of my evening without meeting anyone from outside the professional middle class. It was as if a Serbian militia had rampaged through this corner of the East End and cleansed it of the polluted poor.

The illusion lasted until nine or 10 p.m. when the poor world met the rich. Cleaners struggled in from the deck-access council flats of the London beyond the bomb-resistant glass. A minority were white or black British. Most were immigrants from

Eastern Europe or West Africa, the men and women who service London's service industries through the night.

Banks and newspapers maintain their competitiveness by keeping them in drudgery. The logic of the market demands that they must get the lowest price possible by putting cleaning contracts out to tender. Labour is the biggest cost for the cleaning companies. The best way for an operator to win a contract is to keep wages and benefits down.

At HSBC's annual meeting in Canary Wharf on 30 May 2003 an anomalous figure described the social consequences. Telco, an alliance of East End charities, had bought a few shares for Abdul Durrant, a cleaner employed by the company with the contract to keep the bank clean. Most of his colleagues wouldn't dare speak in public for fear of losing their jobs. But Durrant is a brave man. He stood up, ignored the curious stares and addressed Sir John Bond, the executive chairman of HSBC, thus:

> Sir John Bond, distinguished ladies and gentlemen, my name is Abdul Durrant, I work in the same office as the board members, the only difference is I don't operate computers. My function is to operate a mop and bucket. Yes, I am one of the invisible night cleaners. You may be wondering what the hell is a night cleaner doing here: we're supposed to be invisible. Well, I am here on behalf of all the contract staff at HSBC and the families of East London. We receive £5 per hour – a whole £5 per hour! – no pension, and a measly sick pay scheme. In our struggles, our children go to school without adequate lunch. We are unable to provide necessary books for their education. School outings in particular they miss out on. In the end, many of our children prefer a life of crime to being a cleaner … Sir John, we have met before. Will you consider your previous decision not to review the cleaning contract with OCS, so that I and my colleagues receive a living wage?

Durrant, like most of the other cleaners, supplemented his income with work for another cleaning company once his night shift had finished. At the weekends, he drove a cab. He didn't have many days off. The contrast between his circumstances and those of the HSBC directors on the stage was stark, to put it gently. The bank had recently bought Household International, a loan company that lends to 'sub-prime' – or poor, as we used to say – customers at extortionate rates. It persuaded William Aldinger, the head of Household International, to join HSBC with a package of £23 million over three years and the promise of a hefty pay-off if he was fired in the interim.

Sir John lived more frugally on a salary of £1.88 million, and at least had the decency to agree to meet the contract cleaners, and the Telco workers and religious leaders who were trying to help them. Everyone gave him credit for that, but the meeting was a clash of two uncomprehending world views. Accusations of rapacity baffled Sir John. Didn't the voluntary sector applaud his bank for its strong sense of civic and social responsibility? Did it not contribute generously to many deserving causes and charities?

'Sir John,' interrupted Thomas McMahon, the Catholic bishop of Brentwood, 'we don't want charity; we want justice.'

And that Sir John couldn't give. HSBC's profits were $6.88 billion, so the company could afford to raise the cleaners' pay to the £6.50 an hour that Telco and the trade unions calculate is the minimum wage that Londoners need. But the 'world's local bank' could no more make a concession to the drudges who clean up its mess than to the uncompetitive call centre staff in Swansea and Birmingham whose jobs it was shipping east. In the interests of profit maximisation, it must seek the cheapest labour possible, whether in Bangalore or Bethnal Green. Keeping rates down was a point of principle for the board. If workers in Canary Wharf received privileged treatment, Sir

John explained, HSBC workers all over the world would want it – and then where would the bank be?

How much money is needed to stop the poor being poor is a matter of heated debate, although you'd never guess it from the Canary Wharf press. The Reverend Paul Nicolson, an extraordinary figure who could only be an Anglican vicar, has been trying to force Whitehall to accept that the minimum wage and tax credits don't begin to level Britain's mountainous inequality, and that Labour must put more pressure on firms such as HSBC.

Nicolson is the real Vicar of Dibley, in that the BBC filmed the series in his church in the Buckinghamshire village of Turville. But instead of going on about whether his bum looked big in a cassock, Nicolson infuriated Chiltern Tories by refusing to pay the poll tax and arranging holidays in the village for deprived children. He then retired to the inner city and, with undiminished energy, organised a coalition of sixty-five charities, trade unions and churches to demand that everyone enjoys a civilised minimum income. The leaders met the prime minister, and were pleased that he gave them a fair hearing.

Unfortunately, a fair hearing was all they got. All they can do now is gaze at the towers of Canary Wharf, where the windows never open, and the CCTV camera lenses never close, and reflect that the invisible workers who move in at night can't be given a living wage because of the shocking precedent it would set. Keeping them poor is 'the best – indeed the only – way' of doing business.*

Observer, October 2003

---

* Along with other sub-prime banks, HSBC's Household International enticed poor Americans to buy homes with low 'teaser rates', then whacked up the interest payments when it had ensnared them. It repackaged its loans as bonds, and sold them on to gullible investors looking for high returns in an

era of low interest rates. It did not occur to any of the masters of the universe involved anywhere down the line that the reason why sub-prime customers were sub-prime was that they would not be able to afford to meet their mortgage payments when rates rose. Rates duly rose. The borrowers duly defaulted. Their houses duly flooded the US housing market, which duly crashed, thus making the banks' collateral worth less than the loans they had so rashly granted. In February 2007 HSBC announced that it would not be able to meet its profit forecast for the first time in its 142-year history, and was writing down $10.6 billion of sub-prime debt. By November 2007, the world's banking system was facing its worst crisis since the thirties. HSBC told its shareholders it had wasted yet more of their money and was writing down another $3.4 billion of debt. Still, at least its executives could boast that they had earned their seven-figure salaries by standing firm against cleaners' demands that the shareholders pay them £6.50 an hour, and that was the main thing.

Casino Capitalism

IT WAS COMMONPLACE to say in the twentieth century that the Labour Party owed more to Methodism than to Marxism. In the twenty-first, it will owe nothing to either. The Nonconformist tradition contained much hypocrisy, but among its virtues was an abhorrence of gambling. The fleecing of gullible punters was a great evil to the reformers of late-Georgian Britain, particularly when governments took a cut of the profits. In 1807, after his first parliamentary success in the fight to end slavery, William Wilberforce turned to his fellow evangelical Henry Thornton.

'Well, Henry, what shall we abolish next?' he asked.

'The lottery, I think,' Thornton replied.

These were not frivolous men and Thornton was not joking. By the 1820s, Christian protests had done for the lotteries.

Whatever you think about religious objections to gambling – it encourages the worship of money and persuades people to place their faith in chance rather than God – on one point atheist and believer must agree: there are few means more efficient for redistributing wealth from the poor to the rich. The connection Wilberforce made between gambling and slavery wasn't entirely incredible: slavery is the giving of labour for nothing; on most occasions gambling is the giving of money for nothing. Opposition to the exploitation of credulity united Methodist and Marxist.

No longer. The descendants of the worshippers at chapel and kirk have rebelled against their pious ancestors by reviving the taxation policies of the Georgian oligarchy. Labour kept the lottery John Major revived and is using it to fund the pleasures of its civilised supporters – the Royal Opera House, the art theatres showing unpopular plays – and to pay for the training of Olympic athletes whose success delights the masses. Meanwhile the party is planning to go farther than the Tories by reviving the casino industry and turning it into an instrument of urban renewal and an essential source of income to a Chancellor who would rather milk the foolish than tax the rich.

In the coming weeks, Tessa Jowell, the culture minister, will be considering responses to her White Paper on the 'modernisation' of casinos. It is her misfortune to be stuck with the public image of a nannying prig. Her friends say the charge is the baseless creation of upper-class Tories, whose prejudices against strong women were formed when their heartless mummies abandoned them to the care of sadistic servants. In this, Jowell's defenders are surely right. There is nothing nannyish about her views on gambling. She is its most permissive champion in Labour history.

The tributes to the late Roy Jenkins's reform of the laws on homosexuality and abortion gave the impression that the 1964–70 Labour government created the swinging sixties. But Jenkins's liberalism had its limits and he cracked down hard on gambling. His Gaming Act of 1968 slashed the number of casinos in Britain from roughly one thousand to about a hundred. He assumed that gambling and the Mob went together. The *Sunday Telegraph* confirmed his suspicions by reporting that London casino managers had flown to meet Meyer Lansky and other Mafia bosses in Miami to lament the damage Labour had done to their joint ventures in the West End.

Little changed over the next thirty years. In 1995, the Gaming Board for Great Britain was repeating received wisdom when it warned that a relaxation of restrictions would encourage gangsterism because casinos allow organised crime to launder stolen money. When New Labour came to power in 1997, George Howarth, then a junior Home Office minister, said he was happy to keep the 1968 Act as it was. Continued regulation of the sacred market was, however, too much for Howarth's boss, Jack Straw, who asked Sir Alan Budd to report on the gaming laws.

Budd was a telling choice. As a Treasury civil servant in the seventies, he was one of the loudest proponents of monetarism. When the Thatcher government implemented his theories, manufacturing industry was devastated and unemployment rose to 3 million. In an interview with the BBC in 1990, Budd admitted to a bad conscience about all the wasted lives. He had a recurrent 'nightmare' that many of Margaret Thatcher's ministers

> never believed for a moment that [monetarism] was the correct way to bring down inflation. They did however see that this would be a very good way to raise unemployment. And raising unemployment was an extremely desirable way of reducing the strength of the working classes. What was engineered – in Marxist terms – was a crisis of capitalism which re-created the reserve army of labour, and has allowed the capitalist to make high profits ever since.

For all his belated misgivings, guilt has not paralysed Budd. He has found a new way to hit the incomes of the lowly. With the working class back in work, he wants nearly all restraints on the gambling conglomerates removed.

There must be a twenty-four-hour delay between applying for and receiving membership of a gambling club at present. It is a slight protection against criminal infiltration of casinos because clubs demand proof of identity. It also allows a cooling-off period so that novice gamblers cannot stagger in drunk and throw their money around. Budd said that everyone over eighteen should be able to gamble in a casino straight away. Once on the gaming floor, nothing should prevent them gambling, even when drunk. Casinos should be free to keep them that way by serving them alcohol because current restrictions on the sale of booze were a restraint of trade. Befuddled losers will be able to run up ever higher losses because Budd wants the prohibition on casinos accepting credit cards lifted as well.

If casinos aren't to your taste, Budd has an alternative. At present, fruit-machine owners must limit jackpots to £10. Budd wants the ceiling abolished. In future, you may have to get used to watching dead-eyed dupes robotically feeding money into machines as they chase the faint chance of a big win. (Perhaps they won't be using coins. Sir Alan also wants fruit-machine manufacturers to be free to install slots for credit cards.)

In theory, Jowell is carefully considering the public responses to the White Paper that Budd's findings inspired. In truth, she has made up her mind. Where she can deregulate without parliamentary approval, she has already done so. She has agreed to allow the sale of alcohol on gaming floors and rejected the one tightening of the gaming laws even Budd said was essential. Britain is the only country in Europe that allows children to gamble on fruit machines in cafés and fast-food joints. Budd said there was no excuse for picking the pockets of the young, but Jowell dismissed his concerns. It is a strange nanny who lets her charges waste their pocket money on one-armed bandits, but then these children's parents cannot afford hired help.

As ever when this government meets a well-financed vested interest, there's a ripe smell in the air. The big casinos' campaign was led by the Gambling Consultancy Ltd, run by the son of a Labour peer who told the *Guardian* that he had got to know

Labour ministers through his father, whom, incidentally, he keeps on a Gambling Consultancy retainer.

Perhaps Jowell's critics run the risk of making too much of their lobbying and seeming nannyish themselves. Everyone likes a flutter, after all, and who but killjoys want to stop a bit of fun? The best response comes from dissenting voices within the gambling industry. They are as worried as the most fervent churchgoers. Brian Lemon is general secretary of the Casino Operators Association, which represents the few clubs that are not under the control of the gambling conglomerates. He said his members were 'vehemently against permitting alcohol on the gaming floor'. He accused the government and the new, business-friendly Gaming Board of 'abrogating their social responsibility'. Lady Littler, chairwoman of the Gaming Board from 1992 to 1998, warned Jowell about gambling debts being added to the public's enormous credit-card arrears. 'Many individuals and their families are tempted by easy access to credit, cannot manage their finances and juggle between credit cards,' she said in a memo to the minister. 'Some cards are issued irresponsibly; some have no limits.'

The nannying that most people resent is the excessive duties on alcohol and tobacco. There has been no public demand to make gambling easier because it is already easy enough to gamble. Bookies are everywhere and spread-betting is flourishing. British casinos cash £3.5 billion worth of chips a year. According to the Gaming Board, no other capital city in the world has as many casinos as London. The Gaming Act 1968 struck a sensible compromise between prohibition and permissiveness that anyone who wants to tackle the epidemic of theft and murder caused by the prohibition of drugs should look to as a model.

Officially, the government wanted to replace it because the growth of Internet betting is taking tax revenues offshore. This does indeed threaten the bookies and the public purse, but no one in the gaming industry believes that casinos will be hit. Brian Lemon said the government had capitulated before commercial pressure. David Beeton, director general of the British Casino Association, which represents the gambling conglomerates, couldn't believe his luck: 'It has come as quite a shock to see how radical the changes might be.' Even the government has given up on the pretence that it is protecting a threatened industry from technological change. It now sees gambling as a source of new revenue for the Treasury. Jowell seems certain to remove the controls that keep casinos in city centres. Soon they will be everywhere. Northern Labour MPs boast that their ministers will revive Blackpool by allowing Trevor Hemmings, a Channel Islands tax exile, to build Pharaoh's Palace – a £130 million casino with 3000 slot machines. Becoming rich by making others poor is a sunrise industry in the new century.

There's a fair chance that Britain will end up like Australia. As controls on fruit machines were lifted, the share of Australians' disposable income thrown away on 'pokies' grew from 1.8 per cent in 1990 to 3.6 per cent in 2000. Australians lose about £5 billion each year by gambling – £350 for every adult or twice as much as the government spends on universities. Church groups have monitored the divorces, bankruptcies and suicides that have followed. But state governments cannot respond to their concerns because they are dependent on gambling taxes – New South Wales gets 10 per cent of its revenue from taxes on pokie players. If they clean up gambling, how will they make up that shortfall?

The British government is almost as needy. The long decline in sales of Lottery tickets should be reason for rejoicing. Our fellow citizens are finally realising it is not worth wasting money on a game where the chances of hitting the jackpot are 14 million to one.

To Jowell, however, the sight of the elderly, the careworn and the poor spending their money wisely is a calamity. She warned

Camelot that New Labour would break with all its principles and nationalise the Lottery if it did not find more effective ways to extract money.

As for William Wilberforce, the memory of his campaign against governments going into the gambling racket is forgotten everywhere except in his native East Yorkshire. Hull City Council announced last year that his papers and portraits will be housed in a new archive that will honour the region's greatest sons and daughters. The money for the museum will come, inevitably, from the Lottery.*

New Statesman, January 2003

---

* A rare uniting of protestors from left and right stopped the introduction of super-casinos, but the victory was more apparent than real. Labour introduced 'regional' casinos, which were far bigger than anything seen before, and allowed deregulated bookmakers to become mini-casinos.

Natural-Born Billers

AFTER TWO DECADES of working for large and small management consultancies, David Craig had seen every variety of
human greed. The director of an international consulting firm
gave him one that, try as he might, he could never shake from
his mind. The director boasted about how much time he spent
in brothels at his clients' expense. He was not a man entirely
without principle and explained, 'Good sex means inflicting
pain and you wouldn't want to do that to someone you loved.'
I'm sure his wife was grateful to him for thinking of her.

A few years before, Craig helped sell a project to a
health authority that involved bringing over two consultants
from America, even though there were plenty of people in
Britain who would have done the job just as well. In addition to
their fees, the NHS agreed to pay for their food, the rent on their
flats in Hampstead and Kensington, the cost of hotel rooms
when they were out of town, their children's private schools,
taxis to take their wives to and from teas at the Ritz and train
fares to take the husbands to and from their wives at the
weekends. Only when the consultants hired a private plane to
bring them back from a holiday did the NHS find the nerve to
object.

Whether the receipts they submitted were as straightforward
as they appeared was another matter. Consultancies are bulk
buyers that can demand discounts of about 40 per cent from

airlines and hotel chains. Last year, PricewaterhouseCoopers paid $54.5 million to settle a case brought by American retailers who said that the consultancy firm's rebates from travel and credit card companies weren't passed on to them. PwC said if it had not taken the money, its bills would have been higher.

When Craig was working for another firm, he received a memo from a colleague that read: 'Here's how we do it every time. We bill them for your air-travel expense. Then we get a kickback on your air ticket. But we don't give the client the kickback.'

Over-billing – fraud, to put it crudely – was commonplace. Craig worked in the London office of an international firm that charged clients for the equivalent of 300 support staff, when in reality a mere fifty were in the building. He concluded that for all the jargon it spouted to clients, the enterprise was 'dedicated to the noble cause of further enriching consultancy directors'. Further riches flowed from charging clients for time spent looking for new business elsewhere, or time spent on the consultancy's own business, or time spent on the golf course.

And very rich the billers have become in the process. The management consultancy game is worth £60 billion. Craig began consulting straight out of university with expert knowledge of nothing apart from romantic poetry. A graduate who does the same today costs the client £7000 a week. Directors are multimillionaires who do not get out bed for less than £25k.

Craig had enough of it and spilled the bean-counters' beans in *Rip-Off! The Scandalous Inside Story of the Management Consulting Money Machine*. For once, the usually overheated marketing pitch that this was a book they didn't want you to read was true. He published it himself because business book publishers wouldn't go near him for fear of offending the industry.

Craig once wrote satirical novels and there is a gruesome relish in his descriptions of how consultants get their claws into companies. More pertinently he answers a question that baffles employees and shareholders alike: why do managers let consultants get away with it? Many executives are over-promoted plodders who have become corporate fashion victims, Craig replies. They fall for the consultants' jargon because they are 'fad-surfers riding the crest of the latest management wave and then paddling out again just in time to ride the next one'.

For a long time, Craig was not troubled by the scams he saw. When a big company threw money at consultants, who was hurt? He changed his mind only when he returned home after years of living abroad, and saw what had happened to British government. For the first time in years, the cynical Mr Craig was shaken.

He accepts that managers can get good work from consultants if they hire them to run a tightly defined project. And of course not all consultants are greedy charlatans. But in general, the old rule applies: a manager who needs to hire a management consultant shouldn't be a manager. New Labour's managers have hired thousands of them. They have put David Bennett, a former McKinsey partner, in charge of the Downing Street policy unit, where he works alongside John Birt, the former director general of the BBC, who gave tens of millions to management consultants, who promised they could create an efficient internal market. Predictably, administration costs ballooned – up by £140 million – while staff numbers were cut. Birt moved on to McKinsey and provided 'blue-skies thinking' for Tony Blair as a sideline.

I remember the young Alan Milburn lashing the Tories for allowing management consultants to 'cash in' when Labour was in opposition. In 1994, when he delivered his fiery polemics, the Conservatives were giving consultants £500 million a year. In 2004, New Labour handed over £1.9 billion. I think I know why Blair did it. In his first term, the battle to 'reform' public services left 'scars on his back'. His second was dominated by al-Qaeda and Saddam Hussein. He turned to the consultants to deliver quick fixes.

If you have any feelings of sympathy, I would beg you to stamp on them at once. His impatience was understandable but he ought to have known better. Every politically aware person has had ample time to learn that consultants have been a disaster for the civil service. Repeatedly, they have advised ministers to spend on new IT systems for the Immigration and Nationality Department, the Passport Office and the Probation Service, which came in late and over budget, if, that is, they came in at all. The benefit card payment system was scrapped after about £700 million had been squandered, the Child Support Agency (CSA) wasted £450 million on a system that did not work, while the program the consultants promised would allow doctors to book hospital places for their patients managed to make sixty-three appointments in 2004 – against a target of 205,000 – but still cost £200 million. Current estimates suggest that NHS computerisation may cost £30 billion, five times its original projected cost. The oncoming car crash of the national ID card data bank promises to see £6 billion or £10 billion or £15 billion pounds lost in the wreckage, depending on which outside authority you believe.

Craig is fascinating on why the public has lost so much money. Civil servants are used to dealing with each other, he argues. Whatever interdepartmental rivalries they have, they assume that the people they meet have the country's best interests at heart. They are not prepared for negotiations with consultants whose guiding principle is often how to hit the client for as much money as possible. They do not understand a world where the acronym Afab – 'Anything for a buck' – is thrown around with sniggering nonchalance. Even those who have learned the score after hard-won experience can't use their knowledge because the line from Downing Street is that they must take private-sector advice.

Afab explains the computer scandals. The government could and should have rented proven technology from other governments or companies that had tried it out and dealt with the teething problems. But there were far more billable hours for the consultants if Whitehall reinvented the wheel every time a new system was needed.

When the immigration computers failed, asylum seekers were left to rot in penury and racial tension rose. If the NHS IT project fails, patients will die. As Craig says, this isn't a game any more. If I were Sir Gus O'Donnell or Gordon Brown or, indeed, Tony Blair, I would read this book and then invite Craig into Whitehall to reveal the many and ingenious ways in which the taxpayers have been compelled to provide welfare for the wealthy.

Observer, June 2005

The Roc's Egg of Great Ladies' Assemblies

IN Charles Dickens's *Little Dorrit*, the high society of Victorian London executes a smart U-turn after Mr Merdle, a banker whose money and hospitality they have enjoyed, commits suicide.

Numbers of men in every profession and trade would be blighted by his insolvency; old people who had been in easy circumstances all their lives would have no place of repentance for their trust in him but the workhouse; legions of women and children would have their whole future desolated by the hand of this mighty scoundrel. Every partaker of his magnificent feasts would be seen to have been a sharer in the plunder of innumerable homes; every servile worshipper of riches who had helped to set him on his pedestal, would have done better to worship the Devil point-blank. So, the talk, lashed louder and higher by confirmation on confirmation, and by edition after edition of the evening papers, swelled into such a roar when night came, as might have brought one to believe that a solitary watcher on the gallery above the Dome of St Paul's would have perceived the night air to be laden with a heavy muttering of the name of Merdle, coupled with every form of execration.

For by that time it was known that the late Mr Merdle's complaint had been simply Forgery and Robbery. He, the uncouth object of such wide-spread adulation, the sitter at great men's feasts, the roc's egg of great ladies' assemblies, the subduer of exclusiveness, the leveller of pride, the patron of patrons, the bargain-driver with a Minister for Lordships of the Circumlocution Office, the recipient of more acknowledgment within some ten or fifteen years, at most, than had been bestowed in England upon all peaceful public benefactors, and upon all the leaders of all the Arts and Sciences, with all their works to testify for them, during two centuries at least – he, the shining wonder, the new constellation to be followed by the wise men bringing gifts, until it stopped over a certain carrion at the bottom of a bath and disappeared – was simply the greatest Forger and the greatest Thief that ever cheated the gallows.

A bit strong maybe – and, of course, the authorities have yet to convict him – but what passes for London society in our day is already forgetting that it ever knew Conrad Black and Barbara Amiel.

If the Devil had cast his net, he could not have hauled in a choicer catch than the crowd that used to gather around them. There were the editors of the *Telegraph, Sunday Telegraph* and *Spectator* showing a prudent respect for their owner's many opinions; there on the board of Black's Hollinger International were Henry Kissinger and Richard Perle; there at his summer parties in Kensington were Princes Andrew and Michael, Elle Macpherson, Joan Collins and every manner of celebrity from A- to Z-list, until, finally, bringing up the rear, was David Blunkett, a Labour politician so enamoured of the Tory press he fell in love with one of its publishers.

Now liberals would need bleeding hearts of stone not to burst out laughing as the deference collapses. The treachery of his friends is worthy of a Molière or a Dickens. Where are the Boris Johnsons and the David Blunketts now that their host is on his uppers?

Although it pains me to say it, Black was not a bad historian, for all his pomposity. He is now learning the old lesson that when great newspapers slip from the hands of a press baron, those who appeared to venerate his every word turn out to have always been more concerned with the contents of his wallet than of his mind. There never was a falser cliché than 'loyalty is the Tory party's secret weapon'. The silence of Black's friends has deepened in inverse proportion to the seriousness of the allegations against him. Nobody knows him when he is down and out, and I mean nobody. According to the *Mail*, his second wife is showing signs of wondering whether it is worth standing by her fourth husband.*

I do not want to spoil the merriment, but the joke is as much on us as him. Although we do not have Dickens's Minister for Lordships of the Circumlocution Office, we do not have a democratic parliament either. The House of Lords is as open to cronyism and corruption as it was 150 years ago.

Tom Bower, Black's hostile biographer, got his target just right when he said of Black's gruelling dinner party monologues, 'While most hosts expected guests to sing for their supper, Conrad Black expected his to listen for theirs.'† None the less, Black could be pithy when he wanted to advance his interests. After gaining control of the *Telegraph* newspaper group in 1986 with some deft financial manoeuvres, he decided that a foreign press baron just off the plane from Toronto was entitled to have a seat in the British parliament without going

---

* To be fair to her, she did what many of her former friends did not have the strength of character to do and stood by Black when a Chicago court sent him to prison. Like many formerly rich and beautiful women who fall on hard times, she was the subject of relentless mockery, but in retrospect, she came out better than I expected from the affair.

† Bryan Appleyard of the *Sunday Times* recalls: 'I met the man three times and never found him anything less than weird. On each occasion he had some specific agenda – porn, opera and how well the French speak French (*really*) – which he pursued irrespective of what anybody else said … Frankly, if he had not been proprietor of the *Telegraph* at the time, I would have whacked him.'

through the indignity of standing for election. Happily for him, Britain is the only country in the world to reserve places in its second chamber for wealthy men who know which strings to pull and backs to scratch. Black phoned Charles Powell, Margaret Thatcher's confidant, and for once in his life decided to be concise. 'What does one have to do get a peerage?' he demanded.

Powell did not reply. Such blunt conversations are not an accepted part of the British Establishment's way of doing business. If Black could have persuaded him to speak frankly, I suspect the candid answer would have been either become a political donor or buy a newspaper and make it as partisan as you dare. Many peers meet the first criterion. In 1993, the admirable diggers at Labour Research calculated that the odds that the Conservatives were not selling peerages were almost infinitely long. They found that executives from the 6.2 per cent of British companies which had given money to the Tories between 1979 and 1992 received 50 per cent of peerages and knighthoods for 'services to industry'. The *Guardian* said that the chance of the correlation being a coincidence was one in ten to the power of 133.

New Labour replaced the Tories and in July 2006 the admirable diggers at the Conservative think tank the Bow Group did to New Labour what the trade unionists at Labour Research had done to the old Tories. 'Statistical analysis shows that 58.54 per cent of all donors giving more than £50,000 to the Labour party receive an honour,' they reported. 'This compares with just 0.035 per cent of non-donors. Large Labour donors are 1,657 times more likely to receive an honour than a non-donor and 6,969 times more likely to receive a peerage. It is almost impossible to avoid the conclusion that the Labour party has been selling honours, including places in the House of Lords.'

As the owner of a Conservative newspaper, Black did not need to empty his bank account. His journalists' support for the party guaranteed that its leaders would lobby to have him sent to the Lords. Shortly after his arrival in Britain, Black told one of his editors that 'the deferences and preferments that this culture bestows upon the owners of great newspapers are satisfying. I mean, I tend to think that they're slightly exaggerated at times, but as the beneficiary – a beneficiary – of that system, it would certainly be hypocrisy for me to complain about it.'

His words were a sickeningly accurate description of the survival of old corruption into the twenty-first century.

He is heading for a Chicago courtroom now, but the selling of seats in Parliament for cash or influence will not die with him. Nor will his disgrace end the warm greetings extended to obvious fraudsters. In the coming months, we are likely to hear from many a freeloading celebrity and Tory politician on how they have been shocked – *shocked!* – by the allegations against Black. Yet it has long been apparent that a visit from the police was on the cards. You did not have to be able to hack into Hollinger's computers to guess that there were 'difficulties'.

Sensible investors on Wall Street and the City had steered clear for years. They had been burnt when Black used inside information to sell shares at the top of the market and were not about to repeat the experience. But their suspicions were forgotten and no one in their circle found it odd that Black and Amiel were living like royalty on the supposed salaries and dividends of a 'business empire' which was not particularly large or profitable when you looked at it closely.

But who around them wanted to look? In *My Name Is Legion*, his novel set in the newspaper industry, A. N. Wilson has the beautiful wife of a monstrous proprietor reflect that people do not scrutinise too closely when money is flowing and jobs are up for grabs. 'No one knew how to check details,' she concludes as she passes off a phoney account of her past. 'This was one of the first lessons Martina had learned when she made the career switch and became a journalist.'

They are checking now. The press has concentrated on stories of investigators into Hollinger discovering that Black and Amiel had billed the company for every penny they could; from £2–£3 million a year for an executive jet to £40 for Amiel's jogging suit. (A petty swindle, if true, by the way, which offers further proof that no one is as tight-fisted as the rich.)

The accounts of expenses fiddles miss a darker picture. The investigators describe how Hollinger became a machine to enrich Black and his associates. 'Behind a constant stream of bombast regarding their accomplishments as self-described proprietors, Black and Radler [his sidekick] made it their business to line their pockets at the expense of Hollinger almost every day, in almost every way they could devise.'

They calculated that Black and Radler received the equivalent of 92.5 per cent of Hollinger's adjusted net income from 1997 to 2002. They sold newspapers, not because the sale benefited the company, but because it offered opportunities for Black and his accomplices to 'divert tens of millions in sales proceeds to themselves'. There were 'massive conflicts of interest', as Black presided over a 'kleptocracy' that 'looted' shareholders unlucky enough to be outside the magic circle.

Black denies everything. But if half of what the investigators allege is true, then Hollinger will join Mirror Group Newspapers, BCCI, Enron and WorldCom and be one of those companies which weren't companies at all but criminal conspiracies. All the usual signs are there: the overbearing boss; the compliant board; and the useless auditors, who are more concerned with flattering the executives who pay their fees than with blowing the whistle.

If a quarter of what the investigators allege is true, then Black may be heading for a prison sentence which will encourage childish journalists to dig out the editorial in Black's *Sunday Telegraph* which denounced the Church of England's bishops for fearing 'the wrath of *bien pensants* more than the wrath of

God' – a failure seen at its most acute when they refused to hold criminals morally responsible for their crimes.*

Observer, September 2004

* The Chicago jury found that about a quarter of what the investigators alleged was indeed true. In July 2007 it convicted him of three counts of mail and wire fraud and one count of obstruction of justice and acquitted him of nine other charges, including wire fraud and racketeering. The judge sent him down for six years.

Primal Screams and Broken Dreams

BBC4 HAS HAD THE bright idea of running a series on the lost world of the seventies left. It has produced films on radical feminists, who did change the world although not in the way they intended, and told the story of one of the many disastrous attempts to create a socialist newspaper, which are always a laugh riot. Both appeal to connoisseurs of leftery, but the first documentary, *Property Is Theft*, by Vanessa Engle, should be watched by everyone. It describes how, just thirty years ago, tens of thousands of people could live independently of the state in British cities for next to nothing. That time, and that possibility, feels as remote today as Anglo-Saxon Wessex.

The now-forgotten squatters' movement began in the mid-sixties. Jim Radford, a former merchant navy seaman, led homeless families into houses abandoned either because the fascist movement in Germany had dropped bombs on them or because the modern movement in architecture had scheduled them for demolition. Radford spotted that the law was on the side of the squatters once they were in. Councils and developers could evict them eventually, but it took a hard struggle. After the disastrous slum clearance programme of the sixties collapsed, many landlords just threw up their hands and let the squatters stay.

By the time Engle takes up the story, in 1974, there were 30,000 squatters in London. She concentrates on one street,

Villa Road in Brixton, just south of the Thames. Lambeth Council had planned to knock down its Victorian terraces and build yet more tower blocks, but the money had run out and so had public patience with brutal high-density housing. Villa Road's terraces stood vacant, and young white radicals, nearly all of them Oxbridge graduates, took them over.

They were clear from the start that they would use the privilege of rent-free accommodation to organise a revolution. It is touching to hear them looking back. '"Dialectical materialism" and "historical materialism" were phrases which tripped off the tongue,' said one. 'We actually thought that we could produce a revolution and increase the power of working people,' said another.

The proletariat was mystified. A working-class girl who hung around the fringes of the squats said she could barely understand the conversation of her superiors. 'It was all Marx, Marx, blah, blah.'

The broadcasters do not tackle the dark side of the Marxists of the '68 generation, and treat the far left with a lenience you rarely see them extending to the far right. Engle mentions that the Workers' Revolutionary Party hung around Villa Road, but does not add that it was a cult organised to worship Gerry Healy, a paranoid bully and rapist who took Saddam Hussein's shilling. Most of the squatters belonged to the International Socialists, and, again, she does not mention that if its Trotskyists had come to power, they would have established a tyranny.

She compensates, however, by showing that when you do not have to worry about the mortgage, revolution is not the only game you can play. The therapeutic obsessions of the 1968 generation had a greater effect in the end than its dialectical materialism, and the conflict between the personal and the political divided Villa Road as surely as it divided the rest of the countercultural movement. All the squatters agreed that the nuclear family was an instrument of oppression. In theory, they believed in free love, but with sex, as with Marx, theory did not translate into practice. The radicals found it was no easy task to free themselves from conventional emotions. Thirty years on, women still talked to Engle with bitterness about rivals who stole their boyfriends – and then refused to do a fair share of the communal cooking and washing up to boot.

Pete Cooper, now a folk singer, recalled that boy could not just meet girl and get on with it. Boy and girl first had to explain themselves to the commune. 'It was agonising,' he said. 'You had to explore the feelings you had and the emotional and sexual pressures on you with the group before you did the deed.'

His long face and weary voice make virginity sound a welcome alternative.

Against the tyrannical ideas of Lenin and Trotsky, the supporters of alternative therapy pitted the equally strange theories of Arthur Janov, a Californian psychotherapist who believed you could recover buried memories of traumas suffered in the womb by taking off your clothes and shrieking at the top of your voice. Once you had released the foetal pain, your troubles would pass, he claimed. Janov's ideas rapidly fell out of favour. One critic from the mid-seventies described primal therapy as 'trendy, simplistic, glib, and potentially very dangerous'. Others deplored its manipulativeness and warned that patients who went through three weeks of intensive counselling, and then joined groups of the converted in consciousness-raising sessions, were allowing therapists to subject them to isolation and suggestion – the archetypal techniques of a brainwasher.

For a few years, however, primal therapy was fashionable – John Lennon and Yoko Ono dabbled, inevitably – and in Brixton, tension grew between the therapists seeking personal liberation, and the Trotsykists seeking political revolution. The best-looking women were in the primal screamers' commune and they had artful ways of diverting comrades from the task of overthrowing the state. Anne Janowitz, now professor of

Romantic poetry at Queen Mary, University of London, alleged that 'the primal screamers sent vixens out on to the street to seduce the handsome boys on the left and got them to scream rather than agitate'.

How disgraceful, but New Age ideas that began in obscure corners of rent-free London have spread everywhere. I have no time for them, but perhaps I am prejudiced. Plenty of people find them a help. I have no time either for the hysterical conspiracy theories or the contempt for democracy of the 1968 Marxists, but again I cannot deny they went on to infect the wider left. In any case, not only bellowing Trots and screaming vixens benefited from cheap housing.

IN 2001 MARTIN AMIS published *The War against Cliché*, a collection of his literary journalism. In the introduction, he says he can barely recognise the younger self who produced the reviews from the early seventies. Literary criticism had domi-nated his life. Getting an argument right for the *Times Literary Supplement* meant everything. His friend Clive James said, 'While literary criticism is not essential to literature, both are essential to civilisation,' and Amis agreed. 'I read it all the time, in the tub, on the Tube; I always had about me my Edmund Wilson – or my William Empson. I took it seriously. We all did. We hung around the place talking about literary criticism. We sat in pubs and coffee bars talking about W. K. Wimsatt and G. Wilson Knight, and Richard Hoggart and Northrop Frye ...'

His world collapsed in 1973. Criticism became the province of obscurantist academics without the talent or inclination to address the public that was paying their wages. From then on, no one trying to make a living as a critic could manage without a private income or a remunerative day job. Amis concluded that a four-letter word killed literary London: Opec. 'In the 1960s, you could live on ten shillings a week: you slept on people's floors and sponged off your friends and sang for your supper – about literary criticism. Then, abruptly, breakfast alone cost ten shillings. The oil hike, inflation and stagflation revealed literary criticism as one of those leisure-class fripperies we would have to get along without.'

Just so. Without cheap shelter, all kinds of ways of living become luxuries. A report in 2004 for Gordon Brown by Kate Barker of the Bank of England's Monetary Policy Committee gave a statistical foundation to Amis's lament. Since 1974, the real prices of British houses had increased at a little over twice the rate of the European average. Periodic property market crashes had not slowed the trend. Each fall stopped on a plateau higher than its predecessor.

Millions are suffering as a result. The Treasury naturally worries about the unemployed who can't afford to pay the rents in the towns and cities where there are job vacancies. But the consequences go far beyond the economics of labour mobility. A great welter of misery and frustration lies behind Barker's figures. Grown-up children are forced to live with their parents; women are forced to put off pregnancy until they can afford the space for children they may, by then, be too old to bear; gifted people abandon their ambitions and take a second-best career to pay for a roof over their heads.

In a dismal echo of the sixties, Lord (Richard) Rogers, who lives in the spacious splendour of Georgian Chelsea, proposed the return of high-density and often high-rise housing built across London. There may be a species that can happily raise families in His Lordship's hutches, but the human race is not it.

The alternative is to build in the countryside. I cannot see the problem when so much of Britain's land is controlled by agribusinesses that have left barely a hedgerow or tree standing. If we were to build homes with gardens of their own, we would not only make people happier but also encourage biodiversity as homeowners replant the trees and shrubs that modern agriculture destroyed.

Barker said Britain needed 120,000 more houses a year to reduce property inflation to the European average. Privileged pundits greeted her findings with primal screams. Sir Simon Jenkins said Barker's 'statistics on Britain's so-called housing "shortage" are among the most mendacious that department [the Treasury] has ever published'. A brass-necked Sir Max Hastings posed for the *Sunday Times* lolling against the gates of his country estate while asking, 'Do we not owe it to our descendants to check our obsession with house ownership before it devastates what is left of rural England?' (To which the only sensible answer was, it depends whose children you are talking about, Sir Max.)

The *Daily Telegraph* declared that the native British didn't need new homes because our birth rate is 'precipitately low'. The government was destroying the green belt not for our sake, but for the sake of immigrants who were coming here and taking our land as well as our jobs. At no point did the *Telegraph* stop to ask itself why the birth rate in Britain was so low.

Not everyone of the right is so lacking in intellectual curiosity. You could tell something was shifting in British Conservatism some time before the election of David Cameron, when Tories started producing interesting books for the first time in fifteen years. The best was *Mind the Gap*, by Margaret Thatcher's former adviser Ferdinand Mount. 'Land ownership in Britain is more concentrated than in any other major country I can think of,' he wrote. The great estates still flourish while 'the small holdings which are such a feature of life on the Continent are the exception rather than the rule'.

Contrary to socialist ideals, the green belts and planning restrictions of the Attlee government's 1947 Town and Country Planning Act forced prices so high only big developers could afford to enter the market. Mount proposed relaxing the planning laws so that agricultural land could be used for housing. Land should be sold in plots to families that wanted to build their own homes, he said, rather than to large construction companies. The British landscape he imagined resulting would be cluttered, but eccentric and individual. This vision of small plots and odd houses is not too far away from the dream of the squatters of Villa Road.

Whether they would embrace Mount as a comrade is another matter. Most have ended up as deep Greens who oppose development of any kind. But they ought to retain enough knowledge of dialectics to recognise that ideas can metamorphose into their opposites. When socialist legislation from the forties protects the interests of Sir Max Hastings and his kind, it should not be too great a leap to accept that Barker and Mount may be on the side of the masses.

New Statesman, January 2006

'Sub-prime' (adjective): Insanely Risky

A TORTURING OF THE English language preceded the crash of the US mortgage market. Finance houses offered 'sub-prime' mortgages to anyone who wanted them. 'Sub-prime', like 'sub-optimal', is a euphemism for 'terrible'. The mortgage sales teams did not mean that their products were terrible, although often they were, but that the borrowers were not of prime quality – terribly risky, in short. They were poor serial debtors or once comfortable people who had become too old to realise that they were signing away valuable assets when they remortgaged their homes.

Borrowers who never could pay off their debts took 'stated income loans', which plain-speaking brokers translated as 'liar loans' because debtors were free to lie about their income. As long as American house prices kept rising, the lending bubble did not burst. Homeowners who ran into trouble could either sell and repay their debt or remortgage. Once prices fell, however, a bad-debt crisis drove borrowers to default and finance companies to the wall. The homes of 2 million are at risk and bankers are warning that defaults on $300 billion of mortgage debt may push America into recession.

The British financial press has viewed the carnage as a foreign story, and it is easy to see why many of my fellow journalists think it couldn't happen here. If you live in a housing hot spot, you will have heard predictions of catastrophe before, but the end has never come, and property prices have kept on rising. My colleagues on the *Economist* joke that 'we've predicted ten of the last three recessions'. Those of us who have long thought that the housing market is demented feel much the same way. We keep saying disaster is imminent, and still the market heads upwards.

Nick Gardner, a rather conservative mortgage broker, told me he felt foolish when he thought back to when he had warned clients against putting legal fees and moving costs on the mortgage. Previous generations would have regarded telling a first-time buyer not to take a 120 per cent mortgage as sensible advice – borrow more than the value of the house and you are immediately in negative equity. But Gardner says that the inflation has been so extraordinary his supposedly reckless borrowers were all now sitting on large paper profits.

He believes the arrival of buy-to-rent investors has pushed prices up permanently. Wealthy individuals and, increasingly, property companies are outbidding first-time buyers and sweeping up homes in London, Bath, Edinburgh – anywhere housing seems a guaranteed generator of generous returns. He imagines a future when two or three housing conglomerates control a large chunk of Britain's most desirable housing stock.

In the US, homeowners facing ruin and mortgage companies and builders facing bankruptcy are cursing the market. In Britain, abandoning prudence and diving in before developers sew it up still seems the best strategy.

Yet the differences between the two countries are not so great. British building societies are offering their own versions of 'liar loans', there are 'sub-prime' sales teams at work here too and already repossession rates are rising. Previously, the price of the average house was three times average earnings, now it is six. Previously, building societies lent you three times your income, now they will lend you five times, six, seven … however much you think you can afford to repay. And people are grabbing all they can because they believe that the more you borrow, the more you make.

Sue Edwards of the National Association of Citizens Advice Bureaux tends to the casualties. She has been a debt worker since the last of the Tory recessions in the early nineties, and it seems as if nothing can shock her. But she is noticing an ominous break with the past. When she began advising potential bankrupts during the worst days of the Major administration, unemployment threatened their security. As might be predicted, the catastrophe of losing your job and not being able to find another one led to the catastrophic consequence of losing your home.

Now she is seeing 'butterfly effects': catastrophic consequences flowing from small changes in circumstances. Unemployment is not the only wrecker of lives today. The loss of overtime, rising tax demands or the break-up of a relationship are causing tightly strung borrowers to snap.

Edwards mainly deals with former council tenants, but her description of debtors with no financial slack applies to many in the middle class, particularly the young. If they have paid an extortionate price for a tiny flat, they have a stake in house prices rising. Indeed, the received wisdom of modern Britain insists that house price inflation is somehow beneficial for all.

But if you are young and confined by debt, you are less likely to pursue an uncertain career or start your own business or a family. You have to look for a secure job because, although you may not realise it, you are funding a vast redistribution of wealth between the generations.

Martin Weale, of the National Institute of Economic and Social Research, tells me he is astonished by how few grasp the basic fact that when a pensioner couple takes the profits from their home and moves to France, their retirement is paid for by the young couple who have burdened themselves with debt to meet an inflated asking price.

From this perspective, a crash is what we need. It would free up the labour market and allow the young to think about having families and taking chances. But you only have to remember how many in Britain are counting on their house as a substitute pension to realise that deflation is no better than inflation.

The British have allowed themselves to become far too dependent on the property market. It matters too much, fills too many of our hopes and fears. Whether it goes up or down, the consequences are likely to be as sub-prime as you can imagine.

Observer, March 2007

The Skull beneath the Skin

TO THE WHITE Cube to see the work that has produced the most excited chatter in artistic London for years: Damien Hirst's skull studded with 8601 diamonds.

The gallery attendants do their best to make visitors feel like peasants worshipping a sacred relic. They escort us into the skull's presence in small groups, and give us only a few minutes to admire Hirst's efforts – perhaps because a longer inspection might prompt hard questions about artistic merit.

The critics have been no less reverential than the curators. The skull shows that 'an artist with the tremendous pathos of Damien Hirst cannot just resign to the inevitability of physical decay', intoned one. 'It has a primitivism that renews art for our time just as Picasso's discovery of African and Oceanic masks renewed art a century ago,' gushed another.

To which the only intelligent reply should be 'give us a break'.

All that interests the art world about the skull is its exorbitant price. The critics applaud Hirst not for making what looks like a prop for an Indiana Jones movie but for asking £50 million for it – the largest sum ever demanded by a living artist. The curators do not attempt to hide their money-worship. After a few obligatory burblings about Hirst's confrontation with death, their catalogue continues with pages of descriptions of his largest diamonds, detailing their every 'main facet' and 'girdle facet' with creepy care.

Hirst might have created the same effect by using fake diamonds. No one apart from jewellers would have noticed the difference, but then no one else would have been interested. As it is, he has produced a brainless celebration of a Britain where reward has lost any connection to worth and work. He isn't criticising a country where kitsch comes with a £50 million price tag, not even ironically. He is revelling in it.

My fellow visitors did not look to me like Tories up for the day from the Home Counties, but otherwise liberal metropolitans. I cannot prove that, as appearances are no guide to status any more, but I can say with certainty that Hirst has had his most fawning reviews from critics who are nominally of the left.

I left the White Cube, walked down to the river and picked up a paper. I read that Nicholas Ferguson, chairman of SGV Capital, had said that private equity managers were 'paying less tax than a cleaning lady' after ten years of a Labour government. I looked over to Westminster, where Gordon Brown recruits those same private equity managers to tell him how to govern; then east to the City, where Labour's Ken Livingstone is allowing speculative developers to destroy the London skyline; and finally west to Chelsea, where house prices have floated off into a make-believe economy.

When the bubble bursts, this fairy tale will not have a happy ending. All that will be left will be mountains of debt, thousands of bankrupts and a glittering skull with an idiot grin.*

London *Evening Standard*, June 2007

---

* His skull's 8601 diamonds were 'ethically sourced', Hirst assured liberals. They weighed 1106.18 carats and were worth around £12 million before he got to work. He took an eighteenth-century skull, replaced everything except the teeth with platinum and studded the diamonds on top. He sold the skull for £50 million in August 2007, by which time the bubble world which so venerated him was being swept away by the financial crisis. There were unconfirmed rumours in the press that his dealers had helped with the purchase to keep their client's stock high.

PART 9

Waiting for the Etonians

'It is of great consequence to disguise your inclination and to play the hypocrite well; and men are so simple in their temper and so submissive to their present necessities, that he that is neat and cleanly in his collusions shall never want people to practise them upon.'

NICCOLÒ MACHIAVELLI,
1513

The Making of the Next
Prime Minister?

THE WEST END success of *Frost/Nixon* is a hopeful sign that British theatre can at last escape from anti-Bush agitprop. Peter Morgan's play is a subtle examination of the first fight between television and politics. On the night I was there, the audience was all against Nixon to begin with – what else could we have been? – but Morgan left us with the unsettling feeling that David Frost's success in forcing the stonewalling Nixon to acknowledge his guilt for Watergate was not the triumph it seemed.

After Nixon cracks, Jim Reston, a left-wing television researcher for Frost, goes to a party where admiring politicians and celebrities surround the chat-show host whom serious journalists had once dismissed as a lightweight. Nixon's humiliation ought to have delighted him, but instead, the glum Reston thinks, 'Maybe, in the end, there is no difference between politics and showbiz.'

It isn't an original thought when everyone else has been saying for years that 'politics is show business for ugly people' and no politician can succeed without looking good on the television. David Cameron may be about to prove them and the playwright wrong by showing that you can have too much of the values of the entertainment industry.

Through no fault of his own, show business made Cameron leader of the opposition. David Davis had the strongest base among activists and MPs. The opinion polls declared Kenneth Clarke the front-runner among the wider public. Neither man was a clear election winner, however. Cameron came from nowhere because BBC *Newsnight* commissioned a focus group run by the American pollster Frank Luntz that appeared to prove that the young politician could be extraordinarily popular. The Conservatives believed its findings. The desperation of the Tories in 2005 produced a leadership election without precedent. A focus group drove a hitherto obscure MP to the leadership of a major political party. Not a focus group hired by party managers anxious to uphold the best interests of their cause, but by a broadcaster as interested in entertainment as reputable research.

By the standards of the old-fashioned journalists who looked down their noses at Frost, Luntz was an astonishing pollster for *Newsnight* to commission. He had spent much of the previous decade helping the Republicans find smarmy ways to spin tax cuts for the rich and dismiss global warming as scaremongering.

Samantha Bee, of American TV's *Daily Show*, persuaded him to parade his devious talents on camera when she gave him controversial phrases to translate from English to PR-speak.

Bee: 'Drilling for oil.'
Luntz: 'I would say "responsible exploration for energy".'
Bee: 'Logging.'
Luntz: 'I would say "healthy forests".'
Bee: 'Manipulation.'
Luntz: 'Explanation and education.'

Add to that the reprimand Luntz received from the American Association for Public Opinion Research for his unsubstantiated claim that 60 per cent of Americans supported the Republicans' Contract with America and you seem to be left with a mediocre propagandist the BBC would never allow near its programmes in normal circumstances.

But as the New York journalist Dante Chinni noted in 2000, the normal judgements of broadcasters never apply to Luntz. He was part of 'a new class of media personality, the celebrity pollster … [who] gets the heavy-hitter treatment, frequently getting called in by the networks to offer colour commentary on politics even when he has no poll to cite'. Producers feted Luntz because he gave television what it wanted: strong opinions expressed with absolute certainty in a populist style.

His celebrity notwithstanding, British pollsters tell me that Luntz's work for *Newsnight* should not have influenced a parish council election, never mind the future of a great party. If you cannot follow their case against him in detail, their overall explanation is easy to grasp. A well-run focus group could never fill fifteen minutes of airtime. It would be too boring. Ordinary focus groups have six to eight members, but six to eight people are not an impressive sight on television, so *Newsnight* had Luntz meet twenty-eight voters. As their name implies, focus groups are also meant to be focused. Market researchers want volunteers from a similar background so strangers will lose their inhibitions about speaking freely in front of each other. But *Newsnight* mixed up people who had always voted Tory with people who had once voted Tory and people who had never voted Tory. The danger of a large and diverse group is that the loudest voices will dominate and a herd mentality takes over. Watch the footage that made Cameron leader and you will see the dynamics of crowd psychology convert everyone in the room to his charms. 'That is the best segment I've ever tested in politics,' enthuses Luntz after collecting responses to a clip of Cameron talking. He sounded genuinely surprised.

The standard way to stop easily impressed participants going along with the crowd is to have secret ballots. Luntz and *Newsnight* did not use them because a show of hands looks better on TV. Finally, focus group organisers are meant to be alert to the danger of pre-programmed responses. Yet *Newsnight* played tapes of Cameron mouthing warm generalities. 'I want us to be optimistic talking to people's hopes and not their fears,' the young candidate fearlessly declared. The reaction of the voters on the hand-held dials that measured their instant responses was overwhelmingly positive. But they would have been as positive if you, I or our next-door neighbours had said the same, which is why serious researchers are wary of instant reactions to smooth sentiments. Cameron promised to end the yah-boo-sucks style of the Commons and to support Tony Blair when Tony Blair did the right thing, not a pledge that was likely to anger the voters. 'There are some who say I'm too young,' continued Cameron, self-deprecatingly. 'Some who say I've just been in Parliament for five years and maybe I don't have the experience to do the job. And in some ways they're right. I am only thirty-eight years old and I have been in Parliament for only five years but I believe that if you've got the right ideas in your head and the right passion in your heart and if you know what this party needs to do to change, then you should go for it.' And when presented with this content-free mixture of youth, bashful charm and steely determination to do something or other, the audience responded by acclaiming him. Which audience would not?

Newsnight produced infotainment, not research.

I'm not suggesting a conspiracy. Luntz needed a splash to break into the British market after the pounding he had taken in America. *Newsnight* needed to make a noise to keep the hands of its fickle audience away from the remote control. Their stunt would not have mattered if lucky timing had not turned the Luntz poll from a party piece into the decisive factor in the Conservative leadership race.

Commentators cannot say anything sensible about the next election until they see how Gordon Brown does as prime minister. But maybe it shouldn't be a surprise that Mori reported in the *Observer* that Cameron's personal ratings collapsed after his honeymoon period because voters didn't know what he believed in. The charge that he is an empty vessel isn't fair in my view, but if you are created by the entertainment industry, you must expect the public to treat what you say as mere showbiz.

Observer, December 2006

'We're from the Tory Party and We've Come to Help'

WHEN I WAS AT UNIVERSITY in the early eighties a friend called James Lyle decided to write his way out of student debt by banging out a Mills & Boon story. He was not always the most romantic of men – as he later proved by moving into the hedge fund business – but he was already a smart operator, and had heard that Mills & Boon paid £4000 a novel, an enormous sum for a student in 1981.

For weeks, the poor chap anaesthetised himself with as much alcohol as he could afford, and forced himself to read a romance a night. As heaving bosom followed manly blush, he decoded the formula. Like the readers, the heroine must be from a humble background: a nurse, a secretary or a governess. Like the readers, she must not be too beautiful. By contrast, the hero must fulfil all the readers' fantasies and be as rugged as they come. Unfortunately, a scheming vamp, who wants only to get her manicured hands on his money, must also be after him, and the naive hero should also be blind to the malice beneath her seductive charms. In a dramatic moment – a car crash, a confrontation with bad men in league with the temptress – the heroine would prove herself by saving him, or the vamp would reveal her true worthlessness by running away and leaving him to die. The hero would see that the first Mrs Rochester or Rebecca figure was not the mate for him, and declare his love for plain Jane Eyre. He would marry her, and make her happy *and* rich. The latter was crucial because the readers had once been happy and in love, but now saw the attractions of being rich, too. Lyle even noticed there was always a sex scene in Chapter 7: not real sweating and panting but a moment when a blouse was torn or a stocking ripped, as the author delicately planted the suggestion in the reader's mind of more clothes being shredded at a mutually convenient moment.

His suffering was awful to watch. But he followed the recipe with the diligence of a dutiful cook, and had every right to expect his reward when he produced his romance. Mills & Boon praised his style. They applauded his understanding of the market. They said they wanted to see more of his work, and then flattened his hopes by telling him that they would not print his first effort because 'we're not sure you believe it'.

'Shit has its own integrity', as the Hollywood saying goes. You can't fool others unless you can first fool yourself. Mills & Boon knew that the public always saw through clever men who try to fake sincerity. Far better writers than Ian Fleming, Barbara Cartland and Jeffrey Archer could never imitate their success however hard they tried, because they did not believe the fantasy. The best best-selling authors always do.

Twenty-five years on, and James Lyle is a financier with offices in Manhattan and the City. According to the Register of Members' Interests, he is also funding David Cameron. You can ask the same question of the new Conservative leader as the Mills & Boon editor asked of my old friend: you are very good, almost convincing, but do you really believe it?

I am the last pundit on the planet with the right to offer an answer. Before the Conservative leadership election, I dismissed him in the *New Statesman* as a hopeless Blair clone – 'Blameron', the headline writer called him. He would disappear without trace, I assured you. The impact of my piece was electrifying. Within weeks, Cameron had won the Tory leadership by a land-slide and taken the party to its first consistent opinion-poll lead since Black Wednesday. It is not for nothing that I am known as the Seer of Fleet Street.

Cameron found success by doing exactly what a Conservative Blair would have done. He triangulated the centre-left by moving into its territory and welcomed interesting and iconoclastic figures – Bob Geldof, Zac Goldsmith – into the Conservative version of Blair's 'big tent'. The Cameron Tories talked sensibly about the environment and Africa, and became the political equivalent of Jehovah's Witnesses for workers in modish causes.

Picture the scene. There the bleeding-hearted were, sitting in their offices at Friends of the Earth or Christian Aid, quietly minding other people's business, when the intercom went and they heard the most unlikely sentence in the English language: 'We're from the Tory Party and we've come to help.' I phoned the usually courteous Patrick Holden, the director of the Soil Association, the other day, and he could not wait to get me off the phone. David Cameron was coming to a reception, he explained, and he did not want to miss one minute of the spectacle. I could hear the excitement in his voice. Alongside Monty Don, the apostle of organic gardening, the Greens' Caroline Lucas, the apostle of organic farming, and Rosie Boycott, the apostle of organic cannabis, would be the leader of the Conservative Party. The novelty value should not be underestimated.

Nor should the political value. The Conservative Party survived to become the oldest political party in Europe because if regaining power necessitated swallowing its principles it would gulp them down like a teenager rushing a meal. Disraeli dropped his opposition to the Corn Laws when it stood in the way of winning an election. After the terrible defeat in 1945, the Conservatives promptly accepted Labour's welfare state and were back in office in 1951. Tony Blair presented the Tories with a far trickier conundrum after he beat them with another landslide victory in 1997.

If David Cameron believes anything, he believes that the old ruling class produces the best rulers of the country. But what change did he have to accept to return the Conservatives to office? The answer did not lie in a change in policies but a vaguer change in style. The Tories had to show that they accepted Britain as it is. Hence the well-publicised visit to *Brokeback Mountain* – the most public sign you can make at the moment that you are a Good Person – the hugging of hoodies and the trips to see the melting ice caps.

Cameron understands that political correctness has replaced old-fashioned manners as the dominant middle-class style. It is easy enough to mock its vast duplicities and double standards, but the Tory Party cannot be too far away from respectable opinion and hope to win power. Nor, if it is being hard headed, should it want to be. There are plenty of natural Conservatives in marginal seats who regard recycling or their visits to the farmers' market as duties – almost spiritual duties – which offer them a kind of salvation from the routine of getting money and spending it. The old Tory Party forgot that Conservatives once believed in conservation and needlessly lost their support. Gay marriage reaffirms traditional values, so where's the problem there? The emancipation of women and opposition to racism do not hurt business, and even those voters who are occasionally sexist or racist no more think it respectable for their leaders to be bigoted than those who hit the bottle think it respectable for their prime minister to be an alcoholic. As for the attendant hypocrisies political correctness brings in its train, Tories of all people should know that you must observe conventional pieties.

It did William Hague no good that he was right about the European single currency in the late nineties. To be anti-European was to be beyond the pale of the civil service and BBC in his time as Tory leader. If, a decade on, the price of stopping the incredulous questions on television news programmes and the endless gags on the satirical shows is taking a trip to a melting glacier or catching a gay cowboy movie, I can see why Cameron thinks that is a price worth paying. His success will depend on whether he can convince the public that he sincerely wishes to pay it.

New Statesman, February 2007

Breaking the Camel's Back

AS THE STOCK MARKET roared ahead, the GMB put out the word that it needed to find a way of dramatising the scandal of how much money had been sucked out of the Automobile Association by Damon Buffini and his fellow private-equity tycoons. 'Call the Severnwye Llama Trekking Company in the Forest of Dean,' a comrade recommended. 'It not only has llamas but a camel called Teifet it rents out to add an Arabian touch to parties and wedding receptions.'

Brilliant, thought the union's press officers. Buffini is a pious Christian. When he leaves the service at his Clapham church, we will shame him in front of the congregation with banners carrying St Matthew's warning – 'Again I tell you it is easier for a camel to pass through the eye of a needle than for a rich man to enter the kingdom of God' – backed up by a real camel.

'The media will love it,' they cried, and headed to the pub.

Few hacks were interested in private-equity capitalists in May 2006. The English notoriously prefer animals to their fellow citizens, and the most excited response the GMB received was a denunciation from Animal Defenders International, which condemned the union for forcing a thirty-year-old camel to 'endure nearly six hours of travel in addition to a three-hour protest'.

Although no one else cared, you might have thought that Gordon Brown would have been on the union's side. Not all the

343

private-equity buyouts of the New Labour years were asset-sweating operations – a study by Nottingham University found that employment rose after some takeovers. Nevertheless, it is hard to see how anyone benefited from the takeover of the AA by the Primera and CVC funds, other than Buffini and his cohorts.

They turned what was once a mutual association for drivers into a machine for generating private profits. When the AA merged with Saga, the travel company for elderly tourists, the bankers behind the deal valued it at £3.3 billion, £1.6 billion more than the private-equity companies paid for it in 2004. Paul Maloney, GMB national secretary for the AA, said that by his reckoning: 'The managing partners stand to make £300 million from owning the AA for less than three years.'

How much tax the partners paid is an interesting question. With the extraordinarily generous taper-relief system which deducted a mere 10 per cent of profits when private-equity capitalists sold on, they probably paid very little. Meanwhile, the AA as an organisation paid no corporation tax in the last financial year and its accounts showed that it somehow ended 2005 and 2006 with the Revenue owing it money. (Your taxes, generous reader, have filled the gap.)

Giving evidence to the Treasury select committee, Buffini justified welfare for the wealthy by saying: 'We are generating business investment and creating jobs in the UK.'

Not at the AA they didn't, where the workforce was cut by 3500 after the private-equity takeover, and the survivors were put on longer shifts.

Nor can customers be said to have done well. *Which?* downgraded the AA from first to third in its list of reliable breakdown organisations and the RAC was left free to run attack ads highlighting the failings of Buffini's cash cow. RAC *Schadenfreude* peaked when one of its centres received an emergency call from the AA pleading with it to rescue a patrol vehicle. It had broken down and the AA couldn't fix its own vehicle.

The taxpayers had lost out, the workforce had lost out and there were reasonable grounds for arguing that AA members had lost out, too. To be fair, pension funds might have profited, but that's about it. I was going to say that the shareholders of the banks who organised the merger of the AA and Saga must have done well, but as the deal was done just before the sub-prime credit crunch, they may be stuck with debt they cannot sell on.

Here, surely, was an unacceptable face of capitalism that even New Labour couldn't smother in kisses.

But the business with which Gordon Brown can't do business has yet to be founded. The prime minister has all but tripped over his shoes in his eagerness to embrace Buffini. Brown has put him on the National Council for Education Excellence, to tell him how to raise standards in schools, and the Business Council for Britain, which tells him how to treat business. The *Mirror* reports rumours in Westminster that Buffini will soon be making a donation to the Labour Party. A knighthood feels as inevitable as Christmas.

Union leaders were furious at the TUC conference. Public recognition of Buffini was one of a series of crass insults Brown has directed at Old Labour which culminated in the tea party in Downing Street for Baroness Thatcher. They told me privately that there were limits to what the unions would take from Brown, but all recent Labour history argues against a public break. New Labour was founded on the assumption that Old Labour had nowhere else to go and that reckoning has survived until now.

Instead of worrying about trade union revolts that are always promised and never arrive, Brown ought to worry about the millions who have paid their taxes and seen him waste far too much of their money. Eventually, they are going to realise that they have been required to subsidise tax breaks for private-equity barons, foreign billionaires and British companies with boltholes in tax havens. As I have said before, we are living in exceptional times. No previous Labour government has put itself on the wrong side of a conflict between the working and middle classes on the one hand and the rich on the other. None has wanted to.

For their latest stunt, the irrepressible GMB press office moved on to the country estate of the new boss of the AA. They hired a local poultry farm so they could do a 'chickens are coming home to roost' number, and brought along Teifet for old times' sake.

Severnwye Llama Tracking assures nervous customers that there is no reason to be frightened of camels. They are mild-tempered beasts who are happy to carry others. That does not mean they cannot turn nasty when provoked.*

Observer, September 2007

---

* After this article appeared the GMB called to say that the camel would not be at the demo because he was, in fact, dead. Animal rights activists had warned that there were only so many protests an elderly dromedary could take, and they had been vindicated. The name of Teifet must now join the Labour movement's long list of martyrs who gave their lives in the struggle against the boss class.

All Passion Spent

SATIRISTS ARE NATURAL conservatives. From the Romans on, they have flourished by pitching an older, superior order against ridiculous and sinister innovations. Juvenal contrasted the solid decency of old Rome with the vulgarity brought by Greek flatterers and Jewish merchants who had so corrupted the eternal city that they left 'no room for honest callings'. All the great satirists followed his example of nostalgia and alarm. Swift hated the Whigs for dragging his peaceful country into the long wars against Louis XIV. The threat of mass society to the old aristocratic order appalled Evelyn Waugh and Anthony Powell. By the eighties, it was the turn of leftists to be conservatives and deliver furious tirades against Margaret Thatcher's destruction of the social democratic values they had assumed to be settled. Norman Tebbit showed he understood the satirical dynamic better than many literary critics when he wrote of the best satire of the Thatcher years: '*Spitting Image*'s creators were rooted in a mid-20th-century "Guardianesque" political consensus, which, at the time, was being comprehensively trashed by the Thatcherite reformers.'

Thatcher won, of course. The targets of satire usually do. Swift no more stopped the Whigs making England a European power than Michael Moore stopped George W. Bush winning the 2004 election. Politicians should not necessarily worry if their opponents have the best jokes. To call satire a conservative art is another way of saying that it is the art of the defeated. Even Orwell's *Animal Farm* became an obituary for Soviet communism only after the fall of the Berlin Wall. Like everyone else in the forties, he imagined the regime carrying on indefinitely, until 'a time came when there was no one who remembered the old days before the Rebellion'.

The exceptions to this rule are the professional satirists who began work in the sixties. They would have written themselves out of a job if they had committed themselves to a cause. Thus *That Was the Week that Was* was against the Wilson government as much as the Macmillan government; it had to be or the show would have gone off air when the government changed. Today Ian Hislop describes his mission as waiting in the hills until the battle is over 'then sweeping down and slaughtering the wounded'. This is a commendably unfair attitude for the editor of *Private Eye* to hold. However, the best satirists are rarely equal-opportunities deriders, but are driven by a partisan anger against modernity. They are a success because they are political failures: outsiders appalled by the course history has taken. While others accept the new world as it is, they rage against the consensus and scan it obsessively for weaknesses which might prompt the complacent to revolt.*

If you were commissioning a satirical series, where would you look for today's outsiders? Who are the people who loathe everything about the new establishment? Blair's acceptance of much of what Thatcher had done and his support for Bush kept the elderly left satirists of the eighties in work. But Blair has

---

* Even *Private Eye* is not the equal-opportunities derider it pretends to be. It also hates novelty. Its staple targets are modern architects who destroy old buildings; modern management consultants who cozen taxpayers out of billions with the help of incomprehensible business-school neologisms; and modern artists pseudily revelling in the shock of the new. The intellectual atmosphere of *Private Eye* is as far as you can get from the ideologies of *Newsnight Review* or McKinsey & Company without crossing the Channel.

gone now, and it turns out he was nowhere near as right-wing as those who mocked him imagined. His administration gave women, ethnic minorities and homosexuals – groups despised for millennia – legal equality, and spent hundreds of billions on public services and relief for the poor. The Tory Party no longer quibbles. Just as New Labour once accepted Margaret Thatcher's settlement, now the new Conservatives have come to terms with the Blair legacy.

The blending of Blairism and Thatcherism is the new order, and in the press and on the Net I can find savage attacks on a spending of public money so immense that Brown has no fiscal tools at his disposal if recession comes, and coruscating assaults on the hypocrisies and injustices allowed by the apparently benign orthodoxy of political correctness. All television can give me is *Headcases*.

ITV billed the first series as the successor to *Spitting Image*. If only this were true. The writers had no energy and no ardour. It did not take long for this viewer to guess that they were happy with the world as it is.

Take their attitude to terrorism. Satirists might concentrate on the government's threat to basic liberties. Alternatively, they might turn on a judiciary whose rulings allow 'Londonistan' to survive. What no one with satirical passion would think of doing is telling tit gags Benny Hill would have rejected as not funny enough. Yet *Headcases* had the animated Gordon Brown explaining to Jacqui Smith that she must show more cleavage as the terror threat increases. When an attack was imminent, she must sound the alarm by appearing topless before the Commons. Meanwhile Brown, a politician who has taxed and spent on a scale beyond the dreams of the left of the nineties, became in ITV's hands a Victorian miser who watched every penny from his counting-house desk. You could almost hear the production saying, 'He is Scottish and a son of the manse so – QED! – we will make him as a skinflint!' Its chief writer explained that he thought the prime minister was 'a very austere, Scrooge-like Victorian gentleman … I mean he uses words like "prudence", which people haven't used for a hundred years!'

A Scrooge-like Victorian gentleman? In the week *Headcases* was launched, David Craig published *Squandered: How New Labour Are Wasting Over One Trillion Pounds of Our Money.* To spell it out, Brown has spent £1,229,100,000,000 above Tory spending targets since 1997 and will have spent £1,700,000,000,000 by the 2010 election. His most tangible monument is 'a political and managerial culture where mistakes are never admitted, failings are always covered up and mind-boggling bungling is rewarded by promotion, honours and generous inflation-proof pensions'.

True satirists would have looked at the NHS, which Labour promised to save in 1997. If they wanted to break with the custom and practice of their craft, they could have begun by being fair and acknowledged that Brown has all but doubled the health budget in real terms to £97 billion, brought down waiting lists and built new hospitals. The niceties dispensed with, they could have got stuck into the waste, which has been out of all proportion to the gains. As Craig points out, the number of managers has doubled to 40,000. The taxpayer gives them sumptuous salaries, even though they are so incapable of doing their jobs they need to spend £600 million a year on management consultants to tell them what to do. Farther down the hierarchy, New Labour struck an incredible bargain with GPs: the taxpayer awarded doctors a 60 per cent pay rise in return for the doctors working fewer hours. What funds were left, the Department of Health then decided to pump into a grandiose computerisation programme that every independent expert on information technology says will never work.

As the money flowed to the professional classes, hospitals became death traps. Rates of MRSA and *C. Diff.* rose far in excess of any other European country. The highest estimate of avoidable deaths the NHS admitted to in 2006 was 34,000. To put that figure in perspective, the United Nations estimated that, in 2006, 35,000 died in the civil war in Iraq.

None of the quangos New Labour has set up to regulate in the public interest, such as the Health Protection Agency (annual cost £252 million) or the National Patient Safety Agency (average salary £55,200), pointed out that, while spending an extra £269 billion on the NHS since 1997, Labour has presided over a sharp cutback in the number of hospital beds. Inevitably the shortage led to the filthy process of 'hotbedding' – throwing one patient out and getting another one into the still-warm bed – and a neglect of basic aseptic techniques to prevent infection during surgery.

Writers with real venom would never have shown Brown as a reassuringly old-fashioned pillar of the kirk, but as a demented spendthrift who stuffed the pockets of bureaucrats, IT salesmen, management consultants and hospital consultants while the patients, whose money he had taken, slowly died in pools of their own excrement.

Conservative readers will blame the broadcasters' liberal bias for ITV's failure to turn to right-wing writers who might wound or even graze. I'm sure there's truth in the charge but suspect that a deeper 'bias against understanding' is at work.

In *The New Elites*, his study of modern culture, George Walden dissected Oxbridge-educated media grandees who make a career out of assuming the masses are ignorant. The makers of *Headcases* proved his point. Before the series began, they unblushingly told *The Times* that they would not pick on Jack Straw, Ed Balls, David Davis and Vince Cable because they did not think the viewers knew who they were. Even if they were right, and I'm not sure they are, Straw is Labour's most devious survivor, while any decent satirist would have thanked the gods for giving him the bombastic, bullying Balls to play with. If their audience did not know who they were, they would *make* them know by the force of their anger and comic invention. Not so the writers of *Headcases*. They presumed that the poor stupid little dears would switch channels if presented with anything outside their comfort zone. All the proles wanted to know about was celebrities, so *Headcases* gave them spoofs of Posh and Becks.

The great satirists despised the powerful. Unless the writers of the second series can find an angry intelligence, we will have to conclude that ITV's satirists despise their audience.

Observer and *Standpoint*, Summer 2008

Attack of the Mulletts

THE BEST CRIME writers foresaw the disaster of Labour's target-driven state by creating heroes unlike any other fictional detectives. It is not the determination of Morse, Tennison, Frost and Rebus which marks them out – Sherlock Holmes was as purposeful. Nor is the loneliness their obsessive devotion to work brings unusual. Inspector Frost has only curries for company at night and Inspector Morse never finds a woman who will stay with him, but Philip Marlowe went home to an empty apartment while Dr Watson said of the only woman Holmes ever admired, 'It was not that he felt any emotion akin to love for Irene Adler. All emotions, and that one particularly, were abhorrent to his cold, precise but admirably balanced mind.'

Modern fictional detectives stand out from their predecessors because they have to deal with managers like no other.

Morse's Chief Superintendent Strange and Frost's Chief Superintendent Mullett are not corrupt, like so many police chiefs in American and Continental thrillers. They are good men by their own lights who would never take a bribe. Nor are they always plodders who rely on the brilliance of a Holmes or Poirot to solve their cases for them. On the contrary, when they need to ingratiate themselves, they show they are clever office politicians.

But in pleasing their superiors they infuriate subordinates. In *Winter Frost*, R. D. Wingfield describes Mullett as a man who 'makes a great show of pushing the pile of papers to one side' when a colleague enters the room. He puts on his 'tired, over-worked, but my staff come first expression' and parrots the latest management-speak to Liz, a new recruit.

> Teamwork, Inspector. That's the key word. 'No cowboys, no Indians, no generals, no privates – all one big team.' These were the words the chief constable had used at yesterday's meeting at which Mullett had nodded his fawning agreement. He was surprised that Liz didn't seem to be doing the same.

Frost and Liz must always watch their backs. From the Chief Superintendent to the Chief Constable, they can't trust their managers to support them or help the victims of crime.

Inspector Frosts are all over the public sector, and not only in the police. Paul Gregg, an economist at Bristol University, and his colleagues looked at who in the workforce were prepared to forgo their own self-interest by working unpaid overtime, and found the 'public service ethos' was not just propaganda union leaders issued when the annual pay negotiations began. Among the teachers, doctors and nurses they studied, altruism and devotion to duty were far stronger in the public than in the private sector.

They weren't all saints. Many happily fiddled the incentive schemes Labour invented in the naive belief that they could micro-manage local services. But so many were prepared to work for nothing, Bristol University estimated the Treasury would need to pay for another 60,000 staff to cover for them if they decided to leave at the end of their shifts.

Despite the increases in taxation and national debt, Britain has not benefited from their selflessness. Labour effectively sabotaged their altruism by overwhelming the public sector with legions of Mulletts.

In 2008, Harriet Sergeant of Civitas described a police service that was close to incapable of doing its job. In a think-tank pamphlet, she delivered a devastating condemnation of an enclosed and self-referential bureaucracy, which operated without regard to the wishes of the people who paid for it.

We now spend proportionately more than any other developed country on policing, she pointed out. The Home Office used targets to run it and delivered funding and bonuses to Chief Constables who filled its 'sanction detention' arrest quotas.

The first perverse consequence was that although the public expected the police to keep the peace, an officer who successfully stopped trouble was not rewarded because no trouble meant no arrests. More seriously, the police played the Home Office game by going for trivial offenders rather than serious criminals. Solving the case of a child who steals a Mars bar earned as many points as solving a murder. It made more sense to arrest rowdy children for 'harassing a tree' than to begin the hard work of tackling a potentially homicidal teenage gang.

Chris Dillow, author of *New Labour and the Folly of Managerialism*, describes Brown's Mullettry as a marriage between Old Labour's Fabian belief in the centralised state and Thatcherites' worship of management consultants. Between them, they have spawned a bureaucracy which despises democratic accountability and, worse, does not and cannot work.

Fabianism, with its loathing for the masses – 'We must exterminate the sort of people who do not fit in,' declared George Bernard Shaw at the turn of the twentieth century – is not the only Labour tradition. The Co-op and guild socialist movements were at ease with democracy, as was radical liberalism. Phil Collins, an occasional speechwriter for Labour politicians, suggested to the Brownites that Labour could find a way out of its crisis by listening to the Fabians' liberal opponents. He cited a warning of Leonard Hobhouse, a liberal intellectual of the early twentieth century, that the 'mechanical socialism' of the Fabians 'applauded the running of the machine merely because it is a machine and is being run'. Hobhouse might have delivered it yesterday.

Brown invited Collins to Downing Street to talk over his ideas. Maybe he is grasping the near-universal public dissatisfaction with what Labour has done in its name and with its money. If so, it's too late.

'Right,' cries Frost to his officers as Mullett approaches. 'Super's going to say a few words. Try and look as if you're paying attention.'

Within days of the Civitas pamphlet, the Chief Constables of Surrey, Staffordshire, Leicestershire and West Midlands showed they no longer even had to pretend to pay attention to Labour. They announced they were breaking with the Home Office and everything it stood for.

'Quite simply, local people's safety, confidence in police and their satisfaction when they call us for help are more important than misleading targets,' explained the Acting Chief Constable of Surrey. He would never have said that when Labour ministers were in the ascendancy. But he's not frightened now because he knows that it's over and the electorate's target is to throw them out.

Observer, June 2008

Tory Isolationism

Review of *Three Victories and a Defeat*
by Brendan Simms

BRITISH EUROSCEPTICS LIVE with a paradox which is as close as anything can be in high politics to tragedy. A determination to disentangle Britain from Europe drives them into public life. Without their dislike, more usually hatred, of the EU they would give up on the banal business of Westminster. To their delight they find that the greater part of public opinion agrees with them and that the idealistic believers in ever-greater integration, who were everywhere in the nineties, have all but vanished. Most Europhiles are like Gordon Brown now: grim-faced men and women who go through the motions with Brussels like a couple sustaining the rituals of a loveless marriage.

Passion, flair and the best democratic arguments are on the Eurosceptic side. Yet parties that oppose Europe always lose elections. However much they agree with them, voters sense a danger and turn away. Bennite isolationism helped wreck Labour in the eighties. But socialism in one country was never going to be popular, particularly when the country in question was Britain. Harder to explain is the failure of the modern Tories. In an age of globalisation, their policy of putting clear blue water between Britain and Europe and looking across the oceans to the trading stations of the old empire sounds practical, but a sympathetic public can never be persuaded to vote in large enough numbers to implement it.

Brendan Simms is too good a historian to exploit the past to score a point about the present. Rather, *Three Victories and a Defeat* is an argument about the constants of foreign policy; about how in the eighteenth century the knowledge that Britain wasn't 'an island entire of itself' made it a superpower, and how the American colonies were lost when the British tried to manage on their own.

Like everyone else who tosses the quotation around, I'd assumed John Donne was talking about the human condition, not the balance of power. But, as Simms points out on his first page, Donne was writing when James I had outraged respectable opinion by failing to help European Protestants. 'No man is an island, entire of itself; every man is a piece of the continent, a part of the main; if a clod is washed away by the sea, Europe is the less …' was written at a time of fear that Catholic Spain would overwhelm the Low Countries and seize the ports it needed for an invasion.

From 1688 through to 1763 statesmen sought to prevent a 'universal monarchy', whether Hapsburg or Bourbon, dominating the continent and thus threatening Britain. With great skill and a light touch, Simms tells the complicated story of how an England that under Charles II and James II was little more than a French satellite, searched for security by becoming involved in the politics of every country from the Ottoman Empire to Sweden, built alliances, switched sides, paid bribes, sent off armies and developed the navy.

As now, resentment at involvement in Europe was ubiquitous. Conservatives loathed the Whig oligarchs for their willingness to spend blood and treasure on the wars of the Dutch William and German Georges. In 1711, Swift asked in his polemic *The Conduct of the Allies* why the English should support the cause of the hated Dutch, fight their battles and pick up their bills. Why bother when the only part of England to benefit was the City – 'that set of people who are called the moneyed men ... whose perpetual harvest is war, and whose beneficial way of traffic must very much decline by a peace'?

To my mind, Simms doesn't acknowledge the force of Swift's questions or the Tory and radical criticisms of the wars and corruption of the Whigs. But I suppose he feels he doesn't have to, because after winning the War of the Spanish Succession, the War of the Austrian Succession and the Seven Years' War between 1715 and 1763, Britain turned her back on Europe, as the Tories had always wanted her to, and the result was catastrophe.

Although a Peterhouse don, Simms has become the most formidable modern enemy of the Conservative tradition in foreign policy. His last book, *Unfinest Hour*, so excoriated the Major government's behaviour during the Bosnian crisis that readers have refused to shake the hand of Douglas Hurd or Malcolm Rifkind after reading it. *Three Victories and a Defeat* does the same to their predecessors. The Tories assumed that Britain could forget about Europe and hide behind the Royal Navy. But because the British stopped diverting France and Spain with military alliances in Europe, their enemies could build up their navies and combine to challenge Britain when the American War of Independence began.

Simms is refreshingly unsentimental about the revolution, seeing it as a clash of imperialisms. Benjamin Franklin and many others had been empire loyalists. When they realised that the Tory policy of avoiding conflict would stop the thirteen colonies expanding into French and Spanish territory, they revolted. Britain was never as alone as it was in the American War of Independence. Even in May 1940, Greece was still an ally. In 1776, there was no one. Prescient men of the day realised the scale of the rout and what England had lost. Horace Walpole predicted that one day Europeans would take instructions from

Americans, while the American delegation in Paris told the French that a great empire would emerge from the scattered settlements on the Atlantic seaboard, and its citizens 'will all speak English, every one of 'em'.

Simms delivers a strong riposte to Linda Colley's argument that the British defined themselves against the European 'other'. Not so, Simms replies, 'Britain's fate' is decided in Europe 'always has been and always will be'. History doesn't repeat itself, but geography doesn't change. We do not live on 'an island entire of itself' but in a European country. Unless Eurosceptics can find Continental allies against Brussels, they are as certain to fail as their ancestors.

Observer, November 2007

The Retreat to Little England

WHEN A GOVERNING PARTY'S time is up, no one cares about the failings of the opposition. Ministers in John Major's Tory administration used to bemoan the easy ride the media gave New Labour. Now it is Labour ministers' turn to stare with disbelieving eyes at the free pass we give the Conservatives.

Scandals which would once have made the news – the Tory energy spokesman's links to Vitol, an oil company which cut deals with Saddam Hussein and Slobodan Milosevic; the Conservative peers who still talk about 'niggers in the woodpile' – are passed over with an embarrassed cough. I know from the experience of writing critical pieces about the Blairites in 1997 that when the national mood swings, few readers want to hear about the faults of the government in waiting.

Like Tony Blair, David Cameron has 'decontaminated' his brand and turned the once burning hatred of the Conservative Party into desultory emotion – more of a habit than a passion. The first aim of the British centre-left is no longer to stop the Tories at any cost.

But in one area Cameron has been more than happy to keep his brand toxic. When he enters Downing Street, Britain will be alone in the world, with few friends and fewer allies. It is only a touch hyperbolic to say that in two years' time we won't have a foreign policy.

In the second half of the twentieth century, talk of Tory isolationism would have sounded ridiculous. The Conservatives took Britain into Europe and were the party of the American alliance. We'll discuss the coming breakdown in our relations with Europe later, but first the notion that the Conservatives will be able to stay on good terms with Washington needs to be humanely dispatched.

It is worth recalling a vignette from the Bosnian crisis of the early nineties because it shows that Tories can be as anti-American as leftists. Douglas Hurd and Malcolm Rifkind used every stratagem not only to stop British troops but troops from any other country intervening to protect the Bosnian Muslims. The then Republican senators John McCain and Bob Dole insisted that an EU which boasted that 'never again' would Europe return to the horrors of Nazism had to mean what it said and fight.

In *Unfinest Hour*, his history of the Bosnian war, the Cambridge historian Brendan Simms quotes the Tory response. Aides to Dole and McCain told him that Rifkind, whose experience of combat was limited to the back-stabbing of the Scottish Conservative Party, cried: 'You Americans know nothing about the horrors of war.' Dole, who had been blown up by a Nazi shell in the Second World War, walked out. McCain, who had been tortured for five years in a communist PoW camp, was so enraged by Rifkind that 'a member of his staff feared he was about to hit him'.

This story is, incidentally, the best reason I know for preferring McCain to Obama, but every time a journalist repeats it, they receive a furious denial from Rifkind. Maybe it has grown in the telling, but no one can doubt what John Fox, of the US State Department, described as the 'vigour and desperation' of Tory ministers. They were 'not just indifferent to American plans, but actively hostile to steps that could prevent ethnic cleansing'.

After Britain helped author a peace treaty which suited Milosevic very nicely, NatWest paid for Hurd and Dame Pauline Neville-Jones, a former Foreign Office civil servant who had been responsible for Bosnia, to fly to Belgrade and sell the happy monster a privatisation package.

Despite Cameron's decision to make Dame Pauline a Tory foreign affairs spokeswoman, the Conservatives say the tantrums of the nineties are behind them. They can now ally with America because George Osborne has good contacts with the neoconservative wing of the Republican Party. But it looks as if there will be a Democrat in the White House when the Conservatives reach Downing Street and I don't think that neocons will have Obama's ear.

In any case, the Tory idea that Britain can choose the US over Europe makes little sense because Americans from all parties want Europe to unite against the challenge of the newly invigorated autocracy of Vladimir Putin's Russia, a demand that Cameron is incapable of accepting.

John Major's government at least tried to maintain good relations with our European allies. Cameron makes no effort. I cannot find one Conservative statement since he became leader praising the EU, however grudgingly.

Anti-conservatism may no longer stir the left, but opposition to Europe burns as brightly on the right. The Tories are committed to pulling out of the European political bloc, which includes Angela Merkel and Nicolas Sarkozy's centre-right parties, because it supports the EU. Tory anti-Europeanism is driving Cameron away from what a generation ago would have been his natural allies, and sending him off into the wilds with the chauvinist parties of Russia and eastern Europe.

Far from standing up to Putin, the Conservatives tried to help a Putin stooge and former KGB officer take over the Council of Europe, which oversees the European Court of Human Rights, of all things. Mainstream European conservatives were as loud in their condemnations of Cameron as mainstream socialists. Caroline Jackson, one of the few Conservative members of the European Parliament who wants to work with Britain's allies, wrote in the *Financial Times* that her Tory colleagues 'now have a bad reputation [rapidly getting worse] for crass and offensive behaviour'.

Denis MacShane, the former Labour Foreign Office minister, was not overstating his case when he said that 'never before has a potential party of government adopted such a hostile public approach to working with allies and partners'.

Look again at the current scandals. Alan Duncan's links with Vitol bring back the worst memories of Hurd and Neville-Jones, while the Conservatives who go on about 'niggers' and 'wops' are not likely to be at ease with foreigners, to put the case against them at its mildest.

A Cameron government will tear up the complex web of alliances and understandings through which Britain exercises her influence. It is about time journalists asked him what he intends to put in their place.

Observer, July 2007

The Great Leap Backwards

FOR A FEW DAYS at the TUC, the gossip among the comrades was all about the presence of David Threlfall on the first of what I am sure will be many demonstrations against child poverty of the recession. Although you only have to glance at the FTSE100 to know that child (and adult) poverty will soon explode, the march was not well attended.

Everyone who turned up was welcome, but old Labour protesters still wondered why one of the stars of *Shameless* had joined them in Trafalgar Square. If you haven't seen it, you haven't missed much. *Shameless*, along with *Little Britain* and *The Jeremy Kyle Show*, is twenty-first-century television's prole porn. Whereas wealthy media executives once sought to investigate poverty or arouse anger against it in documentaries and dramas such as *Cathy Come Home* or *Boys from the Black Stuff*, now they commission programmes that laugh at it.

Threlfall plays a parasitic alcoholic whose delinquent children engage in underage sex, thieving and pigging themselves sick on drugs, booze and junk food. They choose to live this way, runs Channel 4's not-so-subliminal message. Don't feel sorry for them, they're grotesques who indulge in perverse pleasures at the taxpayers' expense.

Richard Exell of the TUC is organising a conference on what modern sociologists like to call 'povertyism' and what more straightforward people call 'class hatred'.

As he printed leaflets which pointed out that half the poor children in Britain have parents who are working in low-paid skivvy jobs rather than scrounging on the dole, he told me: 'Obviously writers and actors must be free to do what they want, but I don't understand why they can't show sympathy for the poor when they laugh at them. Dickens managed to do both, after all.'

Perhaps Dickensian sympathy is about to come back into fashion. Readers who have not felt the fragility of their prosperity must either be very rich or remarkably unimaginative. I know from frenzied conversations that the crash has made those who worry about poverty – politicians, charities, the unions – dizzy with apprehension. Like City dealers, they have watched governments and central bankers make extraordinary interventions, only to find that the markets are still falling.

As yet, we have not reached a firm base where everyone from fund managers to debt counsellors can take a breath and make sensible forecasts about the future. So the following predictions are provisional, and probably overoptimistic, but here we go. Both the TUC and the CBI expect unemployment to go above 2 million and to carry on rising. Construction and financial services are on their knees. Retail is in almost as bad a state and if there's a small business that isn't worried about its credit lines, the *Observer* would like to hear from it.

Even before tax receipts began falling, and the government bailed out Northern Rock, Bradford & Bingley and the wider banking system, the state's finances were horrendous. Ministers would have been hard pressed to find extra help for the needy if the banks had not collapsed. As it is, spending cuts and tax rises are unavoidable in the medium term.

Like the government, consumers are up to their necks in debt, and without the cushion of savings to break their fall, hundreds of thousands are tumbling towards poverty. Millions will stay afloat, but will nevertheless experience a sobering shock, a fearful intimation of what it might feel like to lose everything. In these circumstances, it seems reasonable to join with the TUC in hoping that the jeering of the *Shameless* culture will disappear with the bubble. Unfortunately, the history of economic crises suggests that a revival of common humanity is far from inevitable.

My generation has propagated a romanticised view of the recession of the late seventies and early eighties. To hear us talk, you would think we were all listening to punk and raging against poverty and oppression. In truth, punk was an ambiguous movement, which foreshadowed the rise of the right as well as a revolt by the left; Margaret Thatcher's line that 'there is no such thing as society' might have been the title of a Sex Pistols single.

It was also such a minority taste that I sometimes think more people have written about the history of punk than ever listened to it at the time. As in the depression of the thirties, the overwhelming majority of the British preferred escapism to gritty realism. As in the thirties, they gave the Conservative Party enormous majorities.

Altruism can seem a dispensable luxury when times are hard. Recessions have always had the potential to persuade voters that their interests and the interests of their families must come first. The present crisis, however, has an unprecedented and, in my view, alarming dimension. The crash has come eleven years into the longest-serving left-wing administration in British history, and the Labour government's longevity may work against the interests of those who are already living in poverty and all those who are about to join them. Behind the prole-baiting of the media lies the understanding that taxpayers have already given the government billions to help the poor.

If the recipients of all that charity are still on the breadline, then their poverty is the result of their own laziness. Wider society has done its best, really it has, and can now condemn the ungrateful slobs with a clean conscience.

It is a foolish mistake to believe that a recession will guarantee a revival in social solidarity. There are no guarantees and solidarity will have to be fought for. People may fight harder if they realise that, politically, economically and culturally, the advantage currently lies with their opponents.

Observer, October 2008

POSTSCRIPT

The Reasonableness of Ranters

WRITERS SEEKING LASTING fame are much more likely to find it if they produce romance, children's stories, heist capers, sword-and-sorcery fantasies ... any form imaginable, as long as it is not polemic. Nothing brings home the futility of political writing more forcefully than going through an old newspaper and reading the fulminations of a previous age. The savaged politicians are retired or dead, the scandals that provoked the writer's scorn forgotten. In the British press, editors praise polemical journalists for producing 'good rants' – a backhanded compliment if ever there was one. Polemicists themselves agree with their editors and dismiss their craft as the hasty channelling of emotion which would have been better spent elsewhere. In 1944, a weary George Orwell looked back with regret and wrote that 'in a peaceful age I might have written ornate or merely descriptive books, and might have remained almost unaware of my political loyalties. As it is I have been forced into becoming a sort of pamphleteer.'

Yet a few pamphlets live on long after the battles of their age are over, for two reasons. First, future generations realise that on one big point, if not every detail, the polemicist was right. Scoring in a debate is not enough, though, if a second condition isn't met: the polemicist must touch on universal concerns. However vital they were, no one except economic historians will grapple with the arguments about monetarism in the

369

Thatcher years. Everyone has an interest in the battles of tradition against change, faith against free thought and women's rights against male power because they define the future as well as the past.

The two greatest polemics in English, Edmund Burke's *Reflections on the Revolution in France* and Tom Paine's counterblast, *The Rights of Man*, are great because they define the struggle between conservatism and change. Burke saw how the revolution would lead to a new tyranny, and wrote in 1790 that 'the republic of Paris will endeavour, indeed, to complete the debauchery of the army, and illegally to perpetuate the assembly, without resort to its constituents, as the means of continuing its despotism'. That was prescient. The Reign of Terror did not begin until September 1793. At the time, Paine replied with a bewilderment shared by many and condemned Burke's 'outrageous abuse on the French Revolution, and the principles of Liberty'. His enemy did not seem so outrageous three years later when Robespierre ordered Paine's imprisonment. Meanwhile Paine's argument in favour of democratic republics remains the best defence and means of attack against every form of tyrannical government of that time and since. English radicals of the 1790s were inspired, but the aristocratic rulers of Britain had never encountered such an articulate assault and tried Paine *in absentia* for seditious libel.

The history of successful feminist polemics from Mary Wollstonecraft's *A Vindication of the Rights of Woman* to Germaine Greer's *The Female Eunuch* is one of ridicule – revoltingly violent abuse in Wollstonecraft's case – followed by partial and belated acceptance. George Orwell's condemnations of the indifference of the thirties left to the victims of communism in *The Road to Wigan Pier* and *Homage to Catalonia* were more unpopular still. Now it is next to impossible to write about the thirties without mentioning him. Christopher Hitchens's comparable attack on modern liberal-left apologetics for

Islamism in *Love, Poverty and War* and other essays has made former friends hate him. I think his work is a modern example of polemic at its best and that it will last, maybe along with Robert Hughes's assault on political correctness in *Culture of Complaint* and Naomi Klein's condemnations of corporate power in *No Logo*.

If I am right, all three will eventually have to convince even those who are politically predisposed to dislike them that they had a case. The great polemicists jump this bar with ease. A modern conservative can read Tom Paine and recognise that he was fighting for the best freedoms of our world, while deploring his belief that it is a simple matter to dispense with the past. Left-wingers have every reason to raise their eyebrows at Burke's saccharine laments for the age of chivalry, but can see that he understood how revolution in the name of liberty can beat a path to tyranny that has been trod many times since. By contrast, I cannot imagine anyone now choosing to read *What Is to Be Done?* and Lenin's other polemics before the Russian Revolution. Lenin was a powerful writer, but his ideas about tiny groups of militants seizing power in the name of the working class led to three of the most murderous regimes in history. Among their millions of victims was Lenin's future readership.

The tension between believing you are right and fearing that the world will not listen prompts the anger that fuels great as well as dreadful polemics. But it also produces a respect for argument that those who dismiss all polemic as mere ranting fail to see. If you can feel a need to make an unpopular case – and there is no point in being a political writer if you cannot – you must use your talent to win over a sceptical audience. You must acknowledge doubts and counter-arguments, and above all, you must write clearly. For this reason, and despite being intellectuals themselves, the great polemicists of the English tradition from Swift onwards are anti-academic. Burke loathed the 'sophists, economists and calculators' of the Enlightenment. Robert Hughes denounced the 'kind of wooze, unbolstered by proof or evidence, patched together out of vaguely "radical" apercus', which poured out of the postmodern cultural studies departments of American universities in the eighties. Whether they are from the left or the right, good polemicists are the enemies of obscurantism. They crave to be understood, and suspect that those who place unnecessary obstacles in front of the reader are protecting an established interest from scrutiny.

Is that so terrible? Is that mere raving? It can be. The newspaper columnists who comfort rather than confront their readers' prejudices always claim to be plain speakers. But in better circumstances, polemical clarity isn't philistinism or affectation but a recognition that the unfamiliar is hard to grasp and must be explained with patience if readers' assumptions are to be overcome. Great polemicists have a guilty secret. They rant when they have to but they are also terribly reasonable people.

From *Time Out's 1000 Books to Change Your Life*, June 2007

INDEX